EARLY EXPERIENCES AND EARLY BEHAVIOR
Implications for Social Development

EARLY EXPERIENCES AND EARLY BEHAVIOR
Implications for Social Development

Edited by

EDWARD C. SIMMEL

Behavior Genetics Laboratory
Department of Psychology
Miami University
Oxford, Ohio

ACADEMIC PRESS
A Subsidiary of Harcourt Brace Jovanovich, Publishers

New York   London   Toronto   Sydney   San Francisco

ACADEMIC PRESS, INC.
111 Fifth Avenue, New York, New York 10003

United Kingdom Edition published by
ACADEMIC PRESS, INC. (LONDON) LTD.
24/28 Oval Road, London NW1 7DX

Library of Congress Cataloging in Publication Data
Main entry under title:

Early experiences and early behavior.

    Includes bibliographies and indexes.
    1. Socialization--Addresses, essays, lectures.
2. Infant psychology--Addresses, essays, lectures.
3. Child development--Addresses, essays, lectures.
4. Animals, Infancy of --Addresses, essays, lectures.
I. Simmel, Edward C.
HQ783.E23   301.15'72   79-21421
ISBN 0-12-644080-8

PRINTED IN THE UNITED STATES OF AMERICA

80 81 82   9 8 7 6 5 4 3 2 1

Contents

CHAPTER **6**

**Early Development of Exploratory Behavior and
Dominance in Three Litters of German Shepherds**

JOHN C. WRIGHT

List of Contributors

Numbers in parentheses indicate the pages on which the authors' contributions begin.

ELAINE BAKER (3), Department of Psychology, Marshall University, Huntington, West Virginia 25701

ROBERT B. CAIRNS (79), Department of Psychology, University of North Carolina, Chapel Hill, North Carolina 27514

PETER DE CHATEAU* (109), Department of Pediatrics, Umeå University, Umeå, Sweden

JAMES A. GREEN (79), Department of Psychology, University of North Carolina, Chapel Hill, North Carolina 27514

NORMAN D. HENDERSON (39), Department of Psychology, Oberlin College, Oberlin, Ohio 44074

DENNIS J. MacCOMBIE (79), Department of Psychology, Kent State University, Kent, Ohio 44242

Z. MICHAEL NAGY (15), Department of Psychology, Bowling Green State University, Bowling Green, Ohio 43402

J. P. SCOTT (15), Center for Research on Social Behavior, Bowling Green State University, Bowling Green, Ohio 43402

* *Present address:* Department of Pediatrics, Karolinska Sjukhuset, Fack, S-10401 Stockholm, Sweden

EDWARD C. SIMMEL (3), Behavior Genetics Laboratory, Department of Psychology, Miami University, Oxford, Ohio 45056

JOHN C. WRIGHT (181), Appalachian Canid Research Project, Department of Psychology, Berea College, Berea, Kentucky 40403

Preface

What happens to an individual early in life is a major determinant (in many cases, perhaps, *the* major determinant) of what that individual will become, and possibly remain, thereafter. Whether or not this is always true, it is certainly a widely held and seldom questioned assumption, as attested to by everything from proverbs ("As the twig is bent . . .") to major investments in early childhood education, day-care centers, and the like. Over the past several decades, mountains of data have accumulated showing relatively permanent behavioral, social, and physiological consequences of a variety of both drastic and subtle interventions early in the life of organisms.

However, despite good intentions, complex research designs, and the accumulations of data just referred to, it seems that the major conclusion that can be made at the present time is the lack of a conclusion—the relative paucity of definitive summarizing statements and generalizations that can be made. Why this is so and some suggestions as to what might be done to begin to ameliorate this situation serve as a major theme and purpose of this book.

The original contributions presented in this volume discuss the problems associated with determining the effects of early experiences on later behavior, with emphasis on social development, both in humans and in animals. The overall approach is one of constructive criticism, in that specific problems in methodology and conceptualization are highlighted and promising new approaches are suggested and illustrated.

The book is divided into two parts. Part I deals with methodological, theoretical, and conceptual problems: Recurring problems of methodology and definition are specified; a thorough review of the animal literature in early experiences studies over the past quarter of a century pinpoints certain areas of progress among many other areas where advances have been sparse; and two newer approaches are discussed and supported, namely behavioral metamorphosis and the interactional–developmental approach.

Part II presents two case studies which serve to exemplify a variety of older and newer approaches to the investigation of the effects of early experiences on social development. Though one study deals with human subjects, and the other with animals, there are a number of interesting parallels between them: Both are longitudinal studies beginning immediately after birth; both make extensive use of quantitative and qualitative data from naturalistic observations, and both also employ more traditional controlled tests and measurements. Points raised in several of the chapters in Part I are illustrated in these two chapters.

Another theme tying together the contributions in this book relates to the implications of various early experiences on social development. An extensive array of social behaviors and the variables which could alter their development are discussed, running the gamut from such seemingly simple and basic processes as dyadic interactions and attachment behavior, through aggression and communication, to the processes of socialization. Though the theme of social development is more central to some chapters than to others, fairly direct implications relating to this theme can be found in each chapter. It should be pointed out, however, that the conceptual and methodological critiques and suggestions regarding the investigation of the effects of early experiences on development and on later behavior offered in these six chapters are generally applicable to processes and behaviors in general, rather than to social development alone.

ACKNOWLEDGMENTS

This book could not have appeared without the efforts of a number of individuals, and I am most grateful to all of them. Special thanks are due to Betty Marak, my outstanding manuscript typist, who was virtually a co-editor; to Bill Addison and Jeanne Slattery for preparing the subject index; and to Margie Bagwell, who performed a number of vital editorial chores. I am also grateful to two deans at Miami University: Spiro Peterson of the

Graduate School and C. K. Williamson of the College of Arts and Science, for their kind support. The efficient and creative editorial and production staffs at Academic Press almost make editing a book a pleasure.

EARLY EXPERIENCES AND EARLY BEHAVIOR
Implications for Social Development

PART I

METHODOLOGICAL, THEORETICAL, AND CONCEPTUAL ISSUES: PROBLEMS AND PROMISE

CHAPTER **1**

The Effects of Early Experiences
on Later Behavior:
A Critical Discussion

EDWARD C. SIMMEL
ELAINE BAKER

Transsexuals are highly resistant to any change in their gender identity, which they believe to be incompatible with their anatomical sex. This resistance to change is so great that specialists in this area feel it is easier to change the anatomical sex of the individual through surgery than it is to alter the gender identity through psychological intervention (Money & Ehrhardt, 1972). Gender identity appears to be acquired and fixed by the third year of life and is usually stable and impervious to alteration thereafter. This illustrates how permanent and far-reaching the effects of early experiences *can* be. But are all early experiences necessarily so drastic and unalterable in their effects, and is it always so necessary that effective experiences be early?

Studies on the class of variables categorized under the general label "early experiences" define these variables as those that occur early in an organism's life, and that are often assumed to have a greater impact on later behavior than would the same events at any other time. There are several difficulties with this form of the definition and the assumptions stemming from it. One problem is that the temporal dimension of "early" can vary greatly, ranging from prenatal experiences through puberty or beyond. If the major concern is with an effect that cannot be produced at some later age, then distinguishing early from prior or initial experiences will help to clarify

3

EARLY EXPERIENCES AND EARLY BEHAVIOR
Implications for Social Development

the meaning of "early." We will deal with this problem in a later section of this chapter.

EARLY EXPERIENCES AND EARLY BEHAVIORS

Another problem lies in the distinction between early experience and early behavior. It is helpful to refer to the range of behaviors found during a specific period of development for all members of a species or population *early behaviors*. *Early experiences* refer to deviations from the normal range of environmental events that have potential effects on the later behavior of an organism. This distinction can be an important one: Effects of early experiences (as defined previously) are more meaningful if interpreted against the background of normal early behaviors; conversely, the extent of variation of a given type of early behavior may provide clues to the extent of the effect of a major intervention.

The investigation of early behavior should include more than descriptions of fixed action patterns in precocial species, or a detailing of infant reflexes in more complex organisms. While innate species-predictable behaviors should not be ignored, the extent and sources of individual differences in early behavior are at least as interesting. They are also considerably more important in understanding the adaptive significance of early behavior, since varied phenotypes provide the raw material for the operation of natural selection.

Genetic factors are an obvious source of variance in early behavior. There are some instances of excellent research on this topic; for instance, Henderson's studies with infant inbred mice, and the pioneering work of Scott and Fuller (1965) on development in several breeds of dogs. Unfortunately, in most of its applications to early behavior the term "genetic" is used as a synonym for behavior patterns that are innate and fixed, and thus antithetical to the investigation of individual differences in the early behavior of organisms.

Early learning is a topic where a distinction similar to the one we have discussed between early behavior and early experience could be particularly useful. On the one hand, there are the cases of age-dependent, species-specific learning, in which certain features of the usual environment result in the learning of highly similar responses in all members of a species at a given age. The strongest example of this is imprinting, which describes the age-dependent acquisition of an approach or following response as the result of a brief exposure to a stimulus. Other examples might be the acquisition of song patterns in some species of birds, or even the initial development of language in humans. This category of learning is an instance of (or at least analogous to) early behavior, in that highly similar behaviors occur within a species provided that certain features of the environment are present at the appropriate age level.

Contrasted with this are the many instances of diverse learning that seem to have greater effects on younger, rather than older, organisms. It may be, as Scott, Stewart, and DeGhett (1974) assert, that systems that are not completely organized are more easily altered, since organized systems (i.e., more developed organisms) are more likely to modify input to fit what is already stored in the system. This approach is consistent with Hebb's (1972) neurological explanation of the impact of early learning. According to Hebb, experiences occurring early, for example the acquisition of perceptual abilities, are incorporated more slowly than are later events because of the need for integrating and developing cell assemblies. Once these are established, later events and the behaviors resulting from them become largely a matter of transfer, making use of the cell assemblies established earlier. It follows that, especially in relatively long-lived and complex organisms, the early presence of stimuli that are normally absent from the environment, or the early absence of stimuli that are normally present, can affect learning processes and thus provide a catalytic effect on later behavior.

Even a brief perusal of the research literature on early experiences reveals that most studies conducted today, as well as those done in the past, involve either isolation or deprivation, or some degree of strong stimulus enhancement as the operational definition of *experience*. It is increasingly obvious that we are learning a great deal about how to produce abnormal behavior through early and extreme manipulation of an organism's environment. It is unfortunate that we know considerably less about the actual early behaviors that immature animals exhibit in natural settings on their way to becoming adults. In addition to designing experiments involving unusual treatments or extreme deprivations, we need to investigate the range of naturally occurring early behaviors, the range of conditions that affect them, and the influence they have on later behavior. The information gained could provide a more thorough understanding of the impact of early experiences.

EARLY EXPERIENCES AND PRIOR EXPERIENCES

Early (infantile) experiences are frequently assumed to be most important in their effects on later behavior. To illustrate this point we offer the following quotation from one of the most prolific investigators in this area: "We contend that environmental factors during infancy are more profound in their effects than environmental factors during any other period in the organism's history. In fact, the extent and manner to which an organism reacts to later environmental events is determined to a large extent by environmental conditions which prevail during infancy [Levine, 1962, p. 246]." Although these words were written several years ago, it is likely that the viewpoint expressed is even more generally and more uncritically accepted today. Whereas it seems clear that early experiences can be of major importance for *some* durable effects on *certain* later behaviors, the overgeneralization and the a *priori* nature of their effect claimed in statements such as Levine's can be both misleading and counterproductive.

The importance of infantile environment or specific early treatment for any lasting effect on adult behavior is a *hypothesis*. If it is considered to be an assumption instead, the effect is to encourage the use of incomplete and erroneous experimental designs in which older organisms are not tested. This in turn can preclude the possible finding that prior, rather than early, experiences might be involved in the variables under investigation. The appropriate corrective designs will be discussed in a later section.

In this section, we will consider the effects of prior experiences, and various ways in which they could be confused, or could be kept from being confused, with early experience effects. We will also examine *priming* as a specific type of prior experience that sometimes provides lasting effects on later behavior.

A Case in Point

The Berkeley brain chemistry studies have been a series of far-reaching and well-designed experiments on the effects of genotype and environmental complexity on the quantity, distribution, and interrelationship of various neurotransmitters that had previously been shown to be related to problem solving and learning ability in rats (Krech, Rosenzweig, & Bennett, 1960; Rosenzweig, Krech, Bennett, & Diamond, 1962). In these studies, rats of six different strains, including the descendants of the original Tryon maze-bright and maze-dull strains, were placed in one of three environments for several weeks following weaning at 25 days of age. The environments differed in degree of complexity: Environmental complexity training (ECT) rats were placed in large cages (8–10 rats per cage) with various "toys" that were changed daily; they were also given a maze to explore. Social controls (SC) were placed in groups of three in standard laboratory cages. Isolate control (IC) rats were placed alone in cages providing a constant external environment. The results showed, in general, that brain chemistry changes were proportional to the complexity of the environment in which the subjects were maintained. Especially striking was the cortical: subcortical ratio of cholinesterase (ChE), with greater subcortical: cortical ChE levels in ECT animals. ECT subjects also had greater cortical weight and ChE activity in the subcortex than did their IC littermate controls.

The studies we have referred to so far tell us that experience with complex stimuli affects brain chemicals, which in turn affect behavior. The "experiences" of the rats with their complex or noncomplex environments began at weaning age, so they were *early* experiences. Commendably, the authors do not refer to early experience effects since no data existed, at least initially, to determine whether the earliness of the treatment was critical to the effects obtained. Two members of the Berkeley group performed a series of experiments specifically to determine age effects (Zolman & Morimoto, 1962), comparing complexity experiences begun at weaning with those initiated at 55 days of age (adulthood for a rat). Only one of the brain chemistry changes due to ECT was age-dependent, that is, a true early experience effect, and this was reversible if followed by 30 days of isolation.

Despite the strong evidence for important *prior* experience effects, and the sparse evidence for major *early* experience effects in these studies, they are widely cited in popularized accounts as a prime example of the strong influence of early environment on those neural events that can play a major role in adult behavior. A random but representative example can be found in one of the most widely used introductory psychology textbooks (Ruch & Zimbardo, 1971), one that was published nearly 10 years after the studies summarized above. In this textbook, the Berkeley brain chemistry studies are introduced by the following: "The nature of the early life environment to which an organism must adapt obviously ought to play a determining role in its later behavior [p. 102]." On the following page, the authors do state, "This increased activity of the cortex has been found even in animals first exposed to this enriched setting as adults . . . ," but the attribution of the effect to *early* experiences had already been made. A perusal of other introductory textbooks reveals that this attribution is not unique.

A major danger inherent in the assumption (as opposed to a hypothesis) that early experiences will influence later behavior is that experiments will continue to be performed without adequate controls to test for the effects of prior experiences. Since genuine early experience effects will not be discerned, sound general principles of the nature and mechanisms of early experiences will not develop. We are concerned also with a social risk: the unwarranted belief on the part of the public (and the policymakers) in the overriding importance of early environment can lead to the same sort of fatalistic predeterminism that has occurred because of the widespread misunderstanding of the nature of genetic determinants of behavior.

Designs

Since we have stressed the importance of clearly distinguishing between early and prior experiences as these may affect subsequent behavior, it is worthwhile to review briefly some pertinent, but frequently neglected, points of research design. Obviously, nothing can be done about inadequately designed studies that have found their way into the literature, but the competence of the design, in terms of questions asked and conclusions drawn, should be considered by the "consumers" of this literature: those who are seeking background for the preparation of their own research or for theoretical articles on development and the effects of early experiences; those who have some application in mind; and even (or perhaps, especially) those who are developing or revising courses using this topic.

Of course, the most obvious design problem is to control for *age of treatment.* Since the effect in question is one that is hypothesized to be of the greatest importance early in the life-span of the organism, identical treatment for an older aged group is required. This in turn sets up the need for controls to test for the effects of the interval between treatment and testing. (Remember that we are concerned with effects *of* some specified early treatment *on* some set of behaviors later in the life of the subjects.) We must also be concerned with a possible relationship or interaction between age of treatment and the interval between treatment and testing. A concise but thorough discussion of this can be found in Fuller and Waller (1962), and their suggested seven-group design is given in Figure 1-1. (If one is concerned with determining a "critical" age at which a treatment will have a later effect, the appropriately rigorous design will be truly awesome.)

Perhaps the most interesting and important variable in early experience studies is the *duration of treatment* that is hypothesized to affect later behavior. Only under conditions where subjects receive continuous early treatment is the investigator justified in making general statements attributing later behaviors to "early environment." Continuous treatments may be highly specific, involving one or very few variables, such as ambient noise level or temperature, or they may be more global in nature, such as in the Berkeley rats discussed earlier, with their "enriched" and "impoverished" environments. Obviously, control and specification of which specific aspect of the total environment is having the greatest effect on the organism is most difficult if a continuous, "total environment" treatment is used.

On the other hand, intermittent treatments involve specific and presumably discrete interventions, as in periods of stress, isolation, handling, and so on. The control problem here is with the remainder of the environment, and comparison of similar experiments must take this into account, as Fuller and Waller (1962) aptly point out. There are also combination designs, with

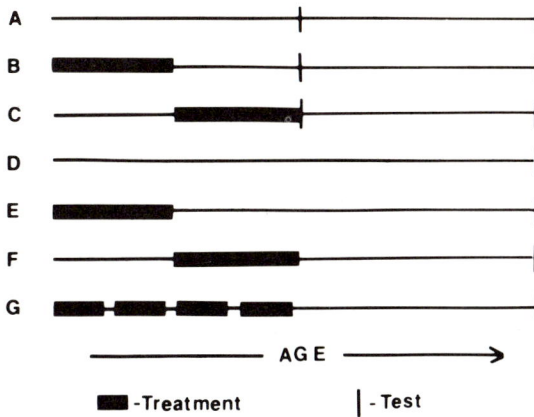

Figure 1-1. Design for analyzing the effects of a continuous treatment at two age ranges, controlling for prior experience and for the interval between treatment and testing. (Redrawn from Fuller & Waller, 1962. Copyright © 1962, Harper & Row, Publishers, Inc.)

intermittent treatments imposed on continuous ones. An example of this is a study by Fuller (1970) in which two breeds of puppies were isolated for 2 months, but with different groups receiving different numbers of "breaks" (10-minute periods with a human handler) per week.

The most limited sort of early experience is the single, brief treatment—a "critical event." Difficult to find, both because of their rarity and the problems of control, single treatments that can be shown to have specific effects on later behavior can be of considerable heuristic and theoretical value. Whether such events are "prior" or "early" experiences, the impact of the single treatment can be striking, as demonstrated by the relatively little-known phenomenon discussed in the following paragraphs.

Priming

One of the more interesting types of prior experience that is an example of such brief, very specific treatments is *priming*. This refers to responses that will occur in a given situation only if certain specific events took place previously; without these events the occurrence of those responses will not occur. An obvious example is the priming for audiogenic seizures (AGS) in certain strains of inbred mice (Fuller, 1975; Fuller & Collins, 1968; Henry, 1967). In these studies it was found that mice of some strains that seemed not to be susceptible to AGS could be induced to have seizures if presented with the auditory stimulus at a specific interval prior to receiving the same stimulus tone. Then, and only then, would the tone result in AGS. This priming phenomenon is highly age-dependent, as are audiogenic seizures themselves.

Another example can be found in a study on the priming for maternal behavior by Noirot (1964). Naive adult female mice that had had brief olfactory and auditory exposure to a 1-day-old pup would show increased maternal behavior, such as retrieval, when later exposed to a drowned pup, a stimulus that does not normally elicit such behavior from naive females. Here, the interval between priming and the later responses is unimportant, with delays of a few minutes or several days showing few differences. In a later study (Noirot, 1969), naive virgin mice were exposed to either olfactory cues from a litter of pups, or to auditory distress cries. When later exposed to 1- or 2-day-old pups, mice primed with the auditory stimuli engaged in more intense nest building than did controls, whereas subjects primed with olfactory cues showed more intense licking of the pups than did the controls. This provides an excellent example of the highly specific nature of the priming stimulus.

The following example shows that, in addition to affecting a specific subsequent response, priming can have a chronic effect on the behavior of the organism—a "personality change." Inbred mice of the LG/J strain are normally docile animals, seldom observed to fight with one another in their home cages or in the arena encounters used to assess the agonistic behavior of mice. However, if 2 male LG noncagemates are placed in an arena with 2 mice of any other strain, but separated from these other-strain mice by a clear plastic partition, the LGs will attack the other mice and each other within 30 seconds after the partition is raised. This was observed by Simmel and Walker (1970) in 26 out of the 26 LGs originally tested. Under various control conditions in the same study (4 LGs separated by pairs; LGs paired with other-strain mice, but with no partition), no fights occurred. The priming condition here is the presence of a strange strain of mice, with no physical contact (social exploration) permitted, for a 10-minute period. Following priming and priming-induced fighting, the LG mice were observed to attack normally unlikely targets, such as cagemates and females, with some instances of this observed as long as 2 months after the original test. Mice retested in the arena began fighting immediately, even several weeks following the priming procedure. Using a slightly different rearing procedure, Wright and Simmel (1976) found that LG mice that fought after the priming procedure attacked opponents much more frequently than did various control animals in a week-long session with several other mice in a seminatural setting. This priming effect seems not to be age-dependent, other than involving primarily young adult (45–70-day-old) animals. It does illustrate the drastic effects on later behavior of a very specific prior experience. Research is currently underway to investigate the neurochemical changes that might mediate this rapid "personality change."

These priming studies show that adult animals can be susceptible to environmental impact, and that brief, albeit highly specific, treatments can result in major alterations of their behavior. Severe and durable effects on later behavior by specific prior experiences are not limited to young organisms.

THE PROBLEM OF CAUSALITY

If all studies purporting to show major and durable effects of early experiences on later behavior were rigorously controlled, clearly pinpointing that the effect is indeed due to early rather than prior experiences, we would certainly have a far greater understanding of this area than we do now. Even if this were the case, however, we would still be only halfway home. No matter how ideally controlled, studies showing early experience effects, whatever the strength, are still merely *preliminary* (Simmel, 1973). They show that an effect exists—that there is a relationship between an intervention at a given age and the presence, strength, or durability of a behavior at a later age—but they do not tell us how or why this occurs. Such data are in effect correlational and are of no greater use in providing explanations that are any other correlational data. Answering the question: "Why are certain monkeys unable to develop normal adult social relationships?" with, "Because they were raised in isolation when they were infants," will not carry our science nearly so far as being able to answer that their early isolation had x effect on them, which in turn resulted in y and z.

We suggest two approaches that might add explanatory power, and thus understanding, to early experience findings. The first (Simmel, 1973) is to design studies so that a sequence of consequences stemming from the initial intervention (the "early experience") can be discerned. What behavioral and physiological events result directly from the initial application of stress, isolation, environmental enrichment, etc.? Do these affect the timing and nature of other developmental processes? Are specific and unique chains of responses set off by the experimental treatment? In many specific experiments, this approach might prove to be quite difficult and expensive, but where it can be employed, it would serve to show how and why particular early experiences affect later behavior.

A second approach is recommended by Cairns (1976): Attempt to find ways of reversing a strong, established early experience effect. For example, Fuller (1970) found that in isolation-reared terrier and beagle puppies, even a 10-minute break per week from isolation over a period of 9 weeks would greatly moderate the effects of early isolation on a number of social and activity measures. This approach requires a good deal of ingenuity and open-mindedness on the part of the experimenter, but it also provides the opportunity to narrow in on the specific or critical variables involved in a given early experience effect. And thus, it can lead to answers to the question, "How?"

SUMMARY

In this chapter, we have tried to emphasize that a changed perspective is needed in the ways in which early experiences and early behaviors are investigated, so that their consequences may be better understood. By way of summary, we feel that the following points are particularly worthy of consideration by both the "producers" and the "consumers" of research in this area:

1. Greater consideration should be given to the investigation of the range of normal stimulus events and normal response patterns that occur early in the life of an animal.
2. It should be recognized that *early experience* refers to a temporal dimension in the occurrence of an event, and is not in itself an explanation for the consequences of that event. Further, the importance of the timing of an event should not be accepted *a priori* as anything more than an hypothesis to be tested.
3. The most useful research designs used in the investigation of the effects of early experiences are those that: (a) clearly control for the effects of prior experiences; and (b) provide a handle for determining just *how* and *why* a particular type of early experience has such an important effect on later behavior.

REFERENCES

Cairns, R. B. 1976. The ontogeny and phylogeny of social interactions. In M. E. Hahn & E. C. Simmel (Eds.), *Communicative behavior and evolution.* New York: Academic Press. Pp. 115–139.

Fuller, J. L. 1970. Genetic influences on socialization. In R. A. Hoppe, G. A. Milton, & E. C. Simmel (Eds.), *Early experiences and the processes of socialization.* New York: Academic Press. Pp. 7–18.

Fuller, J. L. 1975. Independence of inherited susceptibility to spontaneous and primed audiogenic seizures in mice. *Behavior Genetics, 5,* 1–8.

Fuller, J. L., & Collins, R. L. 1968. Temporal parameters of sensitization for audiogenic seizures in SJL/J mice. *Developmental Psychobiology, 1,* 185–188.

Fuller, J. L., & Waller, M. B. 1962. Is early experience different? In E. L. Bliss (Ed.), *Roots of behavior*. New York: Harper & Row. Pp. 235–245.

Hebb, D. O. 1972. *Textbook of psychology* (3rd ed.). Philadelphia: Saunders.

Henry, K. R. 1967. Audiogenic seizure susceptibility induced in C57BL/6J mice by prior auditory experience. *Science, 158,* 938–940.

Krech, D., Rosenzweig, M. R., & Bennett, E. L. 1960. Effects of environmental complexity and training on brain chemistry. *Journal of Comparative and Physiological Psychology, 53,* 509–519.

Levine, S. 1962. Psychophysiological effects of infantile stimulation. In E. L. Bliss (Ed.), *Roots of behavior*. New York: Harper & Row. Pp. 246–253.

Money, J., & Ehrhardt, A. 1972. *Man and woman, boy and girl*. Baltimore: Johns Hopkins University Press.

Noirot, E. 1964. Changes in responsiveness to young in the adult mouse. IV. The effect of an initial contact with a strong stimulus. *Animal Behaviour, 12,* 442–445.

Noirot, E. 1969. Changes in responsiveness to young in the adult mouse. V. Priming. *Animal Behaviour, 17,* 542–546.

Rosenzweig, M. R., Krech, D., Bennett, E. L., & Diamond, M. C. 1962. Effects of environmental complexity and training on brian chemistry and anatomy: A replication and extension. *Journal of Comparative and Physiological Psychology, 55,* 429–437.

Ruch, F. L., & Zimbardo, P. G. 1971. *Psychology and life* (8th ed.). Glenview, Ill.: Scott, Foresman.

Scott, J. P., & Fuller, J. L. 1965. *Genetics and the social behavior of the dog*. Chicago: University of Chicago Press.

Scott, J. P., Stewart, J. M., & DeGhett, V. J. 1974. Critical periods in the development of systems. *Developmental Psychobiology, 7,* 489–513.

Simmel, E. C. 1973. The analysis of the effects of early experiences. *Developmental Psychobiology, 6,* 510.

Simmel, E. C., & Walker, D. A. 1970. Social priming for agonistic behavior in a "docile" mouse strain. *American Zoologist, 10,* 486–487 (abstract).

Wright, J. C., & Simmel, E. C. 1976. Agonistic behavior and social reactivity of LG/J mice in both an arena and a seminatural setting. *Aggressive Behavior, 2,* 11–18.

Zolman, J. F., & Morimoto, H. 1962. Effects of age of training on cholinesterase activity in the brains of maze-bright rats. *Journal of Comparative and Physiological Psychology, 55,* 794–800.

CHAPTER 2

Behavioral Metamorphosis in Mammalian Development

J. P. SCOTT
Z. MICHAEL NAGY

Species whose members live in two radically different habitats during different phases of the life cycle are relatively common in the animal kingdom. Among more primitive animals, certain species of Coelenterates such as *Aurelia* exhibit the phenomenon of alternation of generations, or metagenesis. In the polyp generation, the individual is attached to the substrate and reproduces asexually by budding. In the medusoid or jellyfish generation, the individual is free floating and swimming and reproduces sexually. Whereas Coelenterates are always aquatic, the environments in which the polyp and medusoid forms live are radically different, which means that they must be subject to different sorts of selection pressures.

Among the higher animals most insects exhibit the phenomenon of metamorphosis to some degree. An early larval form, which has no wings, is transformed and reorganized into an individual that is adapted to aerial existence. Some immature forms are aquatic, as in dragonflies, whose nymphs develop for long periods under water before emerging into the air and becoming transformed into flying insects. Other immature insects are terrestrial, occupying various habitats. A common example is the fruitfly, whose larval form lives on fruit, then goes into a pupa stage in which the animal is protected by a tough shell and during which it metamorphoses into a flying insect.

15

EARLY EXPERIENCES AND EARLY BEHAVIOR
Implications for Social Development

One whole class of vertebrates, the Amphibia, typically lays eggs in water, where larval forms develop and eventually undergo extensive metamorphosis into adult forms that can exist on land, although most present-day Amphibia never get far from water. Among frogs, the tadpole larva is vegetarian, swims by means of a tail, and has no limbs. After metamorphosis, the tail is lost, limbs appear, and the adults become carnivorous.

An example that is frequently overlooked includes the nonprecocious mammals, of which the dog is an example. The newborn animals occupy an environment in which almost all functions are performed with the aid of the mother, and all behavior is adapted to that existence. Between 2 and 3 weeks of age the puppies undergo a metamorphosis of behavior that is almost as striking as the anatomical changes undergone in the metamorphosis of the tadpole into a frog. Such a form of development raises many theoretical and empirical problems concerning the effects of early experience, particularly in the neonatal stage.

BEHAVIORAL DEVELOPMENT IN THE DOG

For the first 2 weeks after birth, the puppy is in constant contact with littermates and is given care by its mother around the clock. This means that for the neonatal dog the social environment (consisting of the mother and littermates) is paramount. In contrast, environment for an older puppy includes many contacts with the physical features of the environment and with other living things, as well as a change in the nature of social contacts. The quality of the environment in the neonatal period is thus quite different from that in older animals, and dogs have evolved a distinctly different set of behavior patterns that are adaptive only in early life.

The Neonatal Period

With respect to sensory development, the puppy is born both blind and deaf. The eyes and ears are closed, and there is no response to auditory or visual stimuli. Differential responses are given to olfactory and taste stimuli. The puppies respond to tactile stimuli, pain, and cool temperatures. They give some evidence of responses to internal stimuli concerned with hunger, as poorly nourished puppies are constantly active and vocalize frequently.

Motor patterns are limited. The newborn puppy is capable of sucking, but has no teeth and is unable to chew. The pattern of sucking includes thrusting movements of the head, alternate pushing with the forepaws, and bracing with the hind legs. Locomotion consists of a slow crawl, throwing the head from side to side, that ceases as soon as the puppy's head comes into contact with some soft warm object such as the body of another puppy or the mother's body. Other than this, the puppies are capable of distress vocalization; this can be totally relieved by a combination of warm temperature (30°C) and contact with a soft and warm surface, including a vertical surface. Urination and defecation are reflexive and are normally evoked as a response to licking by the mother. This is obviously an adaptation for keeping the nest area clean.

The social behavior of the neonatal puppies is confined to sucking, distress vocalization, and contact-seeking behavior. Only the last has any degree of importance in older animals.

With respect to orientation, neonatal puppies are only able to find their mother or littermates by random movement. Unlike neonatal kittens, they are unable to locate a nest site by scent. Unlike both kittens and piglets, puppies do not form a teat order. Their position on the mother's teats is random.

Thus the behavior of neonatal puppies is well adapted to a situation in which almost complete care is provided by the mother. Since such care is provided for only a few weeks, one would not expect that the capacity for learning would be well developed. Indeed, learning that does take place seems to be associated primarily with sucking behavior. This suggests that the capacities for carrying over effects of learned experience to later ages are limited in two ways: by the poor development of the sensory, motor, and central nervous systems, and by the fact that the experience is limited to situations that do not ordinarily occur in adult life.

The Transition Period

This period begins with the opening of the eyes and marks the initiation of a brief period of development in which are concentrated major changes in sense organs, motor patterns, eating behavior, and social responsiveness. Compared to adults, puppies in the transition stage are still somewhat handicapped in their sensory capacities. The eyes open gradually, becoming fully open at approximately 13 days. Once they are open, one can obtain pupillary reflexes to light. Nystagmus to lateral movement by the puppy appears, but nystagmus to moving vertical stripes is not found. The retina does not become fully differentiated anatomically until approximately 4 weeks of age (Fox, 1971). Although the development of auditory capacities has not been well studied, the startle response to sound first occurs at about 19 to 21 days of age (Scott & Fuller, 1965). A major change in locomotor behavior also occurs following eye opening; puppies now crawl backward as well as forward. Thus, whereas the sensory capacities of puppies in the transition stage are somewhat inferior to those of adults, by the end of this stage all major senses are functional and the puppies begin to orient toward sounds and sudden movements.

During the week that follows the opening of the eyes, the puppies also show transitions in motor behavior. They begin to walk instead of crawl, their first teeth appear, and they begin to respond to semisolid food, which in the natural state is provided by the mother vomiting food for them.

By the end of the period, at approximately 3 weeks of age, puppies are capable of associative learning in a variety of ways and can be conditioned with a speed approaching that of adults.

With respect to social behavior, the puppies show their first tail wagging and also show the first indications of separation distress when removed from familiar places and individuals.

Development of Learning Capacities in the Neonatal and Transition Periods

What an animal learns, apart from external circumstances, depends on its sensory capacities, motor capacities, and the organization of particular behavior patterns, in addition to any central nervous system capacities for reorganization of behavior in relation to the environment. Each of these capacities can change with development. Discovering what an animal learns is relatively easy, but determining the part that each of the above capacities plays in learning is often extremely difficult. Behavior can change either because of learning or because of maturational changes in the organization of any of the above capacities, including the capacity for learning itself. The usual experimental design is one in which subjects are tested over a period of days or weeks, in which case the changes will reflect both learning and maturation. The factor of maturation can be evaluated separately by starting different groups at successive ages that overlap with previous groups.

As stated above, newborn puppies are responsive to all major classes of sensory stimulation except sight and sound. Both eyes and ears are closed at birth. More than two-thirds of the puppies have their eyes completely open at 14 days (Scott & Fuller, 1965), and they begin to open them several days prior to this, with considerable individual variation. Less than 1% of the animals have their eyes open at 1 week of age, and it can be assumed that the great majority of puppies do not respond to sight before 8 or 9 days. The time of eye opening should be recorded for each individual in every experiment on the development of learning, but it is frequently not reported.

Responsiveness to sound occurs much later. Less than 5% of puppies respond to sound at 2 weeks of age, but nearly 90% respond by 3 weeks.

Auditory function should therefore not be a disturbing factor during the first week of life.

With respect to motor capacities, the mode of locomotion in a neonatal puppy is a slow crawl, swinging the head from side to side. It may move in a circular direction but never backward. Crawling over short distances can be used as a response modified by learning, but oriented responses are quite difficult. In groups of undisturbed puppies, we observed the first walking in any animal at 13 days after birth (Scott & Fuller, 1965). Fifty percent were observed to walk by 20 days.

The most prominent motor behavior of the neonatal pup is the sucking reflex. The full pattern involves pulling and pushing on the nipple with the head, and alternate pushing with the forepaws. The pups also can withdraw the head from an unpleasant taste or odor. Fox (1964, 1971) has described a number of other reflex behaviors that can be elicited in neonatal puppies. In general there are no gross changes in the two major motor capacities of locomotion and sucking before approximately 8 days of age, although the puppies do become stronger and can react more quickly.

As a result of early observations of neonatal puppy development, Scott (Scott & Marston, 1950) stated that the neonatal puppies did not seem to be learning very much; their behavior became faster and better organized, but showed few if any changes with respect to experience. This statement was first challenged by Fuller, Easler, and Banks (1950). They attempted classical conditioning of puppies, using the response of leg withdrawal to the unconditioned stimulus of the pain of an electric shock. They experimented with a variety of conditioned stimuli. Using the arbitrary criterion of 10 responses to the conditioned stimulus, they discovered that no puppies could reach this criterion earlier than 18 or 19 days of age, when there was in each individual a sudden improvement in performance to a level essentially equal to that of adult dogs. Later, Cornwell and Fuller (1960) did a similar experiment using an air puff as the conditioned stimulus, but recording the number of positive responses during each day's performance rather than using an arbitrary criterion. They obtained no responses to conditioned stimuli at 8 days and before, but thereafter the number of responses gradually climbed through 17 days of age. The results of previous training and maturation are confounded in this experiment, but it is noteworthy that the acquisition of the response was much slower than in adult animals, and that even at 17 days of age all the puppies were not giving perfect performances. Therefore, the capacity for learned modification of this particular response appears gradually during the second and third weeks of life.

Similar results were obtained by Klyavina, Kobakova, Stelmakh, and Troshikin (1958). Using auditory stimulation as a conditioned stimulus, they found that puppies at 30 days of age could be conditioned as rapidly as adult dogs. At 15 days they found that it took as many as 80 pairings with the unconditioned stimulus to produce a stable response. These results are somewhat suspect, inasmuch as many puppies do not respond to sound at that age. They also reported that a motor response to food could be conditioned much more rapidly than that to shock, with less than half the number of pairings required. Fuller and Christake (1959) then attempted to condition heart rate change in response to electric shock, supposing that the capacity to modify this response, mediated by the autonomic nervous system, might appear early in development. Actually, they were unable to get stable conditioning before 5 weeks of age. All these results indicate that the maturation of learning capacities is highly specific to the particular response involved and very possibly also to the kind of stimulation that is used as a conditioned stimulus.

At this point Stanley (1970, 1972) and his colleagues theorized that puppies might learn more easily if tested with an instrumental model of conditioning involving an important natural response, sucking. They devised an elegant series of experiments based on starting to train puppies on artificial nipples at 1–3 days of age and continuing daily training sessions for 5–12 days thereafter. Because of the nature of the response, only a small number of trials could be run on any one day, the usual model being five trials per day, one every 2 hours. With this technique, there is no possibility of achieving definitive results on any one day, and comparison of one day's performance with the next may be affected by maturation as well as learning. Stanley was interested primarily in demonstrating that learning would produce differential effects on behavior, and he did not control for maturation.

Stanley has summarized his results in two papers (1970, 1972). For example, the sucking response can be classically conditioned by giving a reward of milk immediately following the insertion of a nipple into the puppy's mouth. Similarly, the withdrawal reflex can be classically conditioned by administering quinine. He also demonstrated instrumental conditioning of approach behavior by training puppies to approach and suck on an artificial nipple (Stanley, Bacon, & Fehr, 1970). One nipple was placed in an area covered by soft terrycloth and the other in an opposite area covered by one-fourth-inch mesh wire hardware cloth. The puppy had to choose the correct nipple (one on which sucking produced milk) on the basis of these tactile stimuli.

In one such experiment the pups showed no improvement between the first and second five-trial blocks, but thereafter performance steadily improved over a period of several days. There seems to be no doubt that the response can be conditioned, although the improvement takes place much more slowly than in adult dogs, who could learn such a discrimination in one or two trials. Also, because there was no control for maturational changes, there is no way of telling how much of the improvement from one day to the next was due to carry over of previous learning or to an increased basic capacity of some sort, although the differential response to the two cues definitely suggests learning. It is fair to conclude with Stanley that the learning capacities of young puppies, while they may be quantitatively different from those of adults, are not qualitatively different.

The one exception to this conclusion is an experiment by Bacon (1971) on reversal learning. In this experiment the puppies found a full or an empty nipple at the end of short alleys that were lined with either terrycloth or wire. In each session the puppy was given two positive and two negative trials. The puppies began to respond differentially after three or four sessions and then gradually improved their speed of crawling to the positive stimulus. In one experiment, puppies were started on Day 3 and trained until Day 7, when the stimuli were reversed. In the alley where the milk had formerly been absent, the puppies improved very rapidly and reached levels higher than those they had previously reached. In the negative alley, the puppies continued to crawl at approximately the same speed for 4 days, the puppies now being 11 days old, and then decreased their times slowly to the previous negative level over the next 3 or 4 days. The puppies thus responded differentially to negative and positive cues after reversal, indicating that their capacity for reversal learning is qualitatively different from that in adults.

In general, these experiments show that the development of learning capacities depends upon the maturation of all four of the general classes of capacities involved: sensory, motor, behavior patterns, and learning. They do not give us information about when the capacity to make associations actually begins, but presumably this might be present before birth in some immature form. The experiments do indicate that the processes for associative learning are much slower in neonatal puppies than in older animals, for whatever reason. This means that a much greater amount of training or experience is required to produce the same effect; neonatal puppies are less sensitive to the effects of experience. They also indicate that what is learned is highly specific to the kind of behavior involved and the situation in which it appears. This implies that, rather than having a general timetable for maturation of learning capacities, the puppy has specific timetables that vary from one behavior and one situation to another. But if such timetables can be pinned down precisely, this should give the opportunity for neurophysiological study of correlated changes in the brain, which in turn should give clues to the physiological basis of learning capacities.

Our latest experiment on the development of learning capacities in puppies (Nagy & Lucas, private communication) dealt with the problem of long- and short-term memory. It used a procedure suggested by Stanley's observation that puppies could be stimulated to crawl using a cold air blast. In this experiment, puppies were placed in the stem section of a T-maze and stimulated by a stream of cold air (8°C) directed to their hindquarters. On the very first trial, the puppies were allowed to escape the aversive cold stimulus by crawling to either the right or left goal box. The first turn at the choice-point was considered to be the puppy's preferred turn, and on each sub-sequent trial, the puppy could escape cold only by reaching the goal box which was opposite the initial choice. If the puppy entered the incorrect goal box, the air stream was reoriented so as to cause the puppy to turn around and crawl toward the correct goal. Each trial ended when the puppy either touched the wall-end of the correct goal box with its nose or if 120 seconds had elapsed before the puppy had reached the choice-point. Following termination of each trial, the puppy was either placed or allowed to remain in the correct goal box for 15 seconds, after which it was placed in a small box under a heat lamp for an additional 45 seconds. This procedure was followed for 25 trials daily for 3 consecutive days, with different groups of puppies being tested at 7–9, 9–11, and 11–13 days of age. Each group was comprised of at least one litter each of beagles, Telomians, and their F_1 hybrids. The numbers of animals in the respective age groups were 18, 17, and 15.

The results showed that this discrimination task was a difficult one. The puppies frequently balked and refused to move. When the puppies actually went to the choice-point and turned, the discrimination was far from perfect. Apart from the discrimination, the pupies could learn that if they moved they were able to get out of the unpleasant situation sooner. Therefore, data were analyzed in two ways, the percentage of no-turn trials (those on which the puppies failed to reach the choice-point within 120 seconds) on successive trial blocks of five each, and the percentage of correct turns based on the total number of turns made.

The percentage of trials in which the puppies failed to reach the choice-point are shown in Figure 2-1. On each day, it is clear that the percentage of such trials decreases over successive trial blocks. Although this might indi-cate short-term memory, it is also possible that such a decrease might simply be the result of increasing activation resulting from repeated stimulation.

Over successive test days, performance is better on the first trial block than on corresponding blocks for the previous test day, except when Days 7 and 8 are compared (Figure 2-2). Comparison of the first trial block perfor-mance across age groups suggests that the capacity for 24-hour recall develops by 9 days of age, about the same age as has been reported by Nagy (1979) for mice on a similar task. Further, naive animals on their first trials perform no better at later ages than at earlier ones, suggesting that im-

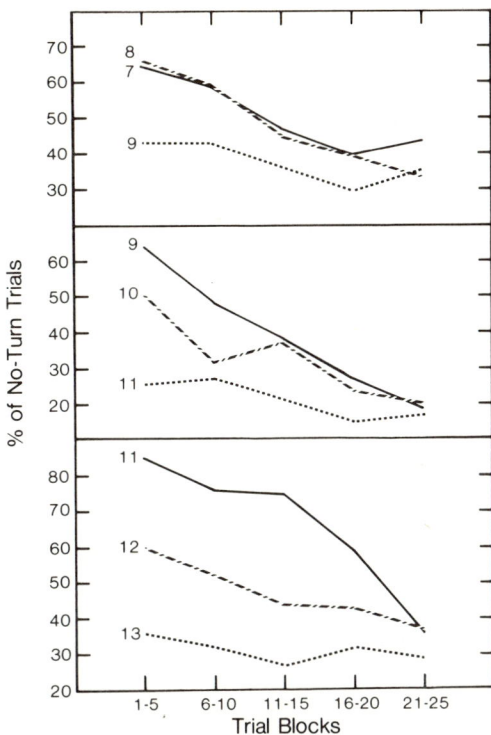

Figure 2-1. Daily performance of puppies in a T-maze, as expressed in percentages of trials in which no choice was made, in three groups of puppies in which training was begun at different ages. Note that improvement was carried over from one day to the next in every case except Days 7 and 8, and that trained puppies were superior to untrained ones on the overlapping days.

provement in performance over days is due to learning rather than to maturation. Indeed, the first trial performance of the 11-day-old group is considerably worse than for groups beginning at 7 and 9 days of age, indicating that factors other than developing learning ability are affecting escape performance with increasing age.

With respect to genetic differences, the Telomians perform better than do either the beagles or F_1 hybrids. This may occur because these animals have the shortest hair and least body fat, or perhaps because they are more agile and begin to walk sooner than do the other two groups of puppies.

With respect to correct choice-point turns, interpretation of these data was difficult in terms of age-related learning abilities. Although most age groups on each test day showed some discrimination learning ability, making around 70% correct choice-point turns, virtually no improvement oc-

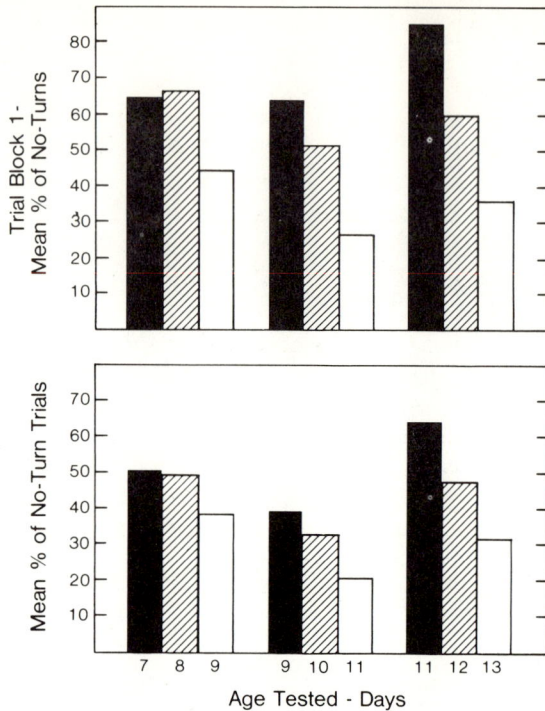

Figure 2-2. Mean performance of puppies in a T-maze, based on same data as Figure 2-1. Upper graph shows Trial Block 1; lower graph shows all trials. Again, performance improves except between Days 7 and 8.

curred over successive trial blocks at any age except on Day 11 for the 11–13-day group. It is clear, however, that this improvement occurred only because this group began so poorly, making only slightly more than 20% correct turns on the first trial block. When considered together with data presented in Figure 2-1, 11-day-old puppies without prior training experience performed very poorly on this task during early trials. Not only did they exhibit the greatest number of trials on which the choice-point was not reached, but they also chose the correct turn least often when a choice had been made. Whereas this performance deficiency might be interpreted as resulting from some age-related factor, such as developing sensory capacities (e.g., gradual opening of the eyes) or changes in the relative aversiveness of the cold air stream or initial response to it, the data also suggest that these factors can be overcome with prior training experience, as evidenced by the performance of the 9–11-day group on its last day of training. On the whole, other than that the capacity to make discriminations appears to be maturing during this age range, relatively little can be said from this experiment about the development of either short-term or long-term memory capacities for this particular task.

In conclusion, the results of this experiment are consistent with the notion that what an animal can learn depends upon the organization of sensory and motor capacities as well as the capacities of the central nervous system at the time of original learning. A neonatal puppy can learn in connection with behavior that is naturally emitted, as Stanley (1970, 1972) has shown. But if this behavior, such as sucking and certain other neonatal reflexes (Fox, 1964), does not persist into later life, or if the puppy is able to learn other responses, such as those in the discrimination task, only with great difficulty, the carry-over of early experience from the neonatal period to later periods of development must be quite limited.

We have only one experiment testing the hypothesis that carry-over from neonatal experience to later life is limited. In many breeds of dogs, tails are normally docked without anesthesia, usually within the first few days of life. In a litter of six cocker spaniel puppies, we followed this procedure on half the animals, leaving the rest as controls. Although the puppies were given a great variety of behavioral and emotional tests (Scott & Fuller, 1965), there were no consistent differences except that the experimental puppies had short tails.

Period of Socialization

During this period, which extends from approximately 3 until 12 weeks of age, the young puppies are behaviorally recognizable as young dogs. The principal organizing process during this period is that of social attachment, which was begun during the transition period. The capacity for making rapid attachments reaches its maximum at approximately 4 weeks of age, continues through 8 weeks, and declines slowly thereafter (Scott, Stewart, & DeGhett, 1974).

Major transformations have already taken place in sensory and motor capacities. During this period further changes take place in the central nervous system. We have pharmacological evidence that a major change in responsiveness to drugs takes place at about 6 weeks of age (Scott, 1978). By 8 weeks the EEG has reached a stage that is essentially the same as in adult animals, indicating that the brain is functionally well developed at this point (Charles & Fuller, 1956; Fox, 1971).

Major changes take place in the relationship of the puppy to its environment. The mother leaves the litter of puppies for longer and longer periods and eventually weans them at approximately 7 weeks of age. She may continue to vomit food for them beyond this period, although this function of providing semisolid and solid food is usually taken over for domesticated dogs by human caretakers. As the teeth develop, the puppy is able to chew solid food more and more successfully, but is so physically awkward that it is unable to hunt. Being able to walk and run, the puppies can now leave the limited environment in which they spent the neonatal and transition periods. In one experiment in which the puppies were allowed unlimited access to the environment, we found that they did not venture more than 20 feet from the nest box area until approximately 12 weeks of age, although the parent animals left to wander more widely (Scott & Fuller, 1965). The puppies themselves remained in visual contact with each other when leaving the nest box. Experiments with separation indicate that the puppies become attached to the site where they live as well as to the other puppies, mother, and any other living beings that may be present, including humans (Scott, 1978).

At approximately 2 months of age, wolf packs move a litter to a spot distant from the original den. This rendezvous site is usually located near a small lake or stream, and the wolf puppies are left to investigate the area as a small pack while the adults go off to hunt in more distant parts. Young animals do not hunt widely until they are at least 4 months of age, which is the time when the second teeth begin to appear.

Nothing of this sort takes place with domestic dogs, but we have found empirically that the age of 8 weeks is the optimum time to remove a puppy from the litter and adopt it into a human family at a different site. As the puppy grows older, it adapts more and more poorly.to primary changes of this sort, and if such a change occurs as late as 6 months of age, the puppy will almost certainly develop the separation syndrome, which consists of exaggerated timidity exhibited toward anything strange.

The latter part of this period of socialization is one that is marked by the development of emotional capacities, particularly fear of the strange, which is first observed at about 7 weeks of age and reaches a peak by 14 weeks. The period from 8 to 12 weeks is also one in which puppies readily learn new tasks, and it is a critical one for adjustment to a new environment. From the viewpoint of practical dog management, this is the age when puppies should be introduced to what will be their future occupation and environment.

In conclusion, the socialization period is marked by gradually lessening dependency upon the mother and other adults, although as highly social animals dogs never become completely independent. The adult behavior patterns emerge in forms that contrast with behavior at the earliest ages. The few neonatal motor patterns disappear rather abruptly. Crawling stops as soon as the pups can walk, and sucking ceases with weaning from the mother, although this neonatal pattern does persist well beyond the transition period. Distress vocalization takes different forms and gradually becomes infrequent. Separation distress does not occur in the neonatal period, but is one of the most prominent features of the socialization period. It declines slowly during the latter part of the period but never entirely disappears, even in adults.

Thus there is discontinuity, both in the behavior patterns and in the nature of the social environment. Since different sorts of behavioral adaptation are demanded in the neonatal stage than are demanded in later periods, the appropriate behavioral patterns should have evolved independently and be modified by different selection pressures. Comparison with other mammals shows that the dog is not unique in this respect.

BEHAVIORAL DEVELOPMENT IN MAMMALS

Marsupials

Excluding the primitive egg-laying mammals, the Class Mammalia is divided into two groups based on mode of reproduction and development. In marsupials, the young are born in a very immature state and spend most of their early lives in a pouch or marsupium. Here they spend most of their time attached to a nipple. By the time they emerge from the pouch, they are developed in most species to a point comparable to newborn placental mammals that are precocious. It is obvious that the marsupial mammals occupy two different habitats during the course of their postnatal development, and that while they are in the pouch they are even more protected than are the most immature of the placental mammals.

Placental Mammals

In the second major group of mammals, the embryos develop a true placenta and hence can be nourished within the uterus for a much longer period than can the marsupials. Development may be precocious, with the young born in a relatively mature state, or nonprecocious like the dog, with the young born in an immature state that demands constant parental protection for weeks, or even months in some cases. A somewhat similar phenomenon exists in birds, except that the precocious birds are not fed by their parents. Here we will discuss only the major orders of the placental mammals.

Rodents.   This is a very successful order in numbers of both individuals and species. In general rodents are small in size. The most successful of them either build nests or dig burrows and have their young born in an immature state similar to that of the dog and consequently exhibit the same phenomenon of behavioral metamorphosis.

Housemice are semiparasitic rodents that usually inhabit human dwellings and hence have no need to dig burrows. They are nest builders and raise their young within these nests. The young emerge at 3–4 weeks, become independent soon thereafter, and are sexually mature at $1\frac{1}{2}$–2 months of age. Compared to dogs, mice show a lower degree of social organization. Adults can live either in a semisolitary fashion or occasionally in very large groups.

In the neonatal period mice are even more immature than dogs, having no hair. They are somewhat more mature in motor development, being able to crawl in a more effective fashion. The transition period involves the first growth of hair as well as major changes in sensory and motor function. Unlike dogs, the ears become functional before the eyes, and also unlike dogs, there is no clear-cut period of socialization. Weaning takes place much earlier, between 3 and 4 weeks of age. Nevertheless, development is similar to that of the dog in that there is an early period in which the social environment is all-important and a later period when it is less so (Williams & Scott, 1953).

Nagy (1979) and his colleagues have done extensive experiments on the development of learning capacities in the mouse, using low levels of electric shock as a motivating stimulus and working primarily with instrumental rather than classical conditioning. Like the dog (Stanley, 1970, 1972), the mouse shows evidence of learning in the neonatal period. Nagy has gone on to study developmental changes in learning capacities and finds striking improvements in 24-hour memory between 8 and 10 days of age. This is the approximate end of the neonatal period as determined by observation, and also coincides with a brain growth spurt (Dobbing, 1968; Epstein & Miller, 1977).

The evidence thus indicates that whereas certain behavioral modifications may occur as rapidly in neonatal mice as in adults, the learned behavior is not retrievable. In addition to the limitations imposed by immature sensory, motor, and patterned capacities, experience in the neonatal period has a qualitatively different effect, limiting carry-over into adult life.

Development in the rat is quite similar to that of the mouse except that, as might be expected with a larger animal, development is somewhat slower. Indeed, morphological, biochemical, electrophysiological (Agrawal & Himwich, 1970; Folch, Casals, Pope, Meath, LeBaron, & Lees, 1959; Kobayashi, Inman, Buno, & Himwich, 1963), and behavioral (Fox, 1965; Nagy, Murphy, & Ray, 1975) evidence suggests that the mouse matures at a somewhat faster rate than does the rat. The development of learning and memory abilities, which also parallels that of the mouse, has recently been summarized (Campbell & Coulter, 1976; Campbell & Spear, 1972).

The guinea pig and related rodents have evolved in the direction of the larger herbivores, and, indeed, some of them are as large as small pigs. In the domestic guinea pig, the young are born in a highly mature state. They begin to take solid food within two days, and the period of nursing is relatively brief. Learning and memory capacities of the newborn guinea pig have been reported to be comparable to the adult (Campbell, Misanin, White, & Lytle, 1974). The cavies do not dig burrows or build nests. The development of other rodents has been summarized by Scott and DeGhett (1972).

Artiodactyla.   These are the even-toed hoofed animals, and many of them are cud chewers or ruminants. In all of them the young are precocious, being able to run and so escape predators within a few hours or days after birth.

In the sheep, young lambs are born in a mature state and begin nursing almost immediately. There is only one transition in function, that from nursing to solid food. Lambs begin to graze within a week or two after birth, but the period of nursing is relatively long, lasting 2 or 3 months. Socialization takes place very soon after birth and is regulated by the behavior of the mother, who will accept only her own lamb.

The development of the pig is different from that of most of the group in that the young are born in litters, the newborn are relatively small, and the mothers build nests for them. In wild swine, the nest is usually built in a cave or some other sheltered spot as pigs do not dig burrows. Newborn pigs are somewhat less mature than lambs, but show evidence of early learning capacities. Mothers soon take their young on foraging expeditions. Unlike the dog, the piglet is acquainted with the outside environment very soon after he is born into the nest. Like the lamb, the chief transition is from sucking to eating solid food, but pigs eat a greater variety of food and do not chew the cud.

Perissodactyla.   This order includes the odd-toed hoofed animals, none of which chew the cud; the domestic horse is an example. Like the lambs, colts are born very mature and begin to run after their mothers within a few hours after birth. There is no specially protected environment in early life, and the chief transition is in the method of nutrition.

Carnivora.   Most of the land-living carnivores are like the dog in that the young are born in a very immature state and are kept in a protected environment in which the mother or other adults take complete care of them. The degree of immaturity varies. This kind of development is adaptive in that it involves a relatively short period in pregnancy when the mother is unable to hunt.

Another large group of carnivores, the seals and walruses, spend most of their adult lives in the ocean. Their feet are reduced to flippers, and they must catch their prey with their teeth. The young are born on land, however, and in a relatively mature state, as in the elephant seal. Development has been little studied, but the land environment is obviously as different from the aquatic environment for seals and walruses as it is for the amphibia who live first in the water and then on land. The young seals have two transitions to make. One is from the land form of locomotion, crawling, to swimming, and the other is from the neonatal form of nutrition to actively catching prey, usually fish. Both transitions are slow and difficult. Elephant seals are weaned a month after birth and grow very rapidly on their mother's milk, but they enter the water very gradually and are unable to catch their own food until they leave the rookery some $2-2\frac{1}{2}$ months later (Reiter, Stinson, & LeBoeuf, 1978).

Cetacea. These are the whales and porpoises, which have inspired a great deal of research because of their high degree of sociality and interesting mode of communication. They are born quite mature in single births, and since they live entirely in the ocean there is no metamorphosis. The only transition is from the neonatal to adult form of feeding.

Primates. Except for man, primates are either arboreal or semiarboreal, and they do not build shelters. The young are born into the habitat that they will occupy as adults, and the only difference is that infants are carried by their mothers. The degree of immaturity varies a great deal.

Primates are born with all senses functional, at least to some extent. Rhesus monkeys are born in a relatively mature state both with respect to motor and psychological capacities. They cling to the mother, just as they will later cling to trees. Thus there is a relatively small degree of metamorphosis and the transition is relatively gradual, as the young rhesus can watch from his mother's arms the environment into which he will enter.

Chimpanzees, which are with the gorilla and orangutan the closest biological relatives of man, spend a great deal of time on the ground. Like human infants, the young chimpanzees are unable to cling to the mother's body by themselves and must be carried in the mother's arms. Compared to the rhesus monkey, they are born in a relatively immature state, but still not as immature as are human infants. Except for the close association with the mother, the chimpanzee infant is born into its adult environment and metamorphosis is relatively slight.

Finally, we can briefly consider human development from the viewpoint of behavioral metamorphosis. Like the great apes, human mothers carry their young, but humans are notorious shelter builders, and they often provide special miniature shelters for their babies. Also, human infants are unusually immature from a motor standpoint and are not even able to crawl for some months. The adult form of locomotion, walking, is not developed until 13 months of age, on the average. This means that the human infant is usually kept in a restricted environment for approximately a year, although it is not as closely restricted as are the neonatal environments of dogs and some rodents. A unique transition in human development is that from the immature form of communication, which has much in common with nonhuman communication in mammals, to the adult form of communication through language (Scott, 1963). This normally occurs at approximately 2 years of age.

Sexual Maturity

Apart from the metamorphosis in behavior that takes place accompanying the transition from the protected neonatal environment to the adult environment, all mammals undergo an internal physiological transformation in connection with sexual maturity. This involves changes in physical appearance and in the function of the sex organs, as well as changes in behavior. While the change is largely internal rather than environmental, it involves the same evolutionary problem: that different times in life are subject to different selection pressures. Particularly in the case of a long-lived animal, this change demands reorganization of behavior that may be deeply rooted in learning. This sort of change, which is not accompanied by an environmental change, may provide a more difficult problem of adjustment than that met with in early behavior.

Summary

From this survey of behavioral development in mammals, it is obvious that two separate but related phenomena are involved: changes in the social (sometimes physical) environment, and transformations in behavioral functions that we have collectively termed behavioral metamorphosis. Some of these phenomena are common to all mammals. As infants, all mammals obtain their nourishment from the mother's milk, and all of them therefore undergo a transition from the infantile form of nutrition to the adult form of ingestive behavior, whatever that may be. This behavioral change is accompanied by anatomical and physiological changes. Teeth appear, and the actual digestive process itself may be modified. Also, all mammals, in common with most of the rest of the animal kingdom, undergo external and internal changes related to the process of sexual reproduction. Following a period of growth, the mammal is transformed physiologically and behaviorally from an animal that is incapable of reproduction to one that can reproduce its own kind.

Most mammals also experience a third early environment within the mother's body (very briefly in marsupials and not at all in the egg-laying mammals). It is during this prenatal period that adaptive behavior first appears. Since the fetus is so well protected, its behavior has almost no function except to promote circulation, to strengthen muscles by exercise, and in other ways to bring about functional differentiation. Nevertheless, behavior that will be functional immediately after birth can be stimulated in the fetus. As in other cases, the sequence of development of behavior provides a safety factor.

Following birth, mammals pass into one of two kinds of social environments. In the animals that are born in an immature state, such as the dog, there is a special neonatal social environment in which the mother gives complete care to the helpless infant. In addition to the general mammalian pattern of nursing, such infants have a variety of other specialized behavior patterns adapted for neonatal existence; they therefore undergo a major transition from the neonatal environment into the adult environment. On the other hand, in those mammalian species in which the young are born precociously, the young animal has contact with the social environment involving adult animals almost from the very first. These species therefore undergo a more drastic environmental change immediately following birth, but undergo relatively little change thereafter.

Whatever the course of mammalian development, it is obvious that it is to some extent discontinuous, and that the changes in both behavior and environment are not always gradual. Some changes, such as those at birth, are quite abrupt. This raises a number of theoretical problems regarding the effects of early experience. Some of the problems are evolutionary, as different environments impose different selection pressures upon the same individual at different times in life. Other problems are experiential; for example, how much is carried over from one kind of environment to the next?

EFFECTS OF EARLY EXPERIENCE

Evolutionary Theory

From the viewpoint of evolutionary theory we would predict that each species, because it evolves independently from all others, provides unique developmental problems and must therefore be studied independently. For example, in the domestic sheep and also in wild species, male lambs are normally reared in a herd with their mothers and other lambs. They have no contact with adult males for several months. If male lambs are artificially reared so that they have contact only with other males, however, they will exhibit as adults sexual preferences for males rather than females. To take another example, in the dog the peak of the primary socialization process occurs at a time in development when the mother begins to leave her pups for long periods. Hence, the puppies have at this time more contact with their littermates than with their mother and become strongly attached to them. This provides a basis for the pack organization of adults, which is essentially a group of peers. Contrastingly, in the human situation, with an individual birth and the peak of the primary socialization process occurring quite early, a baby normally has more contacts with the mother than with anyone else and should develop his primary attachment to her. This correlates with the fact that a feature of human social organization is long continued relationships between older and younger individuals.

Evolutionary theory also predicts that individuals will be selected for their abilities to withstand sudden transitions from one social environment to another. For example, all mammals undergo the shock of emerging from the mother's womb at birth. It would be nonadaptive to maintain a course of development that rendered the newborn organism sensitive to psychological trauma. We would predict that little or no permanent psychological effect should result from the birth experience. This is not to say that infants cannot suffer *physiological* damage at birth under unusual circumstances, but even here the newborn organism should be resistant to a wide range of potentially damaging factors.

Finally, evolutionary theory predicts that where organisms move from one environment into a quite different one during the course of development, there should be independent selection for behaviors that would be adaptive in each situation and that there should be no necessary correlation between such behaviors. This would argue that the effects of early experience in modifying the development of behavior during the neonatal period should be transitory and ephemeral.

This effect need not result from the reorganization of the nervous system, but rather from lost behavioral organization. There is good evidence from nonmammalian species in which drastic reorganization of the nervous system takes place during metamorphosis that the effects of experience in the larval state can be carried over into the adult. If the larvae of certain insects are transferred from the normal food plant to another species, the adults return to lay their eggs on the new plant (Beach & Jaynes, 1954).

More recently, Alloway (1972) found that adult grain beetles performed much better in a T-maze if they had previously been trained in the same maze as larvae. Miller and Berk (1977) obtained similar results with a metamorphosing vertebrate, the clawed frog. While the tadpoles took longer to learn, the information acquired was retained as well across metamorphosis as it was at other times in development.

We are suggesting that in mammals there are at least two reasons why information may not be carried over into adult existence from neonatal life. One is that the learning process is intrinsically much slower and is limited by the poor development of sensory and motor factors; that is, the same amount of experience produces less effect on a neonate than on an older animal. The other factor is that when there is no adaptive relationship between neonatal and later patterns of behavior, there will be no carry-over to the latter. For example, there is little or no evidence from either animal experiments or human observation that the quality of nursing experience of infant mammals has any measurable effect on their behavior as adults (Ross, Fisher, & King, 1957; Sears, Whiting, Nowlis, & Sears, 1953; Scott, Ross, Fisher, & King, 1959).

Organizational Theory

This is based on systems theory. As living systems become organized, they become more and more stable, and the interactions between the component entities become more and more predictable. If behavioral systems become stably organized in the neonatal period, the effects of experience should persist into later periods. On the other hand, if behavior is not stably organized, enduring modification of behavior should result only from later experience. In the neonatal puppy there are no behavior patterns present that are similar to those in adults. Even on the basis of organization through growth and differentiation, the adult behavior patterns are not yet organized. Unless there is a developmental connection between a neonatal pattern and a later adult pattern, there should be no carry-over effects.

A great deal depends on the state of development of learning capacities, as it is through these capacities that the animal organizes its behavior in relation to experience. Most of the experimental work on this point has dealt with the onset of learning capacities. The evidence shows that some form of associative memory appears quite early in development, even in the case of animals that are born in an immature state. The basic capacity for associative learning may be present even before birth. On the other hand, Nagy (1979) has shown that long-term memory is not developed in the neonatal mouse, limiting the retrieval of material learned in this early period.

What is learned, moreover, is limited by behavioral capacities other than learning: patterns of organized behavior and sensory and motor capacities. It is impossible to operantly condition behavior that has not yet appeared, or make associations with events that cannot be perceived. There is also some evidence that the capacity to condition emotional responses does not appear as early as some other capacities (Fuller & Christake, 1959). In short, the development of the ability to be conditioned depends on the behavior that is being conditioned. Early learning is not a general ability and must be studied independently in connection with each behavior. Only in this way can we discover the capacities of an infant organism to become organized through early experience.

Empirical Problems

As we have stated above, the problem of the effects of early experience is a different one in each new species that is studied. Because learning is so important in the postnatal organization of behavior, two basic questions must be answered for every species. The first is: How stable is neonatal learning? This problem is usually attacked in terms of short-term or long-term memory, but we have seen no experiments in which neonatal memories in mammals have been tested in adult life. A second problem, which is particularly pertinent in the human case, is whether early memories can be retrieved. Young infants obviously learn before they can talk, but much of their later memory is organized in terms of language. Most individuals find it impossible to retrieve early prelingual memories. They may be there, but if they are never retrieved, they have no significance. Of course, it is always possible that they could be retrieved through nonverbal cues.

In conclusion, many mammals develop within two distinctly different social environments, an early one in which almost complete care is given by the mother, and a later one in which the young animal must make its own adaptive responses. Being subjected to different forces of selection in these two environments, behavior has evolved independently in the two environments. In the course of transition from one environment to the other, most neonatal patterns of organized behavior disappear completely as the adult patterns begin to appear.

Scott has termed this phenomenon *behavioral metamorphosis*. A major consequence is to limit the amount of learned information that is carried over to later life. Behavior that does not yet exist cannot be instrumentally conditioned, nor can such conditioning be demonstrated on behavior that has disappeared.

The development of changes in the capacity to organize behavior through learning must therefore be carried out in the context of the development of all capacities concerned, as well as the changes in environment. Our best prediction of the outcome of this research, based on conditioning theory and present empirical evidence, is that the lasting effects of neonatal experience in a species that undergoes behavioral metamorphosis should be quite meager, whereas effects of early experience on a precocious mammal might be profound.

ACKNOWLEDGMENTS

We thank the following persons who helped collect the data for the experiment described in this chapter: Dr. Linda A. Lucas, Dr. Alan Schnerson, Kenneth Davis, Mary Ann Nemeth, Arthur Rose, and George Southworth.

REFERENCES

Agrawal, H. E., & Himwich, W. A. 1970. Amino acids, proteins, and monoamines of developing brain. In W. A. Himwich (Ed.), *Developmental neurobiology*. Springfield, Ill.: Thomas.

Alloway, T. M. 1972. Retention of learning through metamorphosis in the grain bettle (*Tenebrio molitor*). *American Zoologist, 12,* 471–477.

Bacon, W. E. 1971. Stimulus control of discriminated behavior in neonatal dogs. *Journal of Comparative and Physiological Psychology, 76,* 424–433.

Beach, F. A., & Jaynes, J. 1954. Effects of early experience upon the behavior of animals. *Psychological Bulletin, 51,* 239–263.

Campbell, B. A., & Coulter, X. 1976. The ontogenesis of learning and memory. In M. R. Rosenzweig & E. L. Bennett (Eds.), *Neural mechanisms of learning and memory*. Cambridge, Mass.: MIT Press.

Campbell, B. A., Misanin, J. R., White, B. C., & Lytle, L. D. 1974. Species differences in ontogeny of memory: Indirect support for neural maturation as a determinant of forgetting. *Journal of Comparative and Physiological Psychology, 87,* 193–202.

Campbell, B. A., & Spear, N. E. 1972. Ontogeny of memory. *Psychological Review, 79,* 215–236.

Charles, M. S., & Fuller, J. L. 1956. Developmental study of the electroencephalogram of the dog. *Electroencephalography and Clinical Neurophysiology Journal, 8,* 645–652.

Cornwell, A. C., & Fuller, J. L. 1960. Conditioned responses in young puppies. *Journal of Comparative and Physiological Psychology, 54,* 13–15.

Dobbing, J. 1968. Vulnerable periods in developing brain. In A. N. Davison & J. Dobbing (Eds.), *Applied neurochemistry*. Philadelphia: Davis.

Epstein, H. T., & Miller, S. A. 1977. The developing brain: A suggestion for making more critical interspecies extrapolation. *Nutrition Reports International, 16,* 363–366.

Folch, J., Casals, J., Pope, A., Meath, J. A., LeBaron, F. N., & Lees, M. 1959. Chemistry of myelin development. In S. R. Korey (Ed.), *The biology of myelin*. New York: Hoeber.

Fox, M. W. 1964. The ontogeny of behavior and neurologic responses in the dog. *Animal Behaviour, 12,* 301–310.

Fox, M. W. 1965. Reflex-ontogeny and behavioural development of the mouse. *Animal Behaviour, 13,* 234–241.

Fox, M. W. 1971. *Integrative development of brain and behavior in the dog*. Chicago: University of Chicago Press.

Fuller, J. L., & Christake, A. 1959. Conditioning of leg flexion and cardio-acceleration in the puppy. *Federation Proceedings, 18,* 98.

Fuller, J. L., Easler, C., & Banks, E. 1950. Formation of conditional avoidance responses in puppies. *American Journal of Physiology, 160,* 462–466.

Klyavina, M. P., Kobakova, E. M., Stelmakh, L. N., & Troshikin, V. A. 1958. On the speed of formation of conditioned reflexes in dogs. *Journal of Higher Nervous Activity, 8,* 929–936.

Kobayashi, T., Inman, O., Buno, W., & Himwich, H. E. 1963. A multidisciplinary study of changes in mouse brain with age. In J. Wortis (Ed.), *Recent advances in biological psychiatry* (Vol. 5). New York: Plenum Press.

Miller, R. R., & Berk, A. M. 1977. Retention over metamorphosis in the African claw-toed frog. *Journal of Experimental Psychology: Animal Behavioral Processes, 3,* 343–356.

Nagy, Z. M. 1979. Development of learning and memory processes in infant mice. In N. E. Spear & B. A. Campbell (Eds.), *Ontogeny of learning and memory.* Hillsdale, N.J.: Lawrence Erlbaum.

Nagy, Z. M., Murphy, J. M., & Ray, D. 1975. Development of behavior arousal and inhibition in the Swiss-Webster mouse. *Bulletin of the Psychonomic Society, 6,* 146–148.

Reiter, J., Stinson, N. L., & LeBoeuf, B. J. 1978. Northern elephant seal development: The transition from weaning to nutritional independence. *Behavioral Ecology and Sociobiology, 3,* 337–367.

Ross, S., Fisher, A. E., & King, D. 1957. Sucking behavior: A review of the literature. *Journal of Genetic Psychology, 91,* 63–81.

Scott, J. P. 1963. The process of primary socialization in canine and human infants. *Child Development Monographs, 28*(1), 1–47.

Scott, J. P. 1978. Critical periods in organizational process. In J. P. Scott (Ed.), *Critical periods.* Stroudsburg, Pa.: Dowden, Hutchinson, & Ross. Pp. 359–367.

Scott, J. P., & DeGhett, V. J. 1972. Development of affect in dogs and rodents. In T. Alloway, L. Kaplan, & P. Pliner (Eds.), *Communication and affect.* New York: Academic Press.

Scott, J. P., & Fuller, J. L. 1965. *Genetics and the social behavior of the dog.* Chicago: University of Chicago Press.

Scott, J. P., & Marston, M. V. 1950. Critical periods affecting normal and maladaptive social behavior in puppies. *Journal of Genetic Psychology, 77,* 25–60.

Scott, J. P., Ross, S., Fisher, A. E., & King, D. J. 1959. The effects of early enforced weaning on sucking behavior in puppies. *Journal of Genetic Psychology, 95,* 261–281.

Scott, J. P., Stewart, J. M., & DeGhett, V. J. 1974. Critical periods in the organization of systems. *Developmental Psychobiology, 7,* 489–513.

Sears, R. R., Whiting, J. W. M., Nowlis, V., & Sears, P. S. 1953. Some childrearing antecedents of aggression and dependency in young children. *Genetic Psychology Monographs, 47,* 135–236.

Stanley, W. C. 1970. Feeding behavior and learning in neonatal dogs. In J. F. Bosma (Ed.), *The second symposium on oral sensation and perception.* Springfield, Ill.: Charles C. Thomas. Pp. 242–290.

Stanley, W. C. 1972. Perspectives in behavior organization and development resulting from studies of feeding behavior in infant dogs. In J. F. Bosma (Ed.), *Third symposium on oral sensation and perception: The mouth of the infant.* Springfield, Ill.: Thomas. Pp. 188–257.

Stanley, W. C., Bacon, W. E., & Fehr, C. 1970. Discriminated instrumental learning in neonatal dogs. *Journal of Comparative and Physiological Psychology, 70,* 335–343.

Williams, E., & Scott, J. P. 1953. The development of social behavior patterns in the mouse in relation to natural periods. *Behaviour, 6,* 35–64.

CHAPTER 3

Effects of Early Experience upon the Behavior of Animals: The Second Twenty-Five Years of Research

NORMAN D. HENDERSON

Twenty-five years ago, Beach and Jaynes (1954) summarized the research available assessing the effects of early experience upon the behavior of animals. Since nearly all of the work reviewed at that time had appeared in the 25-year period prior to 1954, it seems an opportune time for a second quarter-century report on the field. Some indication of the relative success of various research areas may be helpful in providing a long-term perspective of research on the effects of early experience in animals.

The field has not been immune to the exponential growth in research output found in most scientific fields, and a comprehensive review of individual research efforts in the depth originally provided by Beach and Jaynes would now fill several volumes. Even focusing on a more limited number of species, such as laboratory rodents, which represented the largest subgroup of studies reviewed in 1954 (37 papers), the volume of research data is substantial. In Table 3-1 I have listed 13 general research areas involving early experience effects on rodents, along with some recent reviews of the literature in each of these areas. The number of recent comprehensive reviews in these areas is approximately double the total number of original research publications cited by Beach and Jaynes.

Table 3-1, of course, represents only a fraction of the early experience research completed in the past quarter century. An extensive primate litera-

39

EARLY EXPERIENCES AND EARLY BEHAVIOR
Implications for Social Development

TABLE 3-1
Effects of Early Experience on Behavior and Neural Development—Some Active Research Areas

Area	Early treatment/ experience	Typical dependent variables	Some recent literature reviews and critiques
1	Gonadal hormone level manipulation (e.g., administration of androgen, testosterone, progesterone, estrogen; castration)	Adult sexual behavior, maternal behavior, aggression, other social behaviors, food intake	Adler (1974); Beach (1971); Bermat and Davidson (1974); Dorner (1972); Goldfoot (1977); Gorski (1973); Hart (1974); Leshner (1978); Quadagno, Briscoe, and Quadagno (1977); Whalen (1971, 1974); Whitsett and Vandenbergh (1978)
2	Thyroid hormone level manipulation (e.g., administration of triiodothyronine, thyroxine; thyroidectomy)	Spatial and visual discrimination learning, memory, exploratory activity, wheel running, fearfulness, maturation rates, brain catacholamine levels	Balázs, Lewis, and Patel (1975); Eayrs (1971); Kovács (1973); Leshner (1978); Tsujimura, Kariyama, and Hatotani (1973)
3	Adrenocortical hormone level manipulation (e.g., administration of corticosterone and other steroids and growth hormones; adrenalectomy)	Avoidance learning, exploratory activity, wheel running, motor coordination, aggression, water consumption, diet selection, brain DNA levels, adult corticosteroid response to stress	Ader and Grota (1973); Ader (1975); Kovács (1973); Leshner (1978)
4	Modification of synaptic transmitters and modulators (e.g., administration of atropine, chlorpromazine, amphetamines, scopolamine, ACTH, 6-hydroxydopamine, serotonin, MSH, reserpine, taurine)	Spatial and visual discrimination learning, avoidance learning and retention, performance on DRL barpress schedules, locomotor activity, motility; adult norepinephrine, brain amine and dopamine levels	Becker (1970); Gorelick et al. (1975); Murphy and Redmond (1975); Randrup, Munkrad, Fog, and Ayhan (1975)

(Continued)

TABLE 3-1 (Continued)

Area	Early treatment/ experience	Typical dependent variables	Some recent literature reviews and critiques
5	Brain ablations and lesions, ECS	Maze learning, bar press, classical conditioning, spontaneous alternation, maturation rates, aggression, sleep patterns, brain size, DNA levels	Greenough, Fass, and DeBoogd (1976)
6	Malnutrition (e.g., varying litter size, limiting pup access to mother, modifying mother's diet, artificially feeding pups)	Spatial and visual discrimination learning, avoidance learning, bar press, sexual behavior, aggression, growth rate, body and brain size, number of brain cells and synapses in specific brain structures, DNA levels	Crnic (1976); Dobbing and Smart (1973); Leathwood (1978); Plaut (1970); Zamenhof and Van Marthens (1978)
7	Maternal influences (e.g., genotype or previous experiences of mother, modifying olfactory cues of mother, altering degree of tactual or olfactory stimulation of pups)	Body weight, moderating effects on responses to subsequent stressors, dietary and social preferences	Hahn (1979); Joffe (1969); Lehrman and Rosenblatt (1971); Moltz (1971); Russell (1971)
8	Social environment (e.g., varying litter size or sex of littermates, social isolation)	Escape and avoidance learning, position learning, bar press, exploratory and general activity levels, habituation to novel environments, aggression, maternal behavior, adult social preferences, reaction to handling, tail-pinch elicited behaviors	Crnic (1976); Spencer-Booth (1970)
9	Handling, mild to severe stress (e.g.,	Discrimination, escape and avoidance	Ader (1975); Altman, Das, and Sudarshan

(Continued)

TABLE 3-1 (Continued)

Area	Early treatment/ experience	Typical dependent variables	Some recent literature reviews and critiques
	electric shock, temperature change, loud noise, shaking, stroking)	learning, exploratory and alternation behavior, open field behavior, shock-elicited aggression, nest building, plasma corticosterone and norepinephrine levels, adrenal tyrosine levels before and after adult stress, body weight, brown fat layer	(1970); Daly (1973); Denenberg and Zarrow (1971); Hofer (1974); Russell (1971)
10	Exposure to novel tastes or olfactory stimuli; pairing novel odors or tastes with an aversive US	Later preferences for (or aversion to) food or odors involved in previous exposure	Davenport (1976); Galef and Sherry (1973); Hill (1978); Rozin (1976); Rudy and Cheatle (1977)
11	Deprivation or enhancement of visual stimuli (e.g., dark rearing, pattern-free environments, exposure to specific visual stimuli, general visual enrichment)	Visual discrimination learning and information processing, selective attention to visual stimuli, response of single neurons to visual stimuli, retinal cell development; brain ACTH, choline acetyltransferase, tyrosine hydroxylase and serotonin levels	Blakemore (1973); Grobstein and Chow (1976); Hershenson (1971); Hirsch and Jacobson (1975); Mistretta and Bradley (1978); Pettigrew (1978); Tees (1976)
12	Deprivation or enhancement of nonvisual stimuli (e.g., early olfactory bulbectomy, elimination or presentation of specific odors such as male urine, masking of patterned sounds with white noise, exposure to specific sound patterns, plugging ears, removal of vibrissa)	Adult sexual behavior, auditory discrimination, unit activity in superior colliculus during auditory stimulation, changes in somato-sensory cortex	Alberts (1976); Mistretta and Bradley (1978); Rogers and Beauchamp (1976)

(Continued)

TABLE 3-1 (Continued)

Area	Early treatment/ experience	Typical dependent variables	Some recent literature reviews and critiques
13	General environmental complexity or enrichment (e.g., exposure to novel objects, rearing in large cages containing objects to enhance sensory–motor experience)	Visual and spatial discrimination learning, avoidance and escape learning, lever press, locomotor and climbing behavior, food location, fearfulness, body and brain weight, neural development, DNA synthesis, drinking behavior, complex problem solving, reversal learning	Gluck and Harlow (1971); Greenough et al. (1976); Goldman and Lewis (1978); Meyers (1971); Rosenzweig and Bennett (1977, 1978); Walsh and Cummins (1975)

ture exists for nearly all areas shown in Table 3-1, and a considerable amount of research on imprinting, species identification, and cultural transmission (such as song learning typically carried out in birds) is not represented in the table.

It should be noted that in some areas of early experience research listed in the table, rodents are not the species of choice for current research. In the past 5 years, for example, for every study reported involving specific visual deprivation or enrichment effects in rodents, more than four studies have appeared using the laboratory kitten. Similarly, dogs (e.g., Scott, 1977) and sheep (Cairns, 1977) both appear to possess several advantages over rodents for the study of attachment and other social behaviors.

In their 1954 review, Beach and Jaynes attributed motivation for much of the research to one of four sources: (1) examining the relative importance of "maturation" and "practice" on the development of response patterns; (2) tests of Freudian theory; (3) laboratory extensions of ethological observations on the effects of early social stimulation on later behavior in birds; and (4) an examination of the importance of early perceptual learning, stimulated by the ideas of Hebb (1949). A fifth impetus for investigations of early stimulation effects occurred immediately prior to the publication of the Beach and Jaynes review. Weininger's (1953) report of greater weight gain, less fearful behavior, and greater resistance to the stress of total food and water deprivation on rats that had been handled for 10 days following weaning versus control rats triggered considerable interest in the influence of early stimulation on later emotional behavior and thyroid function. Interestingly, Weininger's study had been preceded by 20 years by a far more substantial work in this area (Hammet, 1921), which apparently led to no further research at that time.

Although considerable work was being done in 1954 on the role of hormones on adult behavior, research did not focus on early hormonal influences until Phoenix, Goy, Gerall, and Young (1959) demonstrated that female guinea pigs born of mothers that had been injected with testosterone propionate during pregnancy had masculinized genitalia, whereas males showed no morphological aberrations, and that the early hormone treatment altered the intensity of later sexual behavior in females. Again, one can find in earlier history relevant research on the sexual differentiation of behavior due to early hormonal conditions (e.g., Dantchakoff, 1938; Wilson, Hamilton, & Young, 1941) that failed to trigger the intense research interest generated by a later study.

Some research on the effects of early malnutrition on later behavior had been reviewed by Beach and Jaynes, but the work dealt largely with hoarding behavior and was frequently regarded as an animal model for infant feeding frustration and its relationship to psychoanalytic theory (Hilgard, 1952). The emphasis on feeding frustration as a dependent variable declined steadily, and by the 1960s, research was primarily motivated by an increasing interest in possible cognitive and motivational deficits created by early undernutrition (e.g., Crnic, 1976). Area 4 of Table 3-1—the study of the effects of early administration of drugs that modify neural action—has emerged only recently as an area of early experience research.

Obviously, nearly any categorization scheme is somewhat arbitrary, and that shown in Table 3-1 is no exception. Distinctions between the areas are sometimes blurred, and much of the research on early experience involving multiple independent variables could be placed in more than one of the areas listed. In some cases these factorial designs that cut across categories shown in Table 3-1 consist of some of the most interesting and relevant contemporary research on early experience effects. Examples include the current attempts to determine if enriched environments can overcome deficits created by brain lesions, thyroid manipulations, or infant undernutrition. A survey of much of this work can be found in Walsh and Greenough (1976) and in Goldman and Lewis (1978). The second example of research where a clear rationale exists for choosing independent variables from different domains for simultaneous study involves the current attempts to examine the mediating effects of maternal influences on experimenter handling or stress administered to preweaned animals (e.g., Barnett & Walker, 1974; Bell & Little, 1978). Unfortunately, many factorial designs using manipulations from different areas listed in Table 3-1 are carried out with far less rationale than is at least implicit in these examples. Other investigations overlap two or more areas simply because of the inherent confounding of the experimental manipulation involved. Studies purportedly measuring effects of early undernutrition, infant handling, maternal influences, or early social environments (Areas 6 through 9) often involve nearly identical experimental manipulations, making it difficult to determine the actual causal factors in any subsequent behavioral changes that might be observed.

Some of the literature reviews listed in Table 3-1 did not focus solely on early or infantile experience. In several areas, particularly the first five, research on young animals often represents an extension of active research on mature animals. In some areas listed, such as 13, "early" experiences often begin after weaning whereas in other areas, such as 7 through 9, most studies end early treatments around the time of weaning. In all areas, older animal control groups or parallel experiments with older animals are necessary to separate early experience effects from simple prior experience effects. Surprisingly, a large fraction of the studies in Areas 6 through 13 do not allow a distinction between early and prior experience effects.

RELATIVE PROGRESS IN DIFFERENT AREAS OF EARLY EXPERIENCE RESEARCH

If one "reviews the reviews" of research done in the different areas shown in Table 3-1, it becomes evident that progress in understanding early experience effects differs considerably across areas. Despite its relatively late appearance, for example, the research on the role of gonadal hormones in the development and differentiation of gender differences in sexual behavior, aggression, and, to a lesser degree, avoidance learning has progressed rapidly to the point that both the relationships between early treatment and later behavior and the mechanisms underlying these relationships are rapidly becoming clear (e.g., Whitsett & Vandenbergh, 1978). Research in other areas, however, such as the study of early stress on later behavior, has shown little progress relative to the considerable volume of literature generated during the past 25 years (e.g., Russell, 1971). One can obtain some insight into the reasons for such great differential success by reviewing briefly the typical strategies used in a few of the research areas which have differing histories of success in providing an understanding of early treatment effects on later behavior and of the mechanisms involved. I believe a few principles emerge which suggest a prescription for success in the study of early experience effects in animals. We shall move rather quickly through some of the areas which appear healthy, as a number of comprehensive reviews of this work are available, and devote more space to areas where progress has been disappointing relative to the effort expended.

Areas of Rapid Progress: Early Visual Stimulation and
Gonadal Hormone Manipulation

The study of visual deprivation or enhancement and their effects on later
visual discrimination/information processing and on peripheral and central
nervous system development, brain chemistry, and the response of single
neurons to stimuli has advanced at a rapid pace from the time of the original
experiments on visual enrichment cited by Beach and Jaynes. The work on
rodents, beginning with Lashley and Russell's (1934) study of behavior of
dark-reared rats on the jumping platform, suggested that visually directed
responses of this species were not affected to any great degree by visual
deprivation, whereas at least temporary effects seemed to occur in rabbits,
primates, and birds. Early experience research on the visual system of the
kitten, which is responsible for much of the development of this area, did not
begin in earnest until the late 1950s, when Riesen and Aarons (1959) reared
kittens in the dark for 6 weeks and then measured visual placing response,
depth discrimination, and pupillary reflexes. Many behavioral studies followed, paralleled by the classic experiments of Hubel and Wiesel (1959,
1962, 1963) that helped map the receptive fields and functional architecture
of the visual cortex of the adult cat and of young kittens deprived of visual
experience. The continued work on developmental factors influencing behavior and the formation of feature-extracting neurons in the cat is largely
responsible for recent advances in this area.

More recent research on visual deprivation or enrichment with the rat has
centered on transfer effects of specific early visual stimulation on later visual
discrimination learning (e.g., Ernst, Yee, & Dericco, 1976), effects of dark
rearing on elective attentional and visual information processing mechanisms (e.g., Creighton & Tees, 1975), and attempts to extend some of the
work on early visual experience in kittens to rats (e.g., Corrigan & Carpenter,
1979). The modest success of this and earlier research on visual stimulation
in the rat clearly suggests that such work with this species should be
continued largely for phyletic comparisons and not as an animal model for
early experience research on vision.

I have already referred to the considerable progress of research relating
early gonadal hormone treatments to the understanding of sexual differentiation, its influence on the neuroendocrine system, and subsequent sexual,
maternal, and aggressive behaviors. Several interesting parallels exist between this gonadal hormone research and research involving visual stimulation effects. First, in both fields investigators were aware of major species
differences in amenability to specific experimental manipulations and
allowed these differences to work to their advantage rather than to their
detriment. In spite of its initial use, the rat proved to be a less than ideal

subject for visual enrichment studies. Substantial progress in this field coincided with increased research using the cat and, for certain problems where a closer approximation to the human eye is necessary, primates. Similarly, although the original research was done on guinea pigs, they were not the ideal species for further research involving early gonadal hormone treatments. Because of their relatively long gestation period, sexual differentiation occurs during the prenatal period, making experimental manipulation prior to differentiation difficult. Furthermore, variations in the adult hormonal state of male guinea pigs rarely result in heterotypical sexual responses. For these reasons, the rat turned out to be a better subject for early experience research involving gonadal hormones.

A second parallel between gonadal hormone and visual enrichment research can be found in the considerable body of supporting literature on both behavioral effects and mediating mechanisms involved in various treatments in adult animals. In both research areas the extension to the developing organism opened many new horizons, but investigators had a considerable number of reference points based on data from mature animals from which to interpret results. The visual enrichment research could profit not only from the available understanding of the functional architecture of the visual cortex of the cat (e.g., Campbell, 1973; Blakemore, 1973), but also from an extensive cat psychophysics (Berkeley, 1976) and a growing body of literature on sensory-motor cortex activity associated with visual stimuli in a number of species (e.g., Evarts, 1973). Similarly, a large body of research on hormonal factors in brain function and on neural and hormonal determinants of sexual and mating behaviors of rats (e.g., Goy & Goldfoot, 1973; Pfaff, Diakow, Zigmond, & Kow, 1973; Leshner, 1978) was available to investigators examining the subsequent effects of these hormones when administered early in life. In both fields, one can usually find a clear, logical rationale for the early manipulation used and the subsequent dependent variables to be observed. Furthermore, the stimulus could be defined rather precisely, and the dependent variables usually had inherent construct validity. As we proceed to other research areas, where both treatments and dependent variables are more globally defined and the functional relationship between them is less clear, we find that research progress has been considerably slower.

Areas of Steady but Modest Progress: Thyroid and Adrenocortical Hormone Manipulation and Environmental Enrichment

Research on the effects of different levels of early thyroid and adrenocortical hormones appears to have progressed somewhat more slowly than has research involving early gonadal hormone manipulations. This is hardly surprising since the role of these hormones in specific behavior patterns is not as well understood as is the role of sex hormones on specific sex-related behaviors. Hormones of the pituitary–adrenocortical axis have, for example, been implicated in aggressive behavior, but the effects are not usually as pronounced, nor are they as consistent across species or test conditions as are the effects of gonadal hormones (e.g., Leshner, 1978). Although considerable support exists for Selye's (1956) General Adaptation Syndrome, implicating the pituitary-adrenal hormones in the response to a wide variety of stressors, the relationship of this response to fear-mediated behaviors such as activity and open-field behavior (e.g., Ader, 1975; DiGiusto, Cairncross, & King, 1971) and to measures of avoidance learning and conditioning (e.g., Nyakas, 1973; Van-Toller & Tarpy, 1974; Leshner, 1978) is not clear.

Difficulties concerning the interpretation of avoidance learning and emotional behaviors have posed a problem for several areas of early experience research. Effects of differing early levels of thyroid and adrenocortical hormones on subsequent body growth and in both neural and biochemical maturation of the brain are reasonably well established (e.g., Kovács, 1973), but it frequently becomes difficult to determine whether subsequent behavioral effects of changes in levels of these hormones are not simply due to delayed maturation effects or to reduced body size. Considering the relatively short history of research in Areas 2, 3, and 4 of Table 3-1, it appears that these efforts have been at least moderately successful in beginning to provide an understanding of the effects of alterations in early levels of these hormones and neurotransmitters. On the other hand, the studies attempting to measure constructs such as "emotionality," and "adaptive responses to stress" have in general not been as successful as have been studies using measures closely related to natural behavior patterns that could be more directly related to the early treatments.

Studies of enrichment or environmental complexity and its effects on later problem-solving behavior and neural development would be typical of an area where progress in understanding early experience effects might best be described as moderate, considering the effort expended.

Certainly the long-term and systematic studies of experiential influences on brain that have been carried out for the past 20 years at the University of California at Berkeley (e.g., Rosenzweig & Bennett, 1977, 1978) have produced a considerable amount of consistent data on enrichment effects upon gross brain anatomy, measures of cell density and size, dendritic spine counts, number of synapses, AChE activities, RNA and DNA content, and RNA diversity. Numerous other investigators have continued to extend this research in a number of directions, including an examination of enrichment effects on latency of evoked responses in occipital cortex (e.g., Mailloux,

Edwards, Barry, Rowsell, & Achorn, 1974), enriched versus control group differences in biogenic amine levels in brain (e.g., Riege & Morimoto, 1970), and dendritic branching patterns (e.g., Fiala, 1976; Greenough, 1976). Furthermore, it is now generally acknowledged that most of these effects are not due to experience unique to early life. Most gross anatomical differences and RNA/DNA differences in enriched and social-control animals appear to be age-independent, although microscopic anatomical effects such as dendritic branching may depend on early stimulation (e.g., Greenough, Snow, & Fiala, 1976).

Although the effects of generalized enrichment on brain structure and chemistry appear highly reliable, the mechanisms that mediate production of these cerebral effects have not yet been specified clearly. Part of the difficulty stems from the fact that the enriched rearing conditions allow a variety of unspecified experiences that can have many sensory, motor, cognitive, and emotional effects. Walsh and Cummins (1975) have suggested that cerebral effects may not be totally due to learning or memory changes, but at least in part to a combination of activation of sensory systems and nonspecific activation, or arousal. The basis for this suggestion comes from observations that animals in enriched environments show increased exploration and social interaction when objects in enriched cages are changed, and from evidence that short exposures to environmental complexity have their maximal effect during the nocturnal phase or when the animals are given methamphetamine. Walsh and Cummins (1975) outlined a sequence of cellular events providing a general model for neural response to stimulation mediated by arousal and suggested several tests of their arousal hypothesis.

At present their hypothesis remains viable although a recent experiment (Ferchmin, Bennett, & Rosenzweig, 1975) suggests that arousal may not play a major role since animals reared in an "observer" condition, in which they received a high degree of visual, auditory, and olfactory stimulation in addition to frequent changing from cage to cage, were not measurably different from controls on a number of brain measures, yet were different from rats reared in enriched cages. Additional evidence suggesting that arousal may play only a minor role in the enrichment effect comes from Henderson (1976b). Mice were reared in standard laboratory cages that were either empty or contained enrichment objects. Each day all mice were moved to new cages, some containing identical enrichment objects and some containing new enrichment objects. Animals exposed to different objects each day subsequently performed better on a food-location task than did animals exposed to new versions of the same objects each day or animals moved to new empty cages daily. Arousal may play some role in experiential influences on brain, but at present the role appears to be a modest one. Similarly, training in motor agility alone does not produce cerebral effects similar to those resulting from nonspecific enriched environments (Ferchmin & Eterović, 1977). Recent evidence is thus gradually strengthening the argument that cerebral changes resulting from enrichment are most likely consequences of learning and memory storage.

Studies of enrichment effects on subsequent behavior have been considerably less consistent than have those involving brain measures. Stimulated primarily by Hebb's (1949) neuropsychological theory emphasizing the importance of early sensory experience in the formation of "cell assemblies," a considerable number of studies were carried out attempting to measure the effects of early nonspecific enrichment on subsequent problem-solving behavior. Many of the original rat studies measured problem solving using a modification of the Hebb-Williams closed-field test devised by Rabinovitch and Rosevold (1951). Early results, indicating the superiority of pet-reared and enriched-reared rats in these mazes, have been rather consistently supported in subsequent research. Davenport (1976) found 16 experiments carried out through 1973 that showed enriched animals making fewer errors in this maze than animals reared in either isolated or social control conditions, and only three experiments that reported no treatment differences in Hebb-Williams performance. In one of these latter studies (Woods, Fiske, & Ruckelshaus, 1961), groups were tested under unusually high drive conditions, and in a second (Reid, Gill & Porter, 1968), pretraining and testing conditions differed considerably from those normally used. Results using the Hebb-Williams maze therefore appear to be quite consistent across studies that exposed animals to enrichment over a range of postweaning ages.

Despite the consistency in results, there have been several criticisms that this experimental paradigm is inappropriate for measuring the effects of environmental enrichment on later problem solving. An early criticism was that the measure confounded motivational or exploratory tendencies with learning and memory factors (e.g., Lore & Levowitz, 1966; Woods, Ruckelshause, & Bowling, 1960). The bulk of the current evidence, however, suggests that enrichment effects found in maze performance cannot be attributed to any great degree of differences in exploratory behavior (Davenport, 1976). Gluck and Harlow (1971) suggested that the paradigm of rearing rodents in large cages with enrichment and climbing objects and then testing them in an apparatus such as a Hebb-Williams maze is not appropriate for determining if nonspecific enriched perceptual experience improves overall learning capacity, since similarities of the treatment and subsequent test conditions provide many opportunities for specific transfer effects. Finally, the use of the Hebb-Williams maze as a measure of problem solving has also been questioned. Performance does not appear to improve with age on the test, nor do species differences corresponding with the phyletic scale emerge (Warren, 1965). Thus, despite their consistency, results using the Hebb-Williams maze do not provide unequivocal evidence supporting the hypothesized relationship between early enrichment and later problem-solving capabilities.

The picture becomes further complicated by inconsistent results found with other learning measures. Some nonsignificant effects should be expected if, as Hebb suggested, enriched perceptual experience has a greater impact on complex problem solving than it does on a simple discrimination learning and conditioning. The likelihood of obtaining differences between enriched and standard caged animals has not, however, been highly correlated with the simplicity or complexity of the task used. Apart from the Hebb-Williams maze, enrichment effects seem to be most consistently found on maze learning, especially the Lashley III maze, with somewhat less success on multiple T-mazes and Y-mazes (Davenport, 1976). Visual discrimination tasks only occasionally show positive effects of prior enrichment, and these are somewhat more frequent when visual reversal discrimination is involved. Finally, whereas some positive results have been reported in bar-press and active and passive avoidance situations, the results of most experiments using these measures have been negative. Again, however, slightly better success appears to occur when the measures involve reversal learning as opposed to initial acquisition, or when the measure involves transfer of training from another task (e.g., Davenport, 1976; Henderson, 1972).

It appears then that, quite apart from results using mazes that may allow at least some specific transfer from the enrichment condition, evidence is growing that small positive effects resulting from early enrichment do occur, particularly where the tasks involve reversal learning or transfer of training—two measures that do show orderly improvement over a segment of the phyletic scale. The current body of results also suggests that appetitive tasks may be more likely to produce positive results than do aversive test situations.

A dilemma seems to be emerging in this research area. Many of the enrichment effects found in primates and in dogs originally attributed to cognitive factors have since been re-evaluated, with the conclusion that many of the differences between experimental and control animals could be attributed to heightened emotionality of isolate-reared animals or to deficits in social, emotional, or exploratory activity (e.g., Fuller, 1967; Griffin & Harlow, 1966; Sackett, 1967). Similarly, Walsh and Cummins (1975) have suggested that at least some alteration in arousal occurs in rodents reared in different environmental conditions. To avoid the confounding effects of emergence stress or differences in initial levels of general emotionality or arousal, or, on some occasions, differences in simple levels of motor skill (e.g., Henderson, 1977a), some period of habituation or adaptation to the adult test situation seems necessary. Furthermore, many complex appetitive tasks require extensive pretraining, and many measures require an extended number of test sessions, as in the case of reversal learning or the presentation of a number of different test problems. Under such circumstances investigators will often risk a "wash-out" effect in that, in addition to these procedures equating emotional and other noncognitive factors during habituation or testing, learning and memory differences between enriched and control animals may also be attenuated.

Much of the current research suggests that rather short exposures can produce enrichment effects equal to those that result from constant rearing in enriched conditions. Rosenzweig and his colleagues have, for example, shown exposure to enrichment for only 2 hours a day is adequate for producing standard enrichment effects (Rosenzweig & Bennett, 1978). Henderson (1977b) demonstrated that with the C57BL/10J mouse, only 3 hours of enrichment resulted in measurably improved performance on a complex food-seeking task, and that a total of 12 hours produced effects similar to those of enriched rearing that occurred for the first 60 days of life. Furthermore, a number of short exposures to novel stimulation or enrichment can be considerably more effective in altering subsequent behavior than an equivalent amount of time in a single exposure (Walsh & Cummins, 1975; Henderson, 1976). It thus appears that in the test situations most appropriate for studying enrichment effects, nonenriched control groups will be given the opportunity to gain rapidly many of the experiential advantages accrued by long-term enrichment, thus greatly attenuating experimental–control differences.

Areas of Slow Progress: Malnutrition and Infant Handling and Stress

The study of behavioral consequences of early malnutrition in laboratory rodents has thus far been considerably less successful than have the early experience research areas already discussed. Unlike the situation found in the studies of environmental enrichment, where the majority of studies showed some small positive effects and the others failed to show significant effects, the research on early malnutrition has reported variously that it impairs later learning, has a facilitating effect, or, in most cases, has no significant effects on learning (e.g., Leathwood, 1978). A similar situation exists with respect to the effects of malnutrition on spontaneous locomotor activity and "emotional" behavior. Early research in this field, which attempted to relate early malnutrition to subsequent hoarding behavior as an animal model of infant feeding frustration, also had consistency problems. Attempted replications of the original research showed the effect to be rather fragile (e.g., Hunt, Schlosberg, Solomon, & Stellar, 1947; Marx, 1950, 1952). In reviewing this work Beach and Jaynes (1954) suggested that "in view of the lack of clear cut confirmation by subsequent experimenters, final judgment probably should be reserved." Not long after the 1954 review, the study of early malnutrition metamorphized from one using animal models to test psychoanalytic hypotheses to one using animal models to assess the effects of early protein–calorie undernutrition on cognitive development. Because of the complex number of interrelated variables involved in the "poverty syndrome," uncontrolled field studies of human malnutrition were difficult to interpret; thus, studies on laboratory animal models appeared attractive (e.g., Cravioto, 1968). The apparent simplicity of doing laboratory studies proved to be an illusion.

The animal research has not been particularly successful thus far for two reasons. Paradoxically, the first difficulty for behavioral studies is related to the pronounced morphological, neurological, and delayed maturational effects produced by severe undernutrition. Under such circumstances it becomes difficult to determine if a particular behavioral difference between normal and malnourished animals may not simply be reflecting differences in body weight or a lag in development (e.g., Leathwood, 1978). Similarly, as Altman, Sudarshan, Das, McCormich, and Barnes (1971) have pointed out, malnourished animals are usually passive and weak, and this may be a major contributor to any deficits in their performance.

The second problem found with studies of early malnutrition is evident from an examination of Table 3-1. Experimental manipulations used to produce early malnutrition are often identical with those used in Areas 7, 8, and 9, dealing with maternal influences, early social environment, and effects of handling and stress on subsequent behavior. As a result, most of the typical methods used to vary early nutritional level are likely to be systematically confounded with social, maternal, or handling effects. Since each of these variables has been demonstrated to influence many of the behaviors studied in malnutrition experiments (Crnic, 1976), observed behavioral differences can rarely be attributed specifically to undernutrition. Furthermore, the frequent absence of behavioral differences may be partly due to compensatory effects of increased peer socialization, differences in maternal treatment, or possible beneficial effects of handling. More recent research has attempted to overcome some of these problems of confounding. For example, during separation of the mother and pups to restrict nursing, the mother has occasionally been replaced by a virgin female "aunt" or a nipple-ligated mother able to display most maternal behaviors to maintain nest temperature (e.g., Koos-Slob, Snow, & De Natris-Mathot, 1973;

Schenck, Koos-Slob, & Van Der Werff Ten Bosch, 1978). It appears experimentally possible to eliminate a number of the potentially confounding variables involved in nutritional studies, and now that the importance of including controls for such variables has been repeatedly documented (e.g., Crnic, 1976; Levine & Weiner, 1976; Leathwood, 1978), research in this area should improve substantially.

Obviously, the considerable overlap in experimental manipulations involved in Areas 6–9 inevitably poses problems of confounding for each of these areas. Differing social influences of various litter sizes, for example, are likely to be confounded with both nutritional and maternal care differences. It is hardly surprising therefore that an understanding of the role of maternal influences on later behavior or of the role of early social environment on later behavior has not progressed at a rapid pace. Emphasis on research in these areas, however, has been rather recent and not very extensive. Considerably more discouraging, because of the huge volume of research available relative to the paucity of clear conclusions, has been the effort to determine the behavioral and physiological effects of early handling and stress in rodents.

Although usually grouped together, studies of early handling and studies of more intense infantile stimulation differ, both in the motivation for the original research and in the consistency of findings. Effects of "gentling," or "taming," laboratory rats prior to exposure to test situations was already well known in laboratory lore by the early 1920s. This was in part due to work at the Wistar Institute, which maintained an "experimental colony" of petted and gentled animals, along with their standard stock. In 1921 Hammet described some of the differences in these colonies.

> The behavior of the rats in this latter, i.e., standard group is that of the ordinary laboratory animal. They are timid, apprehensive and high-strung. When picked up they are tense and resistant, frequently exhibiting their natural defensive instincts of fear and rage by biting. *The picture as a whole is one of constant high irritability and neuro-muscular tension.* It is of course not impossible that the high grade of emotional tension ever present in the rats that have not been gentled contributes to the general picture of high tension through mediation of the adrenals.
>
> The behavior of the gentled group is in marked contrast to that of the others. In these animals the defensive instincts have been repressed by the constant handling and petting. This gentling has been carried out for the last five generations. When the animals are picked up they are relaxed and yielding. They are not easily frightened. They give a uniform picture of placidity. The threshold of the neuro-muscular reactions to potentially disturbing stimuli is almost prohibitively high [Hammet, 1921, pp 199–200].

Hammet performed complete thyroidectomies on 90 rats from the standard stock and 96 rats from the gentled stock and found mortality rates of 79 and 13% respectively in these groups after 48 hours. Additional large groups from the two stocks were parathyroidectomized with highly similar results—76 versus 13% mortality within 48 hours. Hammet also took 28 weanlings from the gentled stock and an equal number from the standard stock and reared them under identical nonhandled conditions until 55 days of age. Thyreo-parathyroidectomy on these two groups also resulted in a considerable difference between mortality rates—78 versus 14%—suggesting that the offspring of handled mothers are more resistant to adult stress than are control animals. In another experiment using a split-litter design, half of each of several litters from both the standard colony and the gentled colony were exposed to either postweaning gentling or standard cage rearing. It was found that postweaning gentling produced similar effects in both colony groups.

In addition to the series of experiments, Hammet studied the records of sex, body weight, length, and diet to determine if the factors played any significant role in the results. In essence, Hammet had already carried out in 1920 and 1921 a series of experiments and casual observations that were to be repeated endlessly in varying forms beginning 35 years later. The stimulus for the beginning of this later research would come in part from Hammet's study and other work at the Wistar Institute that was described in its publication *Breeding and Care of the Albino Rat for Research Purposes* (Greenman & Duhring, 1923), and in part from the work of Selye (1950). The quality and scope of Hammet's original research was rarely matched, however. Weininger's (1953) study, which began the flood of rodent handling studies, was based on a total of only seven male rats, in contrast to several hundred used by Hammet; laboratory rearing and experimental controls were considerably less stringent in this later work. Unfortunately, much of the research to follow continued in the Weininger rather than the Hammet tradition. This was in part possible because of the robustness of the handling effects first described by Hammet—the general decrease in fearfulness of laboratory rats placed in a novel test situation and their increased resistance to physiological stress. The striking number of publications involving handling or gentling that have appeared during the past 25 years has demonstrated rather consistently that these effects do indeed occur in rats. Beyond this repeated demonstration, however, few additional consistent and reliable findings have emerged, and the search for mediating mechanisms for the handling effect continues with only modest success.

Interestingly, the data on handling in mice do not provide any evidence that the treatment reduces subsequent emotional arousal or alters adult animals' resistance to stress (e.g., Daly, 1973). It is important to note that this species difference could exist for two reasons. *Rattus* and *mus* may actually differ in their response to the same treatment, but it is also quite possible that the experimental manipulation is in fact a different treatment when carried out in the two species. Size differences alone will often lead to different handling of rat and mouse pups during the first 10 days of life, and the considerable differences in levels of motor activity shown by 12- to 21-day-old rats versus mice usually leads to major differences in how experimenters handle these two species at these ages. One does not read of studies where mice are picked up gently by the body and stroked from head to the base of the tail, nor does one read of studies of rats picked up by the tail using forceps prior to the handling. The term *handling* became reified as a unitary experimental treatment, yet both specific operations and mediating mechanisms can differ considerably as a function of species or age. Capacity for temperature regulation and sensory modalities available for developing organisms changes so rapidly during the first 3 weeks of life that the daily "handling" sessions to which growing animals are exposed may be qualitatively different treatments in terms of the sensory and regulatory systems involved. Under such circumstances it is hardly surprising that many studies involving daily preweaning handling have been unable to elucidate mechanisms creating the effects (e.g., Russell, 1971).

Unlike studies of juvenile handling or gentling, which were based on general questions involving adaptation to novel stimuli and stress, research effects of early noxious stimulation or "infantile trauma" were largely stimulated by a desire to test psychoanalytic theory. In what was the first well-known paper in this area, Hall and Whiteman (1951) regarded their study of infantile auditory stimulation in mice as a direct test of the effect of early trauma on the development of personality. They likened their research to that of Hunt (1941), which involved infant feeding frustration and hoarding behavior, in that both provided animal models to test psychoanalytic theories in a manner that allowed appropriate control groups. The results of a study based on an arbitrarily chosen laboratory species were considered to have general applicability across the phyletic scale—that is, "the specific proposition tested by our experiment is this: subjecting the infant organism to intense stimulation will result in emotional instability in later life [Hall & Whiteman, 1951, p. 61]." Small but significant differences were observed in the frequency of defecation and urination between undisturbed mice and mice exposed to a loud bell for 2 minutes on the fourth through seventh day of life.

The next year Griffiths and Stringer (1952) subjected different groups of rats daily to electric shock, temperature extremes, intense auditory stimulation, or rapid rotation prior to weaning. No differences were found between any of these groups and an undisturbed control group on maze learning, discrimination on a Lashley jumping stand, open field urination/defecation, or susceptibility to audiogenic seizures. Thus began what has been a continuing history of contradictory results concerning effects of intense infantile stimulation on later behavior. These two studies, of course, differed with respect to many particulars, including the species used, the age ranges involved in early stimulation, and the adult testing procedures. Obvious as these factors may now seem, these differences were not regarded as major factors that might have contributed to discrepancies in the results of these studies. Griffiths and Stringer (1952) and Beach and Jaynes (1954) failed to mention any of these as possible reasons for the discrepancies in the results obtained. This was not surprising, given the global nature of the hypothesis: "Trauma to infant organisms alters their later behavior." The specific nature of the trauma, organism, or behavior seemed irrelevant. What is surprising is that many investigators continued to generate broad, all-encompassing statements concerning early experience effects that largely ignored the specifics of the treatment, the organism, and the behavioral measures used.

In retrospect, it may have been unfortunate that research on handling and research on more intense early stimulation did not remain more or less independent. Inevitably, however, investigators began to think of a continuum of stress levels, ranging from isolation through handling, to noxious stimulation and trauma. In one of the earliest of these studies, Scott (1955) assumed that the continuum from gentling to ignoring could be extended by adding the experience of repeated electric shock. In addition to adding further inconsistencies to the relatively small body of literature at the time, Scott's study began the dubious procedure of ranking a series of qualitatively different treatments on a continuum generally called "intensity of stimulation" that has continued to the present. Implicit in this approach is the assumption of a unidimensionality of a "stimulus input" or "stimulus intensity" dimension.

Much effort was later expended attempting to determine whether the relationship between the amount of preweaning stimulation and subsequent emotional behavior was positive, negative, or U-shaped. Thus, for example, Denenberg (1964) put forth the hypothesis that a monotonic relationship would be obtained between amount of stimulus input in infancy and emotional reactivity, in a review remarkable both for its omission of data failing to support the hypothesis and for the fact that none of the studies cited as supporting evidence had manipulated the amount of stimulus input on a unitary dimension. Not surprisingly, contradictory data continued to accrue. At a symposium on emotional behavior, Goldman (1969), in reviewing her own work and other studies of the period, concluded that many of the data were contradictory to the monotonicity hypothesis and that a curvilinear relationship seemed more plausible. At the same symposium Henderson (1969) pointed out that if one does rank different treatments on an intensity-of-stimulation dimension, a second dimension involving the spacing of such stimulation is also necessary for adequate description of treatment effects. Furthermore, the presence of strong genotype by treatment interactions in this research suggested that one cannot generalize across strains within a species, no less across species. At that time some of the beginning research on mediating factors involved in early experience effects looked promising, and it was hoped that continued work in this direction would lead to the demise of dial-twirling experiments of the form "What happens to behavior X in organism Y when I vary Z in early life?" (Henderson, 1969).

Predictions of improvement in the field were unduly optimistic. In a review 2 years later, Russell (1971) cited the often repeated call for attempts to specify the nature of the independent variables in infant treatment studies but concluded that, despite its quantity, the data did not allow one to draw any strong conclusions as to the mediation of treatment effects. Two years later Daly (1973) took exception to the use of an anthropocentric point of view in this research that continued to lead to unfounded statements about the adaptive value of various behavior changes resulting from early stimulation, and the assumption that nonhandled preweanling animals are "deprived of normal stimulation." From an ethological standpoint many of the interpretations and hypotheses in the early experience literature involving such terms as *beneficial, emotionality, adaptiveness,* and *stressful* were rather meaningless.

Two years later Ader (1975), in reviewing the data concerned with the effects of early life experiences on adrenocortical function, concluded that, "while handling characteristically reduces 'emotionality' . . . there is no logical or empirical justification for the assumption that differences in emotional reactivity are mediated by differences in adrenocortical reactivity [p. 26]." The data suggested that the reduction in adrenocortical reactivity of stimulated versus unstimulated animals was independent of the magnitude of the stimulation to which the animals were subsequently exposed. In general, Ader found little support for the hypothesis (Levine, 1970; Denenberg & Zarrow, 1971) that the neonatal rat responds to stimulation by releasing corticosterones from the adrenal cortex that modify neural development in such a way as to reduce emotional and adrenocortical reactivity in response to later stimulation.

Despite a steady stream of research for 20 years, reliable descriptions of the effects of different types or levels of early stimulation were not yet available, nor had there been much success in describing the mediating mechanism for the handling effects, the one reliable phenomenon in the field. In reviewing the effects of generalized enrichment on later learning (Area 13), the majority of studies suggested superior performance of enriched over control animals, and the remaining studies found no differences. In studies of early malnutrition (Area 6), different laboratories occasionally report opposite effects of malnutrition, a more serious problem than the occasional failure to find a treatment effect. A review of research involving early handling or stress, however, reveals that not only do different laboratories produce contradictory results, but that within laboratories, investigators repeating the same methodology will produce direct contradictions to their earlier findings and often report them without comment. This is clearly an area befitting Tolstoy's (1902) comment about science: "a haphazard heap of information, united by nothing."

What is it about much of the research in this area which has led to such slow progress? A detailed examination of a recent example in this field might be instructive on this point. Denenberg, Garbanati, Sherman, Yutzey, and Kaplan (1978) carried out a factorial design in which half a sample of Wistar rats received daily handling prior to weaning and the other half remained undisturbed. At weaning the groups were again subdivided, with half the handled and nonhandled animals housed in enriched environments and the remainder in standard laboratory cages. All rats were placed singly in standard cages at 70 days of age, and at approximately 135 days, four males within a litter were assigned to one of four surgical procedures: left- or right-hemisphere neocortical ablation, sham operations, or no surgery. At 165 days of age animals were tested for 3 minutes in an open field for 4 consecutive days. Among rats not handled prior to weaning, those with brain ablations showed higher activity than did control animals, with no noticeable differences between left- and right-hemisphere groups, Among handled rats, however, right-hemisphere ablated animals showed higher activity levels than did controls if all had been housed in standard laboratory cages after weaning, but they showed lower activity levels than did nonablated animals if all had been housed in enriched environments for 30 days after weaning. Although the significance of the interaction between handling, enrichment, and later surgery was not reported, planned contrasts focusing on right-brain ablated versus control + sham groups were significant at the $p < .05$ level. The authors concluded that "the results show lateralization of the behavioral function in lower mammals and confirm the hypothesis that the effects of early experiences are asymmetrically distributed in the brain. The right brain is a repository for the interactive effect of handling and environmental enrichment, at least as far as open field activity is concerned [Denenberg et al., 1978, p. 1151]." Further, "to our knowledge, our study represents the first report of a major organismic asymmetry in which psychological functions appear to be unequally represented between the two hemispheres within a population of laboratory rodents [p. 1151]," and "these data suggest that lateralization for spatial and affective processes may be phylogenetically older than lateralization for cognitive processes and may also be more developmentally plastic [p. 1151]."

The format of this study is in the general tradition of many contemporary early experience/later emotionality studies in that the handling variable is studied in conjunction with other manipulations shown in Table 3-1. We shall briefly review the study from three perspectives: (1) the rationale for choice of independent variables; (2) the nature of the dependent variable; and (3) the reliability of the evidence of a relationship between these variables.

Is there some theoretical reason to expect an interactive effect of pre-weaning handling and postweaning enrichment on behavior, or higher order interactions between these variables and later brain ablations? The authors review some of the human research reporting differential hemispheric processing of emotional and nonemotional material, indicate that stimulation during infancy modifies a number of adult behavioral and biological variables including emotionality and exploratory behavior, and cite one study which suggested the existence of asymmetry in individual rat brains but found no overall left or right preferential bias in the population. This leads them to the hypothesis that the effects of early experiences are asymmetrically distributed between the two hemispheres and that their experiment will test this hypothesis. The enrichment condition is included because "this treatment reduces emotionality and decreases activity [p. 1150]," a point of some contention (e.g., Davenport, 1976). No predictions are made as to how or why these variables are expected to interact in their influence on the behavior to be measured.

What is being measured by the dependent variable—open-field activity summed over 4 days of testing? The authors state that since all three lines of evidence they cite in their introduction "focus on affective and spatial behaviors, we choose to use the open field activity test, which measures both emotional and exploratory behavior [p. 1150]." Reviews of the extensive literature on open-field behavior, however, have been rather consistent in concluding that locomotor activity in this apparatus has little validity as a measure of either emotionality or exploratory behavior (e.g., Henderson, 1970; Archer, 1973; Daly, 1973; Walsh & Cummins, 1976), although it may be related to a general factor of motor discharge (Royce, 1977). Although considerable discussion has been made of this point, of particular relevance is Denenberg's own history of thinking about this measure. Through the mid-1960s low activity scores in an open field were regarded as an index of heightened emotionality in rats and mice (e.g., Denenberg, 1964). Then, based on his factor analysis of open-field behaviors of an experimentally created set of individual differences in rats (Whimbey & Denenberg, 1966, 1967) and his study of open-field behavior and adrenal steroid levels (Levine, Haltmeyer, Karas, & Denenberg, 1967), Denenberg (1969) concluded that "the interpretation that one gives to activity data when discussing emotional reactivity changes completely from Day 1 to Day 2. On Day 1 high activity indicates high emotionality, while activity after that is indicative of low emotionality [pp. 855–856]."[1] Notwithstanding the difficulty this view posed for some of his earlier interpretations of open-field data, Denenberg began to interpret subsequent data in this manner. Inexplicably, in the 1978 study under review, activity scores were summed across all days of testing, with no mention of differential day-to-day changes. One is thus left to ponder what behavioral construct has been assessed if high scores have opposite meanings on different days of the summed score.

Some clues might have been available if defecation frequencies had been reported, since, despite its modest reliability, the measure appears to have at least a rough monotonic relationship to emotionality or fearfulness in rats and tends to be relatively consistent across sessions or minor variations in the test situation (e.g., Denenberg, 1969; Henderson, 1970; Daly, 1973). These data were not reported, despite their unavoidable, natural availability after each open-field test.

Two questions arise when evaluating the reported relationships between variables—are they reliable and are they interpretable. Aside from an overall surgery effect in which rats with right- or left-hemisphere ablations were somewhat more active than control animals ($p < .05$), the only significant effect reported in this study involved a third-order interaction in which handled animals with right-brain ablations were either more or less active than nonablated animals, depending on postweaning enrichment, whereas no such relationships were found among nonhandled animals. Apart from the perplexing nature of this higher order interaction, its marginal significance level does little to instill confidence in the reliability of the effect, particularly when, in a four-factor design, 14 F ratios are computed to test main effects and interactions and when additional F ratios are computed

[1] Both the reliability of results and the interpretations drawn from them have been questioned for each of the two lines of evidence. The relationship between emotionality and adrenocortical reactivity reported by Levine et al. (1967) has not been observed in other studies (e.g., Ader, 1968; Ader & Plaut, 1968; Hess, Denenberg, Zarrow, & Pfeifer, 1969). In addition, Ader (1975) has questioned whether even the Levine et al. (1967) data provide strong evidence for such a relationship, since differences in corticosterone levels between handled and nonhandled animals decreased with repeated testing while differences in activity levels increased with repeated testing. Henderson (1970) failed to find a major distinction between the first day of open-field testing and testing over 9 additional test days with respect to activity levels. Low positive defecation–ambulation correlations were found on Test Days 1, 5, 7, and 10 and moderate negative correlations found on other days. The data did not support an interpretation that high activity signifies high emotionality on the first test day and low emotionality thereafter. Aitken (1974) reanalyzed the data of Whimbey and Denenberg and concluded that the two factors labeled emotional reactivity and field exploration were essentially test factors. Furthermore, the factorial structure of the data argued against an interpretation of orthogonal dimensions, as originally proposed, but instead suggested a single bipolar factor.

for specific contrasts. It is further troubling that, despite the fact that open-field ambulation has generally been found to have moderate to high heritability (e.g., Broadhurst, 1960), and that this, along with maternal effects and common environmental influences, should combine to produce considerably greater variance between litters than within litters, the reverse occurred in the present study. One is thus left to wonder whether the marginally significant higher order interaction reported represents a reliable but complex relationship between independent variables, or a spurious event—a recurring question in much of the literature in this field. If the results are reliable, one is left with the task of trying to determine exactly what is the combined effect of the three independent variables on spatial and affective processes in Purdue–Wistar rats and what might be the mediating mechanisms for the effect. The points are not discussed by the authors.

Attention was focused on the above study because it is an example of recent research that illustrates three characteristics common to much earlier work in this area. First, several independent variables are chosen to be studied simultaneously in a "let's see what happens if . . ." design. The rationale for the choice of variables tends to be weak or nonexistent, as is information concerning the possible mediating mechanisms involved. Second, dependent variables are frequently used as operational definitions of broad, often anthropocentric, concepts despite little evidence of their construct validity.[2] Third, the evidence for significant early treatment effects is often based largely on unpredicted and unexplained, marginally significant higher order interactions made questionable by their capitalization on chance effects and by "peripheral" experimental outcomes that are incompatible with a body of earlier research. The first two characteristics have been discussed in a number of reviews cited in Table 3-1 and need little further comment. The problem of spurious effects resulting from a combination of inflated F ratios and capitalization on chance is sufficiently serious that it deserves some attention.

Studies involving early handling or stress often involve two or three treatment factors in addition to sex, age, and a repeated measurement, or days, factor. Factorial designs involving from four to six factors are thus not uncommon in this research. A standard ANOVA of a five-factor crossed design can involve the testing of five main effects, 27 interactions, and many contrasts. In most early experience studies, investigators report treatment

---

[2] In addition to open-field activity, the use of avoidance learning performance as an index of emotionality has been widely questioned. Because the relationship between performance and emotionality can be positive, negative, or U-shaped, depending on several factors including task difficulty, shock level, and motor responses required for escape or avoidance, post hoc interpretations of performance in terms of emotionality are not easily made.

effects on several dependent variables, and often one gets the impression that additional variables may have been examined that have gone unreported. About 30 different dependent variables have at one time or another been measured as indices of emotionality in an open field (Walsh & Cummins, 1976), and about 6 of these measures tend to be frequently used simultaneously because of the ease of collecting these data in a standard test situation. Similarly, several measures of activity during habituation as well as escape and avoidance performance are recorded typically in avoidance learning test situations. It is not unusual therefore for investigators potentially to have a large number of dependent variables at their disposal for evaluating early treatment effects, although the effects on only a few variables may ultimately be reported in detail. In a study involving a factorial design with four or more independent variables that examines effects on four or five dependent variables, well over 100 F ratios may be computed.

The problem of spuriously obtaining significant effects is compounded considerably by the fact that, because of experimental limitations, split-litter designs are not often used in infantile stimulation research, but until the late 1960s, most investigators inappropriately analyzed their data using standard crossed ANOVA designs, despite the fact that different litters were nested within each of the experimental treatments. Instead of using between-litter variance as the error term for testing treatment effects (Winer, 1971), an error term averaging within- and between-litter variance was often used. This procedure poses particularly serious problems when scores on the dependent variables are reliable but not monotonically related to Darwinian fitness for the species involved, since additive genetic variation (and consequently the relative magnitude of between- to within-litter variance) is likely to be large in these cases. This is a problem for many variables, such as open-field activity, that are used in early experience research. Open-field ambulation, for example, tends to show considerably higher heritabilities (additive genetic variance) than do mating, nesting, and consumatory behaviors in rodent populations (Broadhurst, 1979).

The improper analysis of nested factors in hierarchical research designs results in F ratios that tend to be inflated in varying degrees depending on the heritability of the behavior in the test population, average litter size, and the number of different litters used in each treatment condition. Assuming even a modest heritability for open-field activity (e.g., .3) and the use of three litters of eight animals each in each treatment condition, F ratios improperly computed will be nearly double those obtained with an appropriate analysis. The inflation of F ratios has differential effects on significance levels, depending on the degrees of freedom (df) associated with the numerator MS. Doubling the F ratio of a main effect test when there are only two treatment levels can change a significance level from $p < .25$ to $p < .10$, whereas the significance of an F ratio involving 8 df in the numerator will change from a $p < .25$ to $p < .01$ with such doubling. In the typical misanalyzed open-field experiment, therefore, various treatment and interaction effects reported significant at the $p < .05$ level may actually represent significance levels in the $.15 < p < .35$ range, depending on the df involved.

It is not difficult to realize that if many significant results reported at the $p < .05$ level are actually closer to the $p < .20$ level and that a large number of F ratios are being computed in each study, investigators will rapidly generate a considerable number of "significant" results entirely due to chance. It is not surprising, therefore, that one can devise nearly any hypothesis concerning early treatment effects and then find a number of experimental results that seem to support the hypothesis.[3] Unfortunately, the field has been left with a legacy of many unreliable results reported in the 1950s and 1960s. The situation has steadily improved with respect to appropriate data analyses, although some investigators persist in ignoring between-litter effects in their analysis (e.g., Wiener & Levine, 1978; Weinberg & Levine, 1977; Weinberg, Krahn, & Levine, 1978).

The described relationship between heritability and degrees of freedom and inflated significance levels leads to two specific predictions with respect to spurious results. First, studying behaviors showing high heritability should result in more spurious significance levels than measuring behaviors showing low heritability. Second, F tests involving several degrees of freedom in the numerator should produce more spurious significant results than tests of effects with few numerator df. In rats and mice, open-field activity measures show higher heritability than open-field defecation measures (e.g., Broadhurst, 1979), and higher order interactions tend to involve more numerator df than do main effects. One would predict then that, in the absence of any actual treatment effects, (1) a larger proportion of significant results would be obtained for open-field activity measures than for defecation measures, and (2) a large proportion of these significant effects should involve higher order interactions. The early experience literature is consonant with both predictions.[4]

---

[3] The volume and diversity of significant findings reported in the literature pose another distinct problem. A contemporary investigator obtaining a spurious result is likely to find at least one prior report describing similar results, leading to the illusion that a particular experimental relationship has been replicated and thus demonstrated to be reliable.

[4] If many "significant" results reported were actually closer to the $p < .20$ level, the question arises whether the proportion of "significant" treatment effects reported prior to 1970 was in fact greater than chance, when well-known sex and age differences and the handling effect are excluded.

SOME LESSONS FROM THE SECOND TWENTY-FIVE YEARS: CHARACTERISTICS ASSOCIATED WITH SLOW PROGRESS

The preceding review has focused somewhat more on difficulties that have impeded success in understanding early experience effects than it has on summarizing progress in each of the areas of research. As a consequence, considerably more space was devoted to areas of research showing relatively little progress than to areas where rapid strides have been made. All areas listed in Table 3-1 are represented by some poorly conceived experiments and inappropriate interpretations of data, and ingenious, well-executed studies exist in even the weakest research areas. Clearly, however, the rate of progress differs considerably in different fields of early experience research. Are there certain basic differences in either the formulation of research questions or research strategies that systematically correspond to differential rates of progress in these fields?

It is difficult to argue that research areas showing relatively less progress are those where the work itself is technically more difficult. The problems may appear more complex in some of these areas, but this may indicate that inappropriate questions are being asked or that inappropriate strategies are being adopted to answer questions. There appear to be five overlapping characteristics that are associated with a failure to clarify the role of some early treatments on subsequent behavioral and neural processes.

The Assumption of a Biologically Neutral Organism

Although most obvious in early research testing psychodynamic hypotheses in randomly chosen rodents, a tendency to overlook inter- and intra-species genetic variation in sensory–motor systems and response patterns (and the relationship of these differences to differences in ecological niche and selection pressures) has been considerably greater in fields showing slow progress. Associated with this is often a failure to appreciate that there is not only little reason to expect two species (or animals in different stages of development) to react in exactly the same way to a similar treatment or test situation, but also that entirely different mediating mechanisms may be involved. Different outcomes of the same treatment in different species or animals of different ages cannot be regarded as evidence of an inconsistency in effect, and a similar effect of early treatment cannot in itself be regarded as evidence of a similar mediating mechanism.

Often overlooked is the fact that often considerable within-species genetic variation exists with respect to reactivity to early stimulation. In some areas of research interactions between genotype and early treatments are sufficiently large as to make any general statements based on a limited genetic sampling questionable (e.g., Erlenmeyer-Kimmling, 1972). In addition, a failure to take into account genetic influences contributing to large between-family differences has resulted in the reporting of a considerable number of experimental findings of dubious reliability. In contrast, recognition of inherent species or strain differences related to experimental manipulations of interest has been used to considerable advantage in some more successful areas. Equally as important as the direct effects of inadequate attention to biological variation are its indirect effects on each of the following characteristics of less than successful research.

The Complex Manipulation of Independent Variables Likely to Act through Several Mediating Mechanisms

The ability to assess early treatment effects seems in part to be related to specificity of the treatment itself. In research where a sensory–motor system, neural structure, or site of action can be clearly implicated by the treatment, progress has been considerably faster than in cases where early treatments involve global, nonspecific stimulation. It is easy to see how, in the latter case, a failure to appreciate biological variability can lead to serious difficulty.

A global treatment administered to organisms of different genetic backgrounds or in different stages of development may be acting in a variety of different ways. In a "handling" study, for example, at any specific preweaning age, the relative influence of different sensory stimuli, effects on thermal regulation, opportunities for conditioning, subsequent maternal treatment, and peer interactions can differ from those occurring at any other preweaning age. The problems of understanding the mechanisms involved in a global treatment administered throughout early development become almost insurmountable when one does not understand the role of each of the systems acting alone at any single age in development, much less the interaction of all systems across all ages. Because some global treatments "work," however, they are incorporated into endless variations of studies whose major impact may be no more than to generate more such studies. Nonanalytic experiments using global treatments does have a place in research. If, for example, one is interested in the effects of enrichment, undernutrition, stress, or other manipulations administered early in life, one may wish to determine if any overall effects are produced as a result of gross manipulation involving several confounded variables before beginning a series of experiments designed to isolate specific mediating mechanisms. One can, however, occasionally carry out a gross manipulation in which effects of two mediating variables produce opposite and cancelling influences on the dependent variable of interest.

The Use of Factorially Complex Dependent Variables of Limited Validity as Measures of Constructs of Interest

Too often dependent variables are chosen because they are convenient to measure or because they have been used in earlier research, even though they may possess little validity as an index of a construct of interest. Frequently an investigator is interested in the effects of specific early treatments on a later general behavior pattern or class of behaviors such as learning or problem solving, emotional responsiveness, maternal behavior, sexual behavior, etc. Most such constructs can be operationally defined and measured in a number of ways, and frequently these differing measures of the same construct are only moderately correlated with each other. This poses few problems when a battery of such measures are used, especially if the behaviors are sequential elements of a complex behavior pattern. McGill (1970), for example, devised a series of 14 measures of male sexual behavior that can be observed in a mating situation. Genetic, experiential, hormonal, and environmental cue factors influence these different measures in somewhat different ways, yet by observing a series of these behaviors, in each of many studies, the effects of different manipulations on this multidimensional behavior are gradually being understood.

In contrast, many complex behavioral constructs are often measured under exceedingly narrow testing conditions. Even if several measures are recorded in an open field, a shuttlebox, or maze, for example, the measures are still related to a single environmental situation. Furthermore, many such measures are factorially complex in that they reflect a number of different underlying behaviors. Locomotor behavior in an open field may reflect in various proportions fearfulness, general activity, exploratory behavior, or novelty seeking, territory marking, "displacement," and escape behavior. Although some of these behaviors may be related to each other as a higher level construct (e.g., Royce, 1977), the use of such a measure in isolation provides little clue as to what is being measured. Unfortunately, when multiple dependent variables are used, there is often an either–or aspect to the final data interpretations. Even if a significant effect is found on only one of several measures all purportedly measuring the same construct, the results are often interpreted as a demonstration of the significant treatment effect on the behavioral construct. More appropriately, such results should be regarded as a failure to support a hypothesis predicting an early treatment effect on a general behavior pattern.

The Formulation of Experiments with Limited
Theoretical or Empirical Foundations

Characteristic of research areas showing modest progress relative to effort expended is a tendency for a large proportion of experimental results reported to be of the dial-twirling variety. An almost random choice of nonspecific early treatments is combined, occasionally with still other manipulations, and their effects are examined on a series of dependent variables having little logical connection with the experimental manipulations. Such experiments often provide little in the way of an animal model for a general experimental paradigm, and they frequently make no ethological sense for the species studied. There is no reason to expect that there will be an absence of significant effects in such experiments, especially when a large number of mechanisms may be involved. Significant findings in such experiments often generate a substantial "spur" line of research of dubious value. Denenberg, Hudgens, and Zarrow (1964), for example, in an experiment of questionable ethological relevance, demonstrated that mouse pups reared by rat mothers differ from normally reared mice. This is not too surprising since the early treatment probably produced major changes in most receptor inputs resulting from substantial differences in maternal behavior, peer socialization, nest temperature, odor, diet, and other factors, whose influence probably changed regularly throughout the preweaning period. In such a situation the number of possible relevant variables and the number of possible interactions between these variables and between age is so substantial that an entire subarea of research can emerge involved with analyzing the mediating mechanisms involved in the "rat foster mother" effect on mice. Inevitably, follow-up research in this area began to appear with the original authors themselves producing at least eight additional papers on the effect through 1973. From a broad perspective, one must question whether such an enterprise, no matter how competently carried out, is an effective means of understanding the relationship between specific experiences early in life and subsequent behavior, especially when the critical combination of variables in these "rat aunt" experiments may be of no ethological relevance to either species involved.

The Overinterpretation of Results

A final characteristic of research areas that have been less than successful relates to the tendency for many experimental findings to be interpreted well beyond the limits of the strength of effects observed, and the variables and organism involved. This of course is a direct consequence of the four problems discussed above. The use of vague terms or constructs such as *beneficial* or *adaptability* give investigators considerable license to interpret specific research outcomes in a manner consonant with broad predictions involving such constructs. Such constructs often merge out of an anthropocentric research orientation and have little validity for the specific organisms or test situations involved (Daly, 1973). In addition, there often seems to be little distinction between significant experimental outcomes that, based on the treatments and measures involved, are logical, interpretable, and consistent with other data, and "surprise" experimental outcomes that possess none of these characteristics. In the absence of an unambiguous replication within the study, and evidence of consistency across other non-contingent dependent variables supposedly measuring the same constructs, "surprise" experimental results, no matter how significant, should best be regarded as a suspicious anomaly, to be replicated before use as supporting evidence or building blocks in a theoretical structure.

CONCLUSION

It should hardly be surprising that characteristics of relative success and failure in early experience research are not very different from those in all behavioral research, and that these characteristics are well known to most persons familiar with animal research. Why then do some fields continue to generate large volumes of research data of limited value in understanding important behavioral problems in their field? Perhaps this has resulted from a focus on technical aspects of research at the expense of concern about the nature or relevance of the issues addressed. In an attempt to avoid addressing "trivial" issues, investigators may have too often raised broad questions that, upon subsequent examination, proved to be totally inappropriate, largely because they diverted focus from more ethologically relevant and specific interrelationships between an early experience and its later effect in their subjects.

REFERENCES

Ader, R. 1968. Effects of early experiences on emotional and physiological reactivity in the rat. *Journal of Comparative and Physiological Psychology, 66,* 264–268.

Ader, R. 1975. Early experience and hormones: Emotional behavior and adrenocortical function. In B. E. Eleftheriou & R. I. Sprott (Eds.), *Hormonal correlates of behavior—I.* New York: Plenum Press. Pp. 7–33.

Ader, R., & Grota, L. J. 1973. Adrenocortical mediation of the effects of early life experiences. In E. Zimmerman, W. H. Gispen, B. H. Marks, & D. De Weid (Eds.), *Drug effects on neoendocrine regulation.* New York: Elsevier.

Ader, R., & Plaut, S. M. 1968. Effects of prenatal maternal handling and differential housing on offspring emotionality, plasma corticosterone levels and susceptibility to gastric erosions. *Psychosomatic Medicine, 30,* 277–286.

Adler, N. T. 1974. The behavioral control of reproductive physiology. In W. Montagna & W. A. Sadler (Eds.), *Reproductive behavior.* New York: Plenum Press. Pp. 259–286.

Aitken, P. P. 1974. Early experience, emotionality, and exploration in the rat: A critique of Whimbey and Denenberg's hypothesis. *Developmental Psychobiology, 7,* 129–134.

Alberts, J. R. 1976. Olfactory contributions to behavioral development in rodents. In R. L. Doty (Ed.), *Mammalian olfaction, reproductive processes, and behavior.* New York: Academic Press. Pp. 67–94.

Altman, J., Das, G. D., & Sudarshan, K. 1970. The influence of nutrition on neural and behavioral development: I. Critical review of some data on the growth of the body and the brain following dietary deprivation during gestation and lactation. *Developmental Psychobiology, 3,* 281–301.

Altman, J., Sudarshan, K. L., Das, G. D., McCormich, N., & Barnes, D. 1971. The influence of nutrition on neural and behavioral development. III—Development of some motor, particularly locomotor patterns during infancy. *Developmental Psychobiology, 4,* 97–114.

Archer, J. 1973. Tests for emotionality in rats and mice: A review. *Animal Behaviour, 21,* 205–235.

Balázs, R., Lewis, P. D., & Patel, A. J. 1975. Effects of metabolic factors on brain development. In M. A. B. Brazier (Ed.), *Growth and development of the brain.* New York: Raven Press. Pp. 83–115.

Barnett, S. A., & Walker, K. Z. 1974. Early stimulation, parental behavior, and the temperature of infant mice. *Developmental Psychobiology, 7,* 563–577.

Beach, F. A. 1971. Hormonal factors controlling the differentiation, development, and display of copulatory behavior in the hamster and related species. In E. Tobach, L. R. Aronson, & E. Shaw (Eds.), *The biopsychology of development.* New York: Academic Press. Pp. 249–296.

Beach, F. A., & Jaynes, J. A. 1954. Effects of early experience upon the behavior of animals. *Psychological Bulletin, 51,* 239–263.

Becker, B. A. 1970. Exogenous drug influences on the developing nervous system: Teratology and perinatal toxicology. In W. A. Himwich (Ed.), *Developmental neurobiology.* Springfield, Ill.: Charles C Thomas. Pp. 613–651.

Bell, R. W., & Little, J. 1978. Effects of differential early experience upon parental behavior in *mus musculus. Developmental Psychobiology, 11,* 199–203.

Berkley, M. A. 1976. Cat visual psychophysics: Neural correlates and comparisons with man. In J. M. Sprague & A. N. Epstein (Eds.), *Progress in psychobiology and physiological psychology.* New York: Academic Press. Pp. 63–114.

Bermant, G., & Davidson, J. M. 1974. *Biological basis of sexual behavior.* New York: Harper & Row.

Blakemore, C. 1973. Developmental factors in the formation of feature extracting neurons. In F. O. Schmitt & F. G. Worden (Eds.), *The neurosciences: Third study program.* Cambridge, Mass.: MIT Press. Pp. 105–114.

Broadhurst, P. L. 1960. Applications of biometrical genetics to the inheritance of behavior. In H. J. Eysenck (Ed.), *Experiments in personality.* New York: Humanities Press. Pp. 3–43.

Broadhurst, P. L. 1979. The experimental approach to behavioral evolution. In J. R. Royce (Ed.), *Theoretical advances in behavior genetics.* Alphen aan den Rign: Sijthoff & Noordhoff.

Cairns, R. B. 1977. Beyond social attachment: The dynamics of interactional development. In T. Alloway, P. Pliner, & L. Krames (Eds.), *Attachment behavior.* New York: Plenum Press. Pp. 1–24.

Campbell, F. W. 1973. The transmission of spatial information through the visual system. In F. O. Schmitt & F. G. Worden (Eds.), *The neurosciences: Third study program.* Cambridge, Mass.: MIT Press.

Corrigan, J. G., & Carpenter, D. L. 1979. Early selective visual experience and pattern discrimination in hooded rats. *Developmental Psychobiology, 12,* 67–72.

Cravioto, J. 1968. Nutritional deficiencies and mental performance in childhood. In D. C. Glass (Ed.), *Environmental influences: Biology and behavior.* New York: Rockefeller University Press and Russell Sage Foundation.

Creighton, T. D., & Tees, R. C. 1975. The effects of early visual deprivation on attentional processes in the rat. *Bulletin of the Psychonomic Society, 5,* 504–506.

Crnic, L. S. 1976. Effects of infantile undernutrition on adult learning in rats: Methodological and design problems. *Psychological Bulletin, 83,* 715–728.

Daly, M. 1973. Early stimulation of rodents: A critical review of present interpretations. *British Journal of Psychology, 64,* 435–460.

Dantchakoff, V. 1938. Role des hormones dans la manifestation des instincts sexuel. *Comptes Rendus Hebdomadaires des Séances de l'Académie des Sciences, 206,* 945–947.

Davenport, J. W. 1976. Environmental therapy in hypothyroid and other disadvantaged animal populations. In R. N. Walsh & W. T. Greenough (Eds.), *Environments as therapy for brain dysfunction.* New York: Plenum Press.

Denenberg, V. H. 1964. Critical periods, stimulus input, and emotional reactivity: A theory of infantile stimulation. *Psychological Review, 71,* 335–351.

Denenberg, V. H. 1969. Open-field behavior in the rat: What does it mean? *Annals of the New York Academy of Sciences, 159,* 852–859.

Denenberg, V. H., Garbanati, J., Sherman, G., Yutzey, D. A., & Kaplan, R. 1978. Infantile stimulation induces brain lateralization in rats. *Science, 201,* 1150–1151.

Denenberg, V. H., Hudgens, G. A., & Zarrow, M. X. 1964. Mice reared with rats: Modification of behavior by early experience with another species. *Science, 143,* 380–381.

Denenberg, V. H., & Zarrow, M. X. 1971. Effects of handling in infancy upon adult behavior and adrenocortical activity: Suggestions for a neuroendocrine mechanism. In D. H. Walcher & D. L. Peters (Eds.), *Early childhood: The development of self-regulatory mechanisms.* New York: Academic Press. Pp. 39–64.

DiGiusto, E. L., Cairncross, K., & King, M. G. 1971. Hormonal influences on fear-motivated responses. *Psychological Bulletin, 75,* 432–444.

Dobbing, J., & Smart, J. L. 1973. Early undernutrition, brain development, and behavior. In S. A. Barnett (Ed.), *Ethology and development.* London: Heinemann. Pp. 16–32.

Dorner, G. 1972. Sex hormone-dependent differentiation of the hypothalamus and sexuality. In K. Lissak (Ed.), *Hormones and brain function.* New York: Plenum Press. Pp. 47–51.

Eayrs, J. T. 1971. Thyroid and developing brain: Anatomical and behavioral effects. In M. Hamburgh & E. J. W. Barrington (Eds.), *Hormones in development.* New York: Appleton-Century-Crofts. Pp. 345–355.

Erlenmeyer-Kimmling, L. 1972. Gene-environment interactions and the variability of behavior. In L. Ehrman, G. Omen, & E. Caspari (Eds.), *Genetics, environment, and behavior.* New York: Academic Press.

Ernst, A. K., Yee, R., & Dericco, D. 1976. Effect of angle stimulation during development on adult discrimination ability in rats. *Animal Learning Behavior, 4,* 241–246.

Evarts, E. V. 1973. Sensorimotor cortex activity associated with movements triggered by visual as compared to somesthetic inputs. In F. O. Schmitt & F. G. Worden (Eds.), *The neurosciences: Third study program.* Cambridge, Mass.: MIT Press. Pp. 327–337.

Ferchmin, P., Bennett, E. L., & Rosenzweig, M. R. 1975. Direct contact with enriched environment is required to alter cerebral weight in rats. *Journal of Comparative and Physiological Psychology, 88,* 360–367.

Ferchmin, P. A., & Eterović, V. A. 1977. Brain plasticity and environmental complexity role of motor skills. *Physiology and Behavior, 18,* 445–461.

Fiala, B. A. 1976. *The effects of enriched or impoverished rearing on development of brain and behavior in rats.* Unpublished doctoral thesis, University of Illinois at Urbana-Champaign.

Fuller, J. L. 1967. Experiential deprivation and later behavior. *Science, 158,* 1645–1652.

Galef, B. G., Jr., & Sherry, D. F. 1973. Mother's milk: A medium for the transmission of cues reflecting the flavor of mother's diet. *Journal of Comparative and Physiological Psychology, 83,* 374–378.

Gluck, J. P., & Harlow, H. F. 1971. The effects of deprived and enriched rearing conditions on later learning: A review. In L. E. Jarrard (Ed.), *Cognitive processes of nonhuman primates.* New York: Academic Press. Pp. 103–119.

Goldfoot, D. A. 1977. Sociosexual behavior of nonhuman primates during development and maturity: Social and hormonal relationships. In A. Schrier (Ed.), *Behavioral primatology: Advances in research and theory.* Hillsidale, N.J.: Lawrence Erlbaum. Pp. 139–184.

Goldman, P. S. 1969. The relationship between amount of stimulation in infancy and subsequent emotionality. *Annals of the New York Academy of Sciences, 159,* 640–650.

Goldman, P. S., & Lewis, M. E. 1978. Developmental biology of brain damage and experience. In C. W. Cotman (Ed.), *Neuronal plasticity.* New York: Raven Press. Pp. 291–310.

Gorelick, D. A., Bozewicz, T. R., & Bridger, W. H. 1975. The role of catecholamine in animal learning and memory. In A. J. Friedhoff (Ed.), *Catecholamines and behavior 2–neuropsychopharmacology.* New York: Plenum Press. Pp. 1–30.

Gorski, R. A. 1973. Perinatal effects of sex steroids on brain development and function. *Progress in Brain Research, 39,* 149–163.

Goy, R. W., & Goldfoot, D. A. 1973. Experiential and hormonal factors influencing development of sexual behavior in the male rhesus monkey. In F. O. Schmitt & F. G. Worden (Eds.), *The neurosciences: Third study program.* Cambridge, Mass.: MIT Press. Pp. 571–582.

Greenman, N. J., & Duhring, F. L. 1923. *Breeding and care of the albino rat for research purposes.* Philadelphia: Wistar Institute of Anatomy and Biology.

Greenough, W. T. 1976. Enduring brain effects of differential experience and training. In M. R. Rosenzweig & E. L. Bennett (Eds.), *Neural mechanisms of learning and memory.* Cambridge, Mass.: MIT Press, Pp. 255–277.

Greenough, W. T., Fass, B., & DeBoogd, T. J. 1976. The influence of experience on recovery following brain damage in rodents: Hypotheses based on development research. In R. N. Walsh & W. T. Greenough (Eds.), *Environments as therapy for brain dysfunction.* New York: Plenum Press. Pp. 10–50.

Greenough, W. T., Snow, F. M., & Fiala, B. A. 1976. Environmental complexity versus isolation: A sensitive period for effects on cortical and hippocampal dendritic branching in rats? *Neuroscience Abstracts, 2,* 824.

Griffin, G. A., & Harlow, H. F. 1966. Effects of three months of total social deprivation on social adjustment and learning in the rhesus monkey. *Child Development, 37,* 533–547.

Griffiths, W. J., & Stringer, W. F. 1952. The effects of intense stimulation experienced during infancy on adult behavior in the rat. *Journal of Comparative and Physiological Psychology, 45,* 301–306.

Grobstein, P., & Chow, K. L. 1976. Receptive field organization in the mammalian visual cortex: The role of individual experience in development. In G. Gottlieb (Ed.), *Studies on the development of behavior and the nervous system: Neural and behavioral specificity.* New York: Academic Press. Pp. 155–193.

Hahn, M. E. 1979. Fuller BWS lines: Parental influences on brain size and development. In M. E. Hahn and C. Jensen (Eds.), *Development and evolution of brain size: Behavioral implications.* New York: Academic Press.

Hall, C. S., & Whiteman, P. H. 1951. The effects of infantile stimulation upon later emotional stability in the mouse. *Journal of Comparative and Physiological Psychology, 44,* 61–66.

Hammet, F. S. 1921. Studies of the thyroid apparatus: I. The stability of the nervous system as a factor in the resistance of the albino rat to the loss of the parathyroid secretion. *The American Journal of Physiology, 56,* 196–204.

Hart, B. L. 1974. Gonadal androgen and sociosexual behavior of male mammals: A comparative analysis. *Psychological Bulletin, 81,* 383–400.

Hebb, D. O. 1949. *Organization of behavior.* New York: Wiley.

Henderson, N. D. 1969. Prior-treatment effects on open-field emotionality: The need for representative design. *Annals of the New York Academy of Sciences, 159,* 860–868.

Henderson, N. D. 1970. Behavioral reactions of wistar rats to conditioned fear stimuli, novelty, and noxious stimulation. *Journal of Psychology, 75,* 19–34.

Henderson, N. D. 1972. Relative effects of early rearing environment and genotype on discrimination learning in house mice. *Journal of Comparative and Physiological Psychology, 79,* 243–253.

Henderson, N. D. 1976. Short exposures to enriched environments can increase genetic variability of behavior in mice. *Developmental Psychobiology, 9,* 549–553.

Henderson, N. D. 1977a. The role of motor learning and cage size in the early enrichment effect in mice. *Developmental Psychobiology, 10,* 481–487.

Henderson, N. D. 1977b. Contact with novel stimuli improves subsequent food-location performance in mice. *Journal of Comparative and Physiological Psychology, 91,* 1320–1325.

Hershenson, M. 1971. The development of visual perceptual systems. In H. Moltz (Ed.), *The ontogeny of vertebrate behavior.* New York: Academic Press. Pp. 29–56.

Hess, J. L., Denenberg, V. H., Zarrow, M. X., & Pfeiffer, W. D. 1969. Modification of the corticosterone response curve as a function of handling in infancy. *Physiology and Behavior, 4,* 109–111.

Hilgard, E. 1952. Experimental approaches to psychoanalysis. In E. Pumpian-Mindlin (Ed.), *Psychoanalysis as science.* Stanford: Stanford University Press. Pp. 3–45.

Hill, W. F. 1978. Effects of mere exposure on preferences in nonhuman mammals. *Psychological Bulletin, 85,* 1177–1198.

Hirsch, H. V. B., and Jacobson, M. 1975. The perfectible brain: Principles of neuronal development. In M. S. Gazzaniga & C. Blakemore (Eds.), *Handbook of psychobiology.* New York: Academic Press. Pp. 107–137.

Hofer, M. A. 1974. The role of early experience in the development of autonomic regulation. In L. V. DiCara (Ed.), *Limbic and autonomic nervous systems research.* New York: Plenum Press. Pp. 195–221.

Hubel, D. H., & Wiesel, T. N. 1959. Receptive fields of single neurons in the cat's striate cortex. *Journal of Physiology (London), 148,* 574–591.

Hubel, D. H., & Wiesel, T. N. 1962. Receptive fields, binocular interaction, and functional architecture in the cat's visual cortex. *Journal of Physiology (London), 160,* 106–154.

Hubel, D. H., & Wiesel, T. N. 1963. Receptive fields of cells in striate cortex of very young visually inexperienced kittens. *Journal of Neurophysiology, 26,* 994–1002.

Hunt, J. McV. 1941. The effects of infant feeding-frustration upon adult hoarding in the albino rat. *Journal of Abnormal and Social Psychology, 36,* 338–360.

Hunt, J. McV., Schlosberg, H., Solomon, R. L., & Stellar, E. 1947. Studies of the effects of infantile experience on adult behavior in rats. I. Effects of infantile feeding-frustration on adult hoarding. *Journal of Comparative and Physiological Psychology, 40,* 291–304.

Joffe, J. M. 1969. Perinatal determinants of emotionality. *Annals of the New York Academy of Sciences, 159,* 668–680.

Koos-Slob, A., Snow, C. E., & De Natris-Mathot, E. 1973. Absence of behavioral deficits following neonatal undernutrition in the rat. *Developmental Psychobiology, 6,* 177–186.

Kovács, S. 1973. The role of thyroid and adrenocortical hormones in the biochemical maturation of the rat brain. In K. Lissak (Ed.), *Hormones and brain function.* New York: Plenum Press. Pp. 53–67.

Lashley, K. S., & Russell, J. T. 1934. The mechanism of vision. XI. A preliminary test of innate organization. *Journal of Genetic Psychology, 45,* 136–144.

Leathwood, P. 1978. Influence of early undernutrition on behavioral development and learning in rodents. In G. Gottlieb (Ed.), *Studies on the development of behavior and the nervous system: Early influences.* New York: Academic Press. Pp. 187–209.

Lehrman, D. S., & Rosenblatt, J. S. 1971. The study of behavioral development. In H. Moltz (Ed.), *The ontogeny of vertebrate behavior.* New York: Academic Press. Pp. 1–27.

Leshner, Alan I. 1978. *An introduction to behavioral endocrinology.* New York: Oxford University Press.

Levine, S. 1970. The pituitary-adrenal system and the developing brain. In D. deWied & J. A. W. M. Weignen (Eds.), *Progress in brain research.* Amsterdam: Elsevier. Pp. 79–85.

Levine, S., Haltmeyer, G. C., Karas, G. G., & Denenberg, V. H. 1967. Physiological and behavioral effects of infantile stimulation. *Physiological Behavior, 2,* 55.

Levine, S., & Weiner, S. 1976. A critical analysis of data on malnutrition and behavioral deficits. *Advances in Pediatrics, 22,* 113–135.

Lore, R. K., & Levowitz, A. 1966. Differential rearing and free versus forced exploration. *Psychonomic Science, 5,* 421–422.

Mailloux, J. G., Edwards, H. P., Barry, W. F., Rowsell, H. C., & Achorn, E. G. 1974. Effects of differential rearing on cortical evoked potentials of the albino rat. *Journal of Comparative and Physiological Psychology, 87,* 475–480.

Marx, M. H. 1950. A stimulus-response analysis of the hoarding habit in the rat. *Psychological Review, 57,* 80–93.

Marx, M. H. 1952. Infantile deprivation and adult behavior in the rat: Retention of increased rate of eating. *Journal of Comparative and Physiological Psychology, 45,* 43–49.

McGill, T. E. 1970. Genetic analysis of male sexual behavior. In G. Lindzey & D. D. Thiessen (Eds.), *Contributions to behavior-genetic analysis–the mouse as a prototype.* New York: Appleton-Century-Crofts.

Meyers, B. 1971. Early experience and problem-solving behavior. In H. Moltz (Ed.), *The ontogeny of vertebrate behavior.* New York: Academic Press. Pp. 57–94.

Mistretta, C. M., & Bradley, R. M. 1978. Effects of early sensory experience on brain and behavioral development. In G. Gottlieb (Ed.), *Studies on the development of behavior and the nervous system: Early influences.* New York: Academic Press. Pp. 215–247.

Moltz, H. 1971. The ontogeny of maternal behavior in some selected mammalian species. In H. Moltz (Ed.), *The ontogeny of vertebrate behavior.* New York: Academic Press. Pp. 263–313.

Murphy, D. L., & Redmond, D. E. 1975. The catecholamines: Possible role in affect, mood, and emotional behavior in man and animals. In A. J. Friedhoff (Ed.), *Catecholamines and behavior 2–neuropsychopharmacology.* New York: Plenum Press. Pp. 73–117.

Nyakas, C. 1973. Influence of corticosterone and ACTH on the postnatal development of learning and memory functions. In K. Lissak (Ed.), *Hormones and brain function.* New York: Plenum Press. Pp. 83–89.

Pettigrew, J. D. 1978. The paradox of the critical period for striate cortex. In C. W. Cotman (Ed.), *Neuronal plasticity.* New York: Raven Press.

Pfaff, D. W., Diakow, C., Zigmond, R. E., & Kow, L. 1973. Neural and hormonal determinants of female mating behavior in rats. In F. O. Schmitt & F. G. Worden (Eds.), *The neurosciences: Third study program.* Cambridge, Mass.: MIT Press. Pp. 621–646.

Phoenix, C. H., Goy, R. W., Gerall, A. A., & Young, W. C. 1959. Organizing action of prenatally administered testosterone propionate on the tissues mediating mating behavior in the female guinea pig. *Endocrinology, 65,* 369–382.

Plaut, S. M. 1970. Studies of undernutrition in the young rat: Methodological considerations. *Developmental psychobiology, 3,* 157–167.

Quadagno, D. M., Briscoe, R., & Quadagno, J. S. 1977. Effect of perinatal gonadal hormones on selected nonsexual behavior patterns: A critical assessment of the nonhuman and human literature. *Psychological Bulletin, 84,* 62–80.

Rabinovitch, M. S., & Rosevold, H. E. 1951. A closed-field intelligence test for rats. *Canadian Journal of Psychology, 5,* 122–128.

Randrup, A., Munkvad, I., Fog, R., & Ayhan, I. H. 1975. Catecholamines in activation, stereotypy, and level of mood. In A. J. Friedhoff (Ed.), *Catecholamines and behavior I—basic neurobiology.* New York: Plenum Press. Pp. 89–107.

Reid, L. D., Gill, J. H., & Porter, P. B. 1968. Isolated rearing and Hebb-Williams maze performance. *Psychological Reports, 22,* 1073–1077.

Riege, W. H., & Morimoto, H. 1970. Effects of chronic stress and differential environments upon brain weights and biogenic amine levels in rats. *Journal of Comparative and Physiological Psychology, 71,* 396–404.

Riesen, A. H., & Aarons, L. 1959. Visual movement and intensity discrimination in cats after early deprivation of pattern vision. *Journal of Comparative and Physiological Psychology, 52,* 142–149.

Rogers, J. G., Jr., & Beauchamp, G. K. 1976. Some ecological implications of primer chemical stimuli in rodents. In R. L. Doty (Ed.), *Mammalian olfaction, reproductive processes, and behavior.* New York: Academic Press. Pp. 67–94.

Rosenzweig, M. R., & Bennett, E. L. 1977. Effects of environmental enrichment or impoverishment on learning and brain values in rodents. In A. Oliverio (Ed.), *Genetics, environment, and intelligence.* Amsterdam: Elsevier/North Holland. Pp. 163–195.

Rosenzweig, M. R., & Bennett, E. L. 1978. Experiential influences on brain anatomy and brain chemistry in rodents. In G. Gottlieb (Ed.), *Studies on the development of behavior and the nervous system: Early influences.* New York: Academic Press. Pp. 289–327.

Royce, J. R. 1977. On the construct validity of open-field measures. *Psychological Bulletin, 84,* 1098–1106.

Rozin, P. 1976. The selection of foods by rats, humans, and other animals. In J. S. Rosenblatt, R. A. Hinde, E. Shaw, & C. Beer (Eds.), *Advances in the study of behavior.* New York: Academic Press. Pp. 21–76.

Rudy, J. W., & Cheatle, M. D. 1977. Ontogeny of associative learning: Acquisition of odor aversions by neonatal rats. In N. E. Spear & B. A. Campbell (Eds.), *Ontogeny of learning and memory.* Hillsdale, N.J.: Lawrence Erlbaum.

Russell, P. A. 1971. "Infantile stimulation" in rodents: A consideration of possible mechanisms. *Psychological Bulletin, 75,* 192–202.

Sackett, G. P. 1967. Some behavioral effects of social and sensory deprivation during rearing on behavioral development of monkeys. *Revista Interamericana de Psicologia, 1,* 55–80.

Schenck, P. E., Koos-Slob, A., & Van Der Werff Ten Bosch, J. J. 1978. Locomotor activity and social behavior of old rats after preweaning undernutrition. *Developmental Psychobiology, 11,* 205–212.

Scott, J. H. 1955. Some effects at maturity of gentling, ignoring, or shocking rats during infancy. *Journal of Abnormal and Social Psychology, 51,* 412–414.

Scott, J. P. 1977. Social genetics. *Behavior Genetics, 7,* 327–346.

Selye, H. 1950. *Stress.* Montreal: Acta.

Selye, H. 1956. *The stress of life.* New York: McGraw-Hill.

Spencer-Booth, Y. 1970. The relationships between mammalian young and conspecifics other than mothers and peers: A review. In D. S. Lehrman, R. A. Hinde, & E. Shaw (Eds.), *Advances in the study of behavior, Volume 3.* New York: Academic Press. Pp. 119–194.

Tees, R. C. 1976. Perceptual development in mammals. In G. Gottlieb (Ed.), *Studies on the development of behavior and the nervous system: Neural and behavioral specificity.* New York: Academic Press. Pp. 281–326.

Tolstoy, L. N. 1902. *What is religion?* (Translation by V. Tchertkoff & A. C. Fiefield.) New York: Crowell.

Tsujimura, R., Kariyama, N., & Hatotani, N. 1972. Disturbances of myelination in neonatally thyroidectomized rat brains. In K. Lissak (Ed.), *Hormones and brain function.* New York: Plenum Press. Pp. 69–78.

Van-Toller, C., & Tarpy, R. M. 1974. Immunosympathectomy and avoidance behavior. *Psychological Bulletin, 81,* 132–137.

Walsh, R. N., & Cummins, R. A. 1975. Mechanisms mediating the production of environmentally induced brain changes. *Psychological Bulletin, 82,* 986–1000.

Walsh, R. N., & Cummins, R. A. 1976. The open-field test: A critical review. *Psychological Bulletin, 83,* 482–504.

Walsh, R. N. & Greenough, W. T. 1976. *Environments as therapy for brain dysfunction.* New York: Plenum Press.

Warren, J. M. 1965. The comparative psychology of learning. *Annual Review of Psychology, 16,* 95–118.

Weinberg, J., Krahn, E. A., & Levine, S. 1978. Differential effects of handling on exploration in male and female rats. *Developmental Psychobiology, 11,* 251–259.

Weinberg, J., & Levine, S. 1977. Early handling influences on behavioral and physiological responses during active avoidance. *Developmental Psychobiology, 10,* 161–169.

Weininger, O. 1953. Mortality of albino rats under stress as a function of early handling. *Canadian Journal of Psychology, 7,* 111–115.

Whalen, R. E. 1971. The ontogeny of sexuality. In H. Moltz (Ed.), *The ontogeny of vertebrate behavior.* New York: Academic Press. Pp. 229–261.

Whalen, R. E. 1974. Sexual differentiation: Models, methods and mechanisms. In R. C. Friedman (Ed.), *Sex differences in behavior.* New York: Wiley.

Whimbey, A. E., & Denenberg, V. H. 1966. Programming life histories: Creating individual differences by the experimental control of early experiences. *Multivariate Behavior Research, 1,* 279.

Whimbey, A. E., & Denenberg, V. H. 1967. Two independent dimensions in open-field performance. *Journal of Comparative and Physiological Psychology, 63,* 500.

Whitsett, J. M., & Vandenbergh, J. G. 1978. Hormonal influences on brain and behavioral development. In G. Gottlieb (Ed.), *Studies on the development of behavior and the nervous system: Early influences.* New York: Academic Press. Pp. 73–106.

Wiener, S. G., & Levine, S. 1978. Perinatal malnutrition and early handling: Interactive effects on the development of the pituitary-adrenal system. *Developmental Psychobiology, 11,* 335–352.

Wilson, J. G., Hamilton, J. B., & Young, W. C. 1941. Influence of age and presence of the ovaries on reproductive function of rats injected with androgens. *Endocrinology, 29,* 784–789.

Winer, B. J. 1971. *Statistical principles in experimental design,* 2nd ed. New York: McGraw-Hill.

Woods, P. J., Fiske, A. S., & Ruckelshaus, S. I. 1961. The effects of drives conflicting with exploration on the problem-solving behavior of rats reared in free and restricted environments. *Journal of Comparative and Physiological Psychology, 54,* 167–169.

Woods, P. J., Ruckelshaus, S. I., & Bowling, D. M. 1960. Some effects of "free" and "restricted" environmental rearing conditions upon adult behavior in the rats. *Psychological Reports, 6,* 191–200.

Zamenhof, S., & Van Marthens, E. 1978. Nutritional influences on prenatal brain development. In G. Gottlieb (Ed.), *Studies on the development of behavior and the nervous system: Early influences.* New York: Academic Press. Pp. 149–186.

CHAPTER 4

The Dynamics of
Social Development

ROBERT B. CAIRNS
JAMES A. GREEN
DENNIS J. MacCOMBIE

Recent advances in theory and research have promoted the establishment of a new interactional–developmental perspective on the problems of social behavior and personality. Our goals in this chapter are to outline some features of this perspective and to examine certain implications it has for the study of social development in children. In addition, because the effects of early experience remain a central concern for the field, we will comment on the limits of social behavior plasticity and on the concept of deprivation.

A DYNAMIC VIEW OF SOCIAL DEVELOPMENT

It is almost true to say that the "new" perspective is not new at all, that it has been in the air for the past 80 years. It has certainly been in the air; unfortunately, most of the time it has been perched in midair, floating beyond the reach of rigorous empirical assessment. This state of affairs has now changed, thanks in part to theoretical realignments within the science and in part to advances in experimental technology. Before outlining these theoretical and empirical changes, some comments are in order on the historical antecedents for the perspective.

79

EARLY EXPERIENCES AND EARLY BEHAVIOR
Implications for Social Development

Antecedents

In the first volume in English that contained the term *social psychology* in its title, James Mark Baldwin (1902) provided a brilliant statement of an interactional approach to social development. Baldwin wrote that "we are members one of another" and that "the development of the child's personality could not go on at all without the constant modification of his sense of himself to suggestions from others. So he himself, at every stage, is really in part someone else, even in his own thought of himself [Baldwin, 1902, p. 30]."

For Baldwin, the key mechanism of modification and change was the *dialectic of personal growth* that was stimulated by imitation. Hence children learn from others, throughout ontogeny, and others learn from them. Each individual's behaviors and attitudes become gradually shaped by the dominant social influences to which he or she is exposed in development; persons become both factors and products in the social organizations of which they are a part.

Baldwin's concept of imitation was more dynamic and interactive than were subsequent statements of the idea, a point emphasized in Kohlberg's (1969) updating of Baldwin's work. Imitation did not involve the mechanical duplication of the acts of other individuals; rather, it involved the concept of what was expected of the individual and what, in turn, others could expect of him. The person's concept of himself thus developed in a social nexus. One unexpected outcome of this view is that there may be as many different "social selves" as there are significant reference groups of which the individual is a part. Unity of self-concept is not automatic; the unidimensional person is likely to be handicapped in the multiple relations of life in which he or she must assume distinct and seemingly contradictory roles.

Baldwin's concept of social interactions and how they develop appears to have been highly influential in the theoretical formulations of symbolic interactionism (G. H. Mead, 1934). Leonard Cottrell (1942, 1969) later elaborated these concepts in social psychology and sociology. Further, the essential concept of the embeddedness of behavior in its social context was independently formulated in other areas of behavioral science, from psychoanalysis to ethology (Bowlby, 1969; Tinbergen, 1972).

The second major conceptual antecedent for the current perspective comes from developmental psychobiology, and the work and thinking of T. C. Schneirla (1966), Z. Y. Kuo (1967), and their colleagues. The essential idea is that a continuing and continuous fusion exists between biological states and behavior during the course of development. As Kuo and Schneirla argued, the relation between behavior and biological structure is a bidirectional one in which states of the young influence their behavior (and those with whom they interact), and behavioral functions can control, to some extent, the course of physical, sensory, and neurological development. The concept of a "fusion" of internal and external sources of control in the regulation of behavior is a key one for the psychobiological view. The fusion is not settled, however, at just a single "magic moment" in time. Bidirectional influences operate throughout the course of ontogeny, as developmental changes affect behavior and vice versa.

Neither Schneirla nor Kuo, nor, for that matter, most of those who were inspired by them, attempted to deal with the special problems of social development in children. (For important exceptions see Sameroff, 1975; Thomas, Chess, & Birch, 1968.) Hence the most compelling empirical support for the holistic view of social development comes from studies of the prenatal and early postnatal development of birds and nonhuman mammals. In an elegant body of studies, Gottlieb demonstrated that the embryonic animal contributes directly to its own socialization, by virtue of the stimuli that it produces for itself in the prenatal environment (Gottlieb, 1971). Further, the bidirectional relation between the behavioral functions of the young organism and its developing structures continues into postnatal relationships, such that the acts of the mother and infant are synchronized by virtue of their biological states and their actions toward one another. As the functions change, so do the structures and vice versa. This "developmental synchrony" is supported, at least in part, by the nature of the hormonal and behavioral events that each—the young and the caretaker—provoke in the other.

Jean Piaget and Heinz Werner pioneered a parallel holistic, developmental emphasis in the study of cognitive development, and some of the central concepts of a developmental approach were introduced into the mainstream of contemporary child psychology. In addition, Lawrence Kohlberg (1969) reminded the field of the earlier and wholly compatible developmental concepts of J. M. Baldwin. For the most part, however, the impact of these proposals was limited to the study of cognitive development.

A pivotal essay by Robert R. Sears (1951) paved the way for the adoption of an interactional perspective in the study of child social behavior. In this article, Sears contrasted the interactional approach to personality and social behavior with the then dominant "monadic" orientation. He argued, in effect, that a focus on the individual instead of the interaction in which the individual was involved served to eliminate primary sources of information. A similar message was communicated by Nowlis (1952) and Cottrell (1942). Nevertheless, the ideas were not given extensive and direct evaluation in studies of social development until the past decade.

The Contemporary
Interactional – Developmental Perspective

Ideas on the nature of interaction and development that were formulated over prior years have, within the past decade, won new attention. Their integration and application to the issues of social development have provided a fresh perspective for contemporary research. The essential features of this perspective can be summarized in five themes, each of which captures a significant feature of earlier proposals. The themes are (1) development as an ongoing process; (2) ontogenetic constraints in social development; (3) organization throughout development; (4) the adaptive properties of behavior; and (5) the relations between social ontogeny and social evolution. Some comments on each theme are in order.

Development as an Ongoing Process. A key proposal for the interactional–developmental perspective is that development is an ongoing process. Kuo's (1967) definition of behavioral epigenesis reflects both the inclusiveness of the concept of development and the influence of biological concepts.

> We shall define behavioral epigenesis as a continuous developmental process from fertilization through birth to death, involving proliferation, diversification, and modification of behavior patterns both in space and in time, as a result of the continuous dynamic exchange of energy between the developing organism and its environment, endogenous and exogenous [p. 11].

Accordingly, the study of social behavior from a developmental perspective should not be limited to the period from birth to adolescence; rather, the appropriate starting point is fertilization, and the terminal point, death. Organisms behave before birth, and the sequence in which sensory capabilities and behavioral patterns appear in the prenatal period has clear implications for our understanding of such basic social processes as species-identification and preference (Gottlieb, 1976a). Similarly, behavioral adaptations do not cease at sexual maturity; changes and modifications in life-style and patterns continue through later maturity and old age. Hence a life-span approach is required if an unbiased picture of development is to be obtained and the pitfalls of selected focus on one ontogenetic stage are to be avoided.

Today, most developmentalists would agree that the early experiences of the child—those occurring during the first 3 years of life—are critical for his social development. The consensus on this matter has not changed greatly over the past 30 years. A second assumption has been added, however, and this change has had a monumental impact on developmental theory and research. That is, now the *subsequent* experiences of the child—those occurring after the age of 3—are seen as potentially important for the organization of social patterns at maturity. In other words, not only are the first 3 years "critical," but so are the next 3, and the following 6, 9, and 12 years, up through adolescence and early maturity. A major concern of contemporary developmental research has been to determine precisely how the developing organism continues to adapt throughout ontogeny and into maturity.

The concern with adaptation and change throughout development has not been limited to studies of children. Indeed, a major impetus for the re-evaluation of the continuity of early experiences has come from studies on nonhuman young raised under various conditions of privation or enrichment. Attempts to "rehabilitate" or reverse the effects of the early isolation can be remarkably successful, if later experiences are appropriately arranged (e.g., Novak & Harlow, 1975).

Ontogenetic Constraints and the Bidirectional Proposal. The idea that the behavior of the organism is constrained by its biological conditions— whether by virtue of its phyletic or ontogenetic status—has waxed and waned in influence with the times. For some investigators, even those at the beginning of the science, the proposition was of great importance. Wilhelm Preyer (1888) explicitly recognized the linkage between structural/ perceptual changes in ontogeny and the form and type of behaviors that could be observed in infants. Investigators who followed Preyer's lead, including Gesell and Thompson (1934) and Shirley (1933), showed a similar sensitivity to the relationship between maturational status and social patterns.

Concern with the establishment of species-general laws of learning led behavioral psychologists to focus on commonalities across species and across ontogenies. Careful comparisons of different species in the same learning situations, however, led to the recognition that there were "biological constraints" on learning, in that some species seemed to be "prepared" to learn relationships more easily than others (Hinde & Stevenson-Hinde, 1973; Seligman & Hager, 1972). Although the role of *ontogenetic constraints* on social performance and learning have been given less attention in the current literature, they may ultimately prove to be even more important for understanding the origins and variations in human social patterns. Because organisms at different age–developmental levels have markedly different requirements for adaptation, it seems entirely reasonable to expect that there will be a developmental synchrony in what is learned and how. Hence, young organisms, by virtue of their peculiar survival requirements and psychobiology, are "prepared" to interact and to learn in ways that are different from how they interact and learn at maturity.

Nor is the relationship between structure and function simply a unidirectional one. A significant proposition that has grown out of contemporary developmental psychobiology is that one's behaviors and experiences are not the outcome only of biological processes, but, as well, behaviors and experiences contribute to the formation and regulation of biological processes.

For instance, one of the more dramatic recent discoveries has been that the sex of the mammalian embryo is not wholly determined at conception (Young, 1961). The male fetus—across the class Mammalia—produces hormones that help to direct its own sexual development, including the formation of male internal and external structures and the inhibition of the formation of female ones. Without this suppression of the feminine and accentuation of the masculine, the infant at birth would have some of the physical features of both male and female.

This phenomenon of the fetus helping to shape its own development illustrates what Gottlieb (1970, 1976b) has called the *probabilistic conception of prenatal development*. According to this interpretation, prenatal behavior is not determined merely by the biological structures of the young. Rather, the relation is a *bidirectional* one between structure and function. Stated more simply, the experiences of the individual, even self-produced ones, can change its biological properties. These changes, in turn, help to control and direct social behavior. Development is a two-way street; it is not just the unfolding of potentials or the shaping by experience.

Organization of Social Patterns.   From birth, the child develops particular styles of social interchange. The interpersonal styles may change from situation to situation, and over time, but they are the stuff of which personality is made. The fact that certain behavior patterns become increasingly predictable and characteristic for individuals is one of the basic phenomena of social development. The social behaviors of the child or even of the infant are more than a patchwork of unrelated sequences that have somehow been drawn together; they ordinarily form distinctive and easily recognizable patterns and networks. It is these patterns that make for individuality—for likes and dislikes, for trust and suspicion, for love and hate.

The interchanges in which organisms become involved contribute to the integration of behavior patterns, as we just observed. But the interchanges themselves are regulated by the broader social network in which the interchanges occur, and by the inherent properties of the individuals, including their action capabilities, developmental status, and prior experiences. In other words, interchanges are embedded in a social system and are controlled by the capabilities of each participant.

The social system "beyond the dyad" has been conceptualized in various ways. The essential point to be made is that the understanding of social development demands going beyond the direct observation of behavior on the part of one or two persons in the same place; it requires examination of multiperson systems of interaction not limited to a single setting and must take into account aspects of the environment beyond the immediate situation containing the subject (Bronfenbrenner, 1977, p. 514).

What kinds of "multiperson" systems must be considered? A primary candidate for developmental analysis has been the family system, consisting of the members of the primary family (father, mother, siblings, aunts, depending on the social organization of the species). Among children, other systems would include those in which the child is involved in school or preschool, peer groups, as well as other, loosely structured groups. On still a broader scale, Bronfenbrenner identifies a "macrosystem" as "the overarching institutional patterns of the culture or subculture . . . [p. 515]." Such macrosystems provide the "blueprints" or the norms for the individuals and subgroups within the culture.

Other "support" for the organization of social behavior is basically structural–biological, and some patterns are established with little or virtually no specific prior experience. The synchrony of the mother–infant relationship in feeding is a case in point. Young mammals, including humans and other primates, can suckle shortly after birth. The hormonal states of the mother and the propensities/activities of the newborn are prepared for the elicitation and maintenance of appropriate feeding activities. There are indeed a full range of activities of the infant that are organized by the time of parturition, including its swimming movements (neonates can effectively swim; see McGraw, 1939), activities that contribute to temperature control (Alperts, 1978), reflexive acts in response to sudden shifts in physical support, and a variety of other basic response dispositions.

More generally, the organization of social patterns reflects the fusion of internal, interpersonal, and sociocultural influences. It is not the case, however, that all activities are determined in an equivalent fashion, or that persons are necessarily equal in how they influence each other, or that the bases for organization are the same across ontogenies or across species. These are matters to be clarified through the direct empirical investigation of the actual foundations for social organization.

Behavior as an Active Adaptation of the Organism. As Scott (1976) pointed out, there are at least two meanings of the word *adaptation*.[1] First, adaptation may refer to the very gradual changes in the biology and be-

---

[1] James M. Baldwin (1902) made the same distinction. He proposed that the term *adaptation* should be reserved for evolutionary changes, and that *accommodation* should refer to modifications in the course of a lifetime. The latter term was adopted by Piaget and others.

havior of organisms during evolution. Second, adaptation may refer to the process by which an organism adjusts to environmental demands during ontogeny.

It is this second meaning of the term, or what Baldwin (1902) has labeled *accommodation,* on which we will focus. During their lifetimes, organisms adjust to the relatively predictable features of their physical and social environments, in part by developing distinctive and idiosyncratic styles of relating to others. Each person develops what Kuo (1967) has called *neophenotypes,* or wholly distinctive and individual patterns of interchanges with others (see also Allport, 1937). Although the content and nature of the accommodations are unique, the processes by which the individual arrives at them during the course of ontogeny are presumably general. It is in the examination of these general principles of social development that one should be able to identify the events that provide for behavioral continuity and change over the course of development.

There is a second type of accommodation that is observed in social behavior. In addition to the relatively enduring patterns of interchange that persons develop over time, there are moment-by-moment and situationally specific adaptations. Hence, much of the variance in social behavior patterns seems to be determined by the powerful immediate interpersonal and contextual controls that operate upon persons in the particular social matrix in which they are observed (Barker, 1963; Cairns & Green, 1979; Lewin, 1935).

A major concern of contemporary personality and developmental theory has been to identify how these two types of accommodation are intertwined. The solutions proposed have ranged from an integrative concept of the *self* (Baldwin, 1902; Cottrell, 1969; Kohlberg, 1969) to a behavior-contingency unit analysis of organismic and environmental controls (Mischel, 1973).

Ontogeny and Phylogeny of Social Interactions.   A final concern is the relation between the ontogeny of social patterns and their evolutionary history (see Gould, 1977; Mason, 1968; Piaget, 1978). The issues are significant ones for both biology and psychology, and represent the reintroduction of issues raised by Darwin in *The expression of the emotions in man and animals* (1872). Three major problems can be identified: (1) whether an evolutionary explanation of behavioral origins is an adequate explanation for development; (2) whether early behavior is "the motor for evolution", and (3) whether variations in the regulation of development can account for major shifts in the adaptive capabilities of descendant species.

One of the issues that has produced no little grief in modern studies of animal behavior concerns the relation between evolutionary explanations of behavioral origins and ontogenetic ones. E. O. Wilson (1975), in his influential *Sociobiology*, observes that a behavior pattern, say aggression, can be traced in the life history of the species in terms of the functions that it has served in enhancing inclusive genetic fitness. Such explanations have been labeled *ultimate causation*. At quite another level of analysis, aggressive acts may be traced to their occurrence in the life history of individuals. The developmental investigator thus is concerned with the integration of hormonal, morphological, and experiential influences that permit, in the ontogeny of individuals, the performance and expression of acts that are hurtful to other individuals. These immediate and lifelong influences have been called *proximal causes*. Is one level of explanation—proximal or ultimate—more basic than the other? That question is still a matter of some controversy. E. O. Wilson, noting the seemingly modest progress made by functional biologists and psychologists in understanding proximal determinants, has proposed that evolutionary causes of social behavior are not only more fundamental but also more likely to yield interpretable outcomes in the foreseeable future. Hence Wilson would "decouple" the study of evolutionary determinants of such social patterns as altruism and aggression from their developmental study, and would place an emphasis on understanding the "ultimate" determinants of these patterns.

Developmental psychobiologists, on the other hand, have proposed that evolutionary and developmental concerns are intimately related. Indeed, an understanding of development might be fundamental to accounting for phyletic changes. Two major propositions have been offered regarding the relation between social behavior ontogeny and phylogeny. One is that behavior is the "motor of evolution" (Piaget, 1978), and that the extreme plasticity of the behavior patterns of young animals heightens the likelihood that they will explore new areas and adapt to new conditions that are foreign to their species. Their descendants, by virtue of selective propagation, will be more favorably prepared for adaptation in the "novel" ecological conditions. (See also Baldwin's [1902] concept of organic selection and Waddington's [1968] "genetic assimilation.")

A second proposition, not inconsistent with the first, is that modifications in the rate of developmental characteristics of descendants can bring about structures and behaviors that differ markedly from those of the ancestors (deBeer, 1958; Gould, 1977). The modification in the timing of developmental features has been called *heterochrony*. Variations in the regulation of development, heterochronies, have been employed to explain why species with great basic similarity in genetic properties differ markedly in structure, capabilities, and behavior (King & Wilson, 1975). One major variation can be in the direction of an extended immaturity, or neoteny. Neoteny would be found, for example, in the extended immaturity of human beings relative to ancestral primates. This may include, according to de Beer (1958), the delayed closing of the sutures of the skull and the concomitant expansion of the brain in humans relative to ancestral primates. Another major type of heterochrony would involve the accelerated development of one characteristic relative to others. Acceleration may be seen, for example, in the more rapid onset of puberty and child rearing in descendants than in the ancestors. It has been proposed that modest changes in the timing of certain characteristics of development—whether of a neotenous or an accelerated sort—can produce multiple consequences in the social behavior patterns as well as in the cognitive and physiological characteristics of descendant generations (see Mason, in press; Cairns, 1976).

Most of the speculation on the relations between ontogeny and phylogeny remains just that—speculation. Nonetheless, as Wilson (1975) and Gould (1977) agree in their influential volumes on evolution and behavior, the relationship remains a central one for both the biological and the behavioral sciences. Further, it seems unlikely that the matter will be resolved until a vigorous attempt is made to trace the similarities and differences among the ontogenies of closely related species.

GOALS OF THE INTERACTIONAL–DEVELOPMENTAL APPROACH

As the area has been redefined in themes and approaches, so have the problems of what are suitable and appropriate goals for the discipline been reexamined. The work of contemporary investigators appears to be relevant to one of three major questions. Hence the goals of interactional developmental study might be said to involve gaining a satisfactory answer to the following three questions:

1. What are the origins of social patterns in the ontogeny of the individual?
2. How are social patterns maintained over the course of development?
3. How are social patterns changed or modified over the course of development?

Answers to these questions demand the detailed study of interchanges across development. The insight is not a new one. Wesley Mills (1899) argued that the basic, and most informative, developmental design would be one in which the investigator traced the behavior of one puppy day and night, from birth to the first birthday. While Mills's design has yet to be undertaken, progress has nonetheless been made in the longitudinal study of social development in children. We turn now to a brief review of some of the findings that seem especially pertinent to the interactional–developmental approach.

SOCIAL DEVELOPMENT IN CHILDREN: SOME RECENT FINDINGS

Significant advances in methodology, including improvements in methods of recording and analyzing interactional data, have permitted a direct evaluation of the utility of the interactional–developmental approach to social ontogeny. These technological and statistical advances have been discussed and critically evaluated elsewhere (e.g., Cairns, 1979a; Sackett, 1978). We need note here only that features of social interchanges heretofore inaccessible have recently become the subject of extensive investigation (Cairns, 1979b; Schaffer, 1977a). In this section, we briefly discuss some of the relevant findings.

The Early Years

During the 1960s and into the 1970s, the theoretical emphasis in socialization research shifted from a stress on how parents "shape" or mold their children toward a stress on the capabilities that infants bring into the world (see, e.g., Bell, 1968, 1971; Stone, Smith, & Murphy, 1973). Part of the reason this shift in orientation came about was because socialization research failed to find consistent relationships between parental socialization practices and child/adolescent behavior and personality (see Yarrow, Campbell, & Burton, 1968). In addition, Bowlby (1958, 1969) and others extended the ethological emphasis on the biological/evolutionary substrates of behavior to the study of human infants.

The issue of how each participant in the child-rearing process contributes to development came to the fore with Bell's (1968) influential paper, suggesting a reversal of the direction of effects in the parent–child relationship. According to Bell, it is as plausible to believe that infants produce individual differences in parental behavior as it is to believe the reverse (see also Bell & Harper, 1977). Other investigators, including some who studied the mother–infant relationship, implied that there was a near balance of control, such that each participant contributed 50%, or equally, to the direction of the relationship. In any case, one goal of recent mother–infant studies has been to determine how "dialogues" or reciprocal interchanges originate and how they are regulated during ontogeny.

The answer to both the questions—that of origins and that of regulation—depends upon the nature of the activity or type of dialogue to be explained. For instance, Kaye (1977) has shown that there is indeed a synchrony in the feeding patterns in which mother and infants engage, from the first day of life onward. The data are less clear with respect to the regulatory roles played by mothers as opposed to infants. Maternal competency in feeding has been shown by Thoman and her colleagues (Thoman, Barnett, & Leiderman, 1971) to determine both weight gains of the infant and duration of feeding episodes. Multiparous mothers (those with previous births) tended to be more efficient and effective than do primiparous mothers (those with no prior births). The most competent of all, however, were the caretakers employed in the neonatal nursery.

Investigations that go beyond the feeding/nursing interaction yield data on interpersonal control and synchrony that is intriguing but preliminary. When very young human infants are placed together, they show little capability to interact with each other in any meaningful or systematic fashion. Such an observation is of some importance because it raises the possibility that some of the interactional synchronies that have been observed in infant–mother interchanges reflect the abilities of exceedingly competent interactors (i.e., adults) to react flexibly and adaptively to subtle cues provided by socially "incompetent" babies.

Perhaps the most informative and compelling evidence on the nature of interactional development comes from longitudinal observations of mothers and infants over significant periods of the first year of life. The outcomes of such studies—which involve an intensive analysis of the changing relations between mother and child—underscore the importance of ontogenetic constraints in determining the quality and quantity of social interactions. To illustrate, Green, Gustafson, and West (1979) report data based on repeated observations of infants interacting with their mothers, at home, for a total of 80 waking minutes at 6, 8, and 12 months of age. The explicit focus of the data collection was the social interaction between mother and infant, defined as periods when one member was directing social behavior toward the other without interruption. The social interactions at each age were then analyzed in terms of frequency, duration, stability, initiators, initial behaviors, and relational themes or goals during the interaction.

The results indicated that changes in several of these properties of social interactions were the result of developmental changes in infants' motor and social skills. Infants initiated an increasing number of interactions from 6 to 12 months, using both behaviors they acquired during this time (e.g., pointing and giving objects) and behaviors used throughout the previous months (e.g., vocalizing at, fussing at). Further, when initiated to, infants more often responded with a socially directed behavior at 12 months. There was a more equal give-and-take between mothers and infants, at least during the initial moves in social interactions.

Analyses of mother–infant games showed that the increasing competence of infants was not limited to their participation in initiations of interactions. Games offer a better social setting in which to study the acquisition of social skills, because the rule-structure of the game is prescribed, and it is known by both the mother and the observers. Gustafson, Green, and West (1979) showed that changes in games paralleled the changes just noted in initiations of interactions. It can be seen in Figure 4-1 that new games appeared as infants acquired new capabilities (give-and-take games, for example) and infants' participation in old games (such as peekaboo and ball) was more often judged as active (see Bayley's [1969] criterion of active participation). Further, games in which the infant's role was explicitly passive declined or disappeared by 12 months. Thus, mothers played games with their infants at 6 months which infants were not capable of fully participating in but which would come, over time, to be a situation in which both members of the pair could anticipate and control the other's behavior.

The social skills of infants must necessarily have an impact on social interactions, but more basic ontogenetic constraints also operate on mother–infant interactions. The development of locomotor skills has been shown to be related to the increase over age in the number of times mothers attempt to terminate or redirect an infant's ongoing activity (Green et al., 1979). Locomotor development also was shown to be related to more general changes in the number of verbal requests by mothers, and decreases

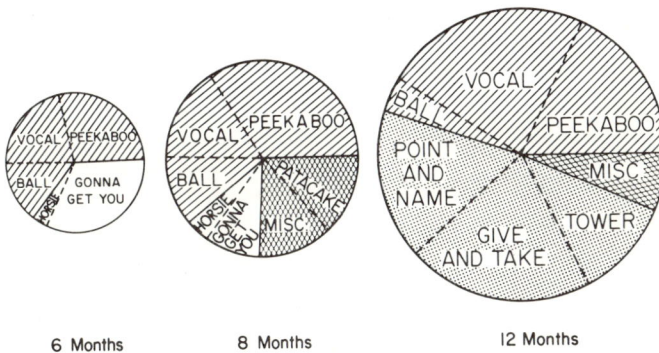

| 6 Months | 8 Months | 12 Months |

Figure 4-1. Mother–infant games played at 6, 8, and 12 months of age (area is proportional to frequency). Stippled areas represent games in which the infant's role is explicitly active; blank areas represent games in which the infant's role is typically passive. Hatched areas represent games played at all ages. Cross-hatched areas represent both active and passive games. (From Gustafson et al., 1979.)

in repositioning, caretaking, and providing toys to infants. These changes in maternal behavior were seen both as age-related trends and as effects of giving nonlocomoting infants the ability to locomote (by placing them in walkers).

Each of these findings supports the proposition that there are ontogenetic constraints operating on interactions at any one time and that changes in the capabilities of the young affect their social environment. Thus, developmental changes in young pace changes in their environments, which, in turn, feedback to produce subsequent alterations in their behaviors.

The picture is not one-sided, however; the role played by the mother in regulating early social development is beginning to gain explicit attention. One of the most detailed treatments of the maternal contribution to interactional structure is given by H. R. Schaffer (1979). His purpose was to review the hallmarks and possible determinants in acquiring the idea of the dialogue. Recognizing that mothers play a pivotal role in early interactions by sequencing their behaviors around those of their infants, Schaffer distinguished six maternal dyadic techniques, ordered on a rough continuum from maternal passivity to activity—phasing, adaptation, facilitation, elaboration, initiating, and control techniques (see also Schaffer, 1977a, 1977b). Schaffer sees the "structural preadaptations" of infants (oral, visual, auditory, and so on) as ensuring a basic compatability between infants and mothers and the "functional preadaptations" of infants (sucking and sleep–wake cycles) as providing the occasions for mothers to use these six techniques to produce "pseudo-dialogues."

Three kinds of prerequisites combine, then, to facilitate the acquisition of dialogues in the first year. Biological prerequisites ensure that there is a basis on which mothers can act to produce pseudo-dialogues (the social prerequisites). Cognitive prerequisites, generated to some extent through repeated participation in pseudo-dialogues, combine with the other two and produce an ability to participate in social interactions characterized by reciprocity of roles and intentionality of communicative behavior. With regard to infants controlling their own development, we note that even in that aspect of development in which the infant must necessarily control certain features— that is, social development—the caregiver is given a role of fundamental importance.

What of other aspects of development and the contributions infants might bring? On certain very basic matters, the infant has very little control. Infants play little role in controlling their own diet or getting vaccinated, and they make little input into decisions about the nature of their daily social environment—full-time home care, day-care, babysitters, siblings, or playmates. They apparently play only a small role in determining aspects of their physical environment, including play materials, hazard-free furnishings, and so on. In general, parents are not only more competent than are their offspring, in terms of regulating social interactions, but they also determine the range of conditions and experiences to which the young are exposed.

Beyond Infancy

Ontogenetic changes in the frequency of complex interchanges between infants and their mothers in the first year might be expected to continue into the second year, and extend to the child's relationship with other, nonparental adults. Despite the common-sense nature of this expectation, at least one study obtained little support for it. Margaret C. Holmberg (1977) found few changes in the frequency of "elaborated" interchanges (complex, extended interactions) between adults and children over the period from 1 to 3 years. Why the apparent failure to change with age? Examination of the interactions between the children of varying ages and adults indicated that the adults tended to modify their actions and role with respect to the children as a function of the youngsters' capabilities to interact. Although the children changed markedly in their ability to initiate and sustain a relationship over this 2-year period, the adults with whom they interacted compensated for the child's early deficiencies and later competence. The upshot was that the two effects balanced, and as many "elaborated" interchanges were observed between adults and 1-year-old children as between adults and 3-year-old children.

How might one avoid the "natural" confounding that occurs by virtue of adults adjusting their behaviors and expectations to fit children of different ages, hence canceling out developmental changes? One alternative that has been used increasingly in studies of children in early childhood has been to study the interactions that occur between peers of the same age. The observations have been taken in both natural conditions of the day-care or preschool and in laboratory conditions where either unfamiliar or familiar children are placed together. The results of the observations, made under two different conditions, have been reasonably consistent across investigations (e.g., Eckerman, 1979; Holmberg, 1977; Mueller & Lucas, 1975; Ross & Goldman, 1977), and together they provide a clear picture of the ontogeny of peer relations in young children.

The main findings indicate:

1. Encounters between peers at 1 year of age are transient and are as likely to yield negative consequences ("coercive," "assertive") as positive ones. These outcomes occur because the interchanges frequently involve attempts to gain possession of an object or a physical position.

2. The proportion of interchanges with negative consequences relative to those with positive ones decreases as a function of age, so that by 42 months, less than 20% of the interchanges with peers are negative ones.

3. The quality and complexity of interchanges between peers show a rapid increase at approximately 24–30 months, when the children are able better to communicate.

4. By $3\frac{1}{2}$ years of age, the incidence of complex or "elaborated" interchanges with other children (i.e., interchanges that involve some turn taking and variation in activity) equals or exceeds the incidence of such interchanges by the same children with adults.

Observations of peers indicate that children take an active role in socializing each other, long before they ordinarily enroll in elementary school. Very early after infancy, the actions of children toward each other begin to take the form and quality of interchanges observed between older children and adults. The rapid growth of the child's capability to form and maintain relationships indicates that an exclusive focus on the mother–infant unit is likely to yield a limited picture of the course of socialization.

Precisely how to do children influence each other, and what is the outcome during social interactions? Recent attempts to answer this question have focused on the nature of the actions and counteractions typically provoked in interchanges. Perhaps the most striking outcome of these analyses has been the finding that children tend to entrap each other in common activities, common patterns of communication, and common feelings and behaviors. There is, in effect, a strong reciprocity evident in the actions of children when they interact with each other. Hence, children who are observed interacting together will typically show similar preferences and participate in the same activities. They effectively funnel each other's behavior along a common theme or pattern. The levels of similarity are often striking and can be identified across several dimensions of responding, including linguistic, emotional, cognitive, and behavioral.

To clarify the developmental course of reciprocity, children of different ages were placed together in pairs (MacCombie, 1978). Within a very short interval, the children joined each other in a common activity. If one child switched an activity, the other typically followed suit within 10 seconds (see Figure 4-2). There is, thus, an *interpersonal bias* whereby children attend to the actions of others and participate with them in a common "plan" for behavior.

Such findings underscore the ability of children to fine-tune their activities so that they are synchronized with the activities of others. They also indicate that the children are likely to be strongly influenced by the actions of the other. The effect is not merely correlational; attempts to program the

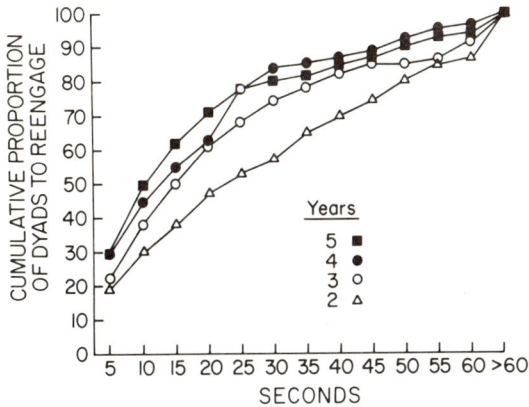

Figure 4-2. Amount of time required for two children to re-engage in a common activity after one of them moves to another task. In all ages tested (from 2–5 years old), there was a strong tendency for the children to rapidly become involved in the same activity. (From MacCombie, 1978.)

activity of the "other" have been successful in recruiting the attention and joint participation of the child (Hall, 1973; MacCombie, 1978). This work underscores the power of the social system in directing and controlling the acts of children.

The ubiquity of reciprocity does not ensure that relationships among children are always benign and mutually agreeable, however, since children entrap each other in negative interchanges as well as positive ones (see Patterson, 1979; Raush, 1965). One of the major problems of socialization appears to be the establishment of constraints against the escalation of interchanges in a negative trajectory, given the strong propensities of children (and adults) to reciprocate hostile themes or actions initiated by others in relationships. Precisely how children escape from synchrony is as significant for socialization as the development of mutually agreeable and integrated relationships. The interactional analyses of Patterson and his coworkers have been of special interest in determining the controls of coercive familial patterns.

Summary of Recent Empirical Findings

To conclude this brief summary of recent empirical studies of interactional development in young children, the following points can be offered:

1. Behavior is organized throughout development, from early infancy onward. High levels of interactional organization can be identified in the early maternal–infant relationship, and the level of synchrony

appears to depend on the nature of the activity and the extent to which the activity is controlled by internal sources.

2. The developmental course of synchronous acts depends upon the capabilities and activities of the person who interacts with the child. Different developmental curves may be found, for instance, in interchanges with adults than in interchanges with same-age peers.

3. In the second year, the acts of peers assume increasing importance in regulating the direction, nature, and outcome of the child's activities. Reciprocities in the social patterns of children are ubiquitous across response systems, and can be observed in motor, cognitive, linguistic, and emotional patterns.

4. There is considerable relational and situational-specificity in social behavior patterns beyond infancy. This specificity seems to reflect, in part, the powerful constraints provided by the acts of other individuals. Nonetheless, some individual difference consistencies in interpersonal patterns can be identified across short-term intervals and across situations. A primary mediator for the continuity appears to be the consistency of the acts of others (Green et al., 1979).

5. As important as synchrony is in accounting for the development of social patterns, a major achievement occurs when children develop interpersonal strategies that permit them to escape from synchrony. The achievement is of particular importance in promoting ways for the child to avoid becoming entrapped in sequences that result in escalating, hostile interchanges.

SOME IMPLICATIONS FOR UNDERSTANDING THE EFFECTS OF EARLY EXPERIENCE

In the last part of this chapter, some comments are in order on the implications of the interactional approach for two issues central to understanding the effects of early experience on social behavior. One matter concerns the problem of the limits of social behavior plasticity in the young, and who controls whom: parent or child? The second issue concerns the effects of deprivation and whether there is a single course of normal social development.

Limits of Plasticity

For social development, first in occurrence is not always first in importance. Empirical documentation for this generalization has been accumulating over the past 2 decades (see other chapters in this volume; Cairns, 1977,

1979b). Useful as this insight may be in clearing the way for studies of influences that operate over the life-span of the individual, it is essentially a negative statement. By discarding the assumption that early experiences are always primary or foundational, it leaves open the question of what, indeed, influences social patterns in ontogeny. Two general positions seem to have been entertained in recent discussions of this matter. One is that variations in early experience are relatively unimportant because of the formative impact of preprogrammed or constitutional differences among persons. Such *canalization*, according to R. S. Wilson (1978), can override many variations in individual experience. A second general explanation for frequent failures of the primacy assumption is that social patterns are dynamic and capable of modification at various stages of life. Hence ontogenetic changes in individuals, and in the social systems of which they are a part, promote modifications in social patterns at each stage of development. This proposal, which is the backbone of the interactional–developmental perspective, holds that social patterns are not irrevocably fixed, either by genes or by early experience (Fuller, 1966).

Although the interactional–developmental perspective is open with respect to the critical issue of how much weight must be assigned to the influence of infants in interactions, it provides guides as to how one might determine the relative weight of influence, and who controls whom. It thus provides a basis for specifying the degree of plasticity that might be shown by each interactor, and it permits one to assess how, and whether, these influences may be preserved or modified. Accordingly, the limits of plasticity depend upon, among other things, the nature of the response patterns involved, the relative difference in the competence of each member of the relationship to perform the action pattern, and the age–ontogenetic status of each of the participants.

Consider the nature of the response pattern. Some activities reflect primarily internal sources of control and, once elicited, provide the conditions for their own maintenance. Crying is one such positive feedback system in that the behavior provides stimuli for its own recurrence. Punishment for crying will, paradoxically, perpetuate or intensify the behavior instead of eliminating or inhibiting it. Suckling in the neonate is another instance where there is a "circular reaction," in that the occurrence of the behavior supports its recurrence. A primary function of external stimulation in suckling is to provide the manipulanda necessary for the performance of the activity. Provided with a nipple or nipple-like object, suckling proceeds in a highly organized and adaptative fashion in infancy. The "design" of the birth equipment of the infant (including the rooting reflex) and the maternal condition of the mother promotes a close synchrony between them in the feeding interchange.

Even in this fundamental interchange, however, there is some opportunity for behavioral plasticity. Infants appear to learn rapidly to discriminate what events are readily integrated with feeding patterns, including what and when and where to suckle. Following a period of indiscriminate sucking, virtually all mammalian infants form preferences in these matters. (See conditioning studies of newborn puppies [Bacon & Stanley, 1970], newborn rats [Hall & Bennett, personal communication, 1979], and infant kittens [Rosenblatt, 1972].) This "internally organized" activity must itself benefit from the early social experiences of the infant in order to achieve heightened efficiency and adaptability.

Although less attention has been given to what the mother learns in this fundamental relationship, the information available indicates that mothers also learn a great deal. Not only do parturient females of most mammalian species learn to distinguish their own infants from others (and thus form a strong attachment preference for them), but mothers also acquire information about feeding patterns and how to find or avoid their offspring. These lessons appear to influence the mothers' behaviors in the next rearing cycle, in that multiparous females are typically more efficient, capable, and successful in rearing young than are primiparous ones (Lehrman, 1961). Whatever is learned becomes fused with psychobiological conditions. Even in the absence of hormonal states required to bring about maternal behavior, learned modifications may support the continuance of maternal care (Lehrman, 1961). Through learning processes, behavior patterns of mothers toward their offspring can be conserved and maintained beyond infancy.

Our information about what human mothers learn in the early infant–mother relationship is even less complete. Nonetheless, there appears to be support for the proposition that mothers learn a great deal about their infants and how to respond adaptively to their several moods, needs, and actions. For example, experienced mothers are more efficient in feeding (and promote more rapid weight gains) than do inexperienced mothers (Thoman, Barnett, & Leiderman, 1971).

In addition to acquiring information about how to handle specific behaviors of their infants, human parents also have a bigger picture of what the future holds and how to plan for it. Parents thus can learn how to arrange situations and contingencies so as to promote desired states and activities in their offspring. Planned variations in how the infant's world is designed can also promote multiple learning opportunities for infants, including new schedules of feeding, new activities, and new preferences. Hence parents and infants not only affect each other directly by virtue of immediate behaviors, but they influence each other indirectly by creating new conditions for living and by determining to what each must adapt. It is in the structure of environmental and relational contingencies that the parents usually have the upper hand. The parent–infant relationship is thus unbalanced to the extent that the parents exercise control over the nature of the lessons to be learned, and when and how they are presented to the child. Yet the balance in the parent–child relation is not constant over time. Shifts in the nature of influence occur as a function of age–developmental status over the first 3 years. In their interactions with peers and adults, children demonstrate an increasing ability to influence, and to be influenced, by others.

The upshot of recent studies of social development is to expose the fallacy of considering the earliest stages of life to be the only ones in which enduring interactional adaptations occur. There are indeed significant lessons to be learned early in postnatal life. But the actions that are learned may be relatively specific ones—such as when and how and what to suckle—with little direct relevance to later behaviors. The present evidence suggests that it is not until the child reaches relatively advanced levels of cognitive development that interchange experiences will have a continuing influence on the nature and quality of his social patterns (Kagan & Moss, 1963).

One hypothesis that arises from recent studies of social continuity is that the "critical" periods for malleability are not necessarily in the infancy or youth of the *organism*, but in the "infancy" of the social (or sexual) *pattern*. Although some interchange patterns may be consolidated early in life, the relationship between consolidation and age is not a necessary one. Sexual preferences and actions, for instance, may be determined in large measure at the time in which these patterns are established and consolidated at puberty and early adulthood. More generally, psychobiological, cultural, and cognitive influences collaborate to determine when specific patterns are likely to be established in ontogeny. Changes in these factors may, in turn, promote social behavior change and modification. Hence, attempts to account for the distinctive features of personality and social behavior must be concerned with the life-span of the individual, not merely with the events of infancy or with those present in the contemporaneous setting.

Deprivation Re-evaluated

No single concept has been assigned a more central role in developmental theory and research over the past quarter century than has deprivation. Nor has one been more susceptible to misunderstanding. The concept of *deprivation* has been used by investigators who work in a variety of research areas; it has been employed in the analysis of early childhood psychopathology (*maternal deprivation*), in studies of sensory functioning (*visual deprivation*), and in investigations of conditioning in children (*social reinforcer deprivation*). The interactional–developmental approach provides a new perspective on this old concept. But before exploring the implications of the view for understanding phenomena assigned to various kinds of social deprivation, we need to comment upon the problems that have been associated with it. Perhaps the major difficulty has been that the concept has been employed with several different shades of meaning. They share in common the implication that the organism has had something essential withheld from it, but they differ in specifying the nature and presumed consequences of the relevant experimental operations. At least three different operational definitions of deprivation can be identified.

1. Deprivation may be defined in terms of experimental operations whereby there is a *decrease* (qualitative or quantitative) in the properties of a "normal" experience relative to when that experience is supposed to occur in development. Hence, maternal deprivation points to the decrement in the quality or quantity of maternal care relative to the norm for its species or society. Typically such deprivation is produced by removing the infant from its mother for various periods of time.

2. Deprivation may refer to the *retardation* in the timing of an experience relative to when it normally occurs. The experience remains the same, but it is delayed. Thus infants may be deprived of exposure to patterned or meaningful visual stimulation until after some presumed critical period for the establishment of patterned vision has past. That is, exposure may come after the time in development that the relevant neural pathways have been established.

3. Deprivation may refer to a relative *change* in the nature of stimulation, regardless of when it occurs in development. Hence there is a decrease in the ongoing levels of social approval during periods of "social reinforcer deprivation" (Gewirtz & Baer, 1958). This usage of deprivation is sometimes contrasted with the concept of *privation,* which refers to the complete absence of stimulation of some type instead of variations in its quality. Hence maternal deprivation, for Gewirtz (1961), would be reserved for instances where children were once exposed to maternal care, and then it was withdrawn; maternal privation would refer to instances where children were removed from maternal care at birth.

Deprivation, however introduced, has been assumed to produce either a slower rate of development than is normal, a lower outcome at maturity than is normal, or a greater sensitivity to stress than is normal. In each instance, the deflection in development is relative to normal course, and in the direction of rendering the individual less capable of performing adaptive behaviors and functions. The deprivation concept thus implies that there exists, for the species, an optimal trajectory for normal social development.

Deprivation operations have often been contrasted with *enrichment*. Whereas the nature and functions of enrichment experiences have been less extensively discussed, it has been generally assumed that enrichment will produce effects that are opposite to deprivation. Hence enrichment should facilitate development relative to a normal course, either in the quickening of the rate of development or in the achievement of new levels of functioning. But whether one or both outcomes may be expected has seldom been explored. Should, for instance, early childhood cognitive enrichment lead to more rapid development of reading and vocabulary skills, to higher levels of achievement at 18 years of age, or to both more rapid development and higher terminal achievement levels? Without attempting to answer this question (although it seems that both changes in rate and in outcome are usually anticipated), we can observe that enrichment also appears to presuppose an optimal rate of normal development, and that under some circumstances, the normal trajectory can be exceeded to produce supranormal capabilities.

The experimental operations of deprivation and enrichment have provided significant insights on the development of sensory mechanisms and sensorimotor coordination (see chapters in Gottlieb, 1976c). There is considerable evidence now that experimental fine-tuning occurs in sensory systems during ontogeny, and that this adjustment within the sensory system and between systems can be disrupted by the omission of species-typical stimulation. The unsolved problems, now being vigorously investigated, concern such matters as the pervasiveness of the deficits, and how permanent they are.

Social deprivation experiments have yielded less coherent results. As in the case of sensory deprivation and enrichment research, significant outcomes in social interchanges can be produced by varying the nature of the social experiences to which the young are exposed in development. But it is unclear whether these deprivation experiences produce organisms that are "retarded" or "deficient." For example, socially deprived male cowbirds are *more* effective in eliciting mating in females than are "normal" males (King & West, 1977). Similarly, male mice reared in isolation are *more* dominant, aggressive, and likely to mate than are nonisolated male mice (Cairns, 1973).

Such reversals in the direction of deprivation effects—where isolation leads to superior social performances rather than inferior ones—point to a more general problem in applying the deprivation model to the understanding of social development. The problem is that the interactional–developmental perspective contradicts the assumption that there is only a single trajectory of "normal" social development. There are, potentially, multiple trajectories. As the interactional demands change, so must the actions that are deemed adaptive or optimal. Hence one might expect as many "optimal" courses of development as there are social systems into which the young must be integrated. Accordingly, deprivation operations describe only one of a population of conditions to which the young can adapt, one in which some seemingly critical features of stimulation have been omitted. The interactional orientation focuses attention *on the nature of the social system to which the young must adapt instead of on the one of which he is deprived.* It points to the relativity of what might be judged normal and adaptive to the particular features of the social context of which the individual is a part. This idea was stated in a more general form by Michel and Moore (1978) when they wrote:

> The environment is not only a good provider, giving sustenance for growth, as the predeterminist would have us believe; it is also a source of structure for the developing organism. There are trace effects of experience woven into all aspects of the developing organism. In other words, the organism does not unfold from some preformed blueprint but rather derives its organization, as it progressively changes, from what it is at present and from the stimulative context within which it behaves. . . . It is possible, from this viewpoint, to envision a multiplicity of alternative developmental outcomes and to see that one outcome might be reachable by different pathways. This view is to be contrasted with the one that asserts that there is one path and one outcome, dictated by an unfolding of previously encoded instruction [p. 52].

In other words, social interchanges reflect the operation of ongoing processes that are responsive to both interpersonal and intrapersonal influences. To think of a social pattern as a "structure" of the individual—one that is described by an optimal normal growth pattern that can be facilitated or retarded—is hardly consistent with the extensive body of information on the importance of interpersonal regulation of behavior, from infancy onwards. Social patterns are necessarily dynamic, reversible, and capable of change throughout ontogeny, even though the biological structures upon which they ultimately depend are relatively enduring. James Atz (1970, p. 69) provided a succinct statement of the matter when he observed that "to think of behavior *as* structure has led to the most pernicious kind of oversimplification."

A FINAL COMMENT

Historically, accounts of social development and personality have begun their task by inventing ways to simplify the explanatory chore. Social learning approaches began with a denial of organismic changes and development; cognitive approaches, with a rejection of emotional and irrational sources of control; evolutionary approaches, with a decoupling of idiosyncratic events and experiences to which the individual is exposed in ontogeny. Psychoanalytic theories, despite fanciful motivational speculations, have captured some of the emphases of each of the above approaches. The individual, in a dynamic neo-Freudian perspective, is active and reactive, a complex mosaic of internal and interpersonal sources of control. The developmental–interactional perspective might rightfully be seen as the descendant of each of the above models of man, but not wholly determined by any one of them. Because it has grown out of psychobiological studies of human and nonhuman young, it maintains a close and immediate linkage to the empirical science. The orientation may achieve its most useful service if it provides a framework for understanding how early experiences are fused with later ones in the regulation of social patterns.

REFERENCES

Allport, G. W. 1937. *Personality: A psychological interpretation.* New York: Holt.

Alperts, J. R. 1978. Huddling by rat pups: Group behavioral mechanisms of temperature regulation and energy conservation. *Journal of Comparative and Physiological Psychology, 92,* 231–245.

Atz, J. W. 1970. The application of the idea of homology to behavior. In L. R. Aronson, E. Tobach, D. S. Lehrman, & J. S. Rosenblatt (Eds.), *Development and evoluation of behavior: Essays in memory of T. C. Schneirla.* San Francisco: Freeman.

Bacon, W. E., & Stanley, W. C. 1970. Reversal learning in neonatal dogs. *Journal of Comparative and Physiological Psychology, 70,* 344–350.

Baldwin, J. M. 1902. *Social and ethical interpretations in mental development: A study in social psychology* (3rd ed.). New York: Macmillan. (1st ed., 1897.)

Barker, R. G. (Ed.). 1963. *The stream of behavior.* New York: Appleton-Century-Crofts.

Bayley, N. 1969. *Manual for the Bayley Scales of Infant Development.* New York: Psychological Corporation.

Bell, R. Q. 1968. A reinterpretation of the direction of effects in studies of socialization. *Psychological Review, 75,* 81–95.

Bell, R. Q. 1971. Stimulus control of parent or caregiver behavior by offspring. *Developmental Psychology, 4,* 63–72.

Bell, R. Q., & Harper, L. V. 1977. *Child effects on adults.* Hillsdale, N.J.: Erlbaum.

Bowlby, J. 1958. The nature of the child's tie to his mother. *International Journal of Psychoanalysis, 39,* 350–373.

Bowlby, J. 1969. *Attachment and loss. Vol. 1.: Attachment.* New York: Basic Books.

Bronfenbrenner, U. 1977. Toward an experimental ecology of human development. *American Psychologist, 32,* 513–531.

Cairns, R. B. 1973. Fighting and punishment from a developmental perspective. In J. K. Cole & D. D. Jensen (Eds.), *Nebraska Symposium on Motivation* (Vol. 20). Lincoln: University of Nebraska Press.

Cairns, R. B. 1976. The ontogeny and phylogeny of social interactions. In M. E. Hahn & E. C. Simmel (Eds.), *Communicative behavior and evolution.* New York: Academic Press.

Cairns, R. B. 1977. Beyond social attachment: The dynamics of interactional development. In T. Alloway, P. Pliner, & L. Krames (Eds.), *Attachment behavior.* New York: Plenum.

Cairns, R. B. 1979a. *The analysis of social interactions: Methods, issues, and illustrations.* Hillsdale, N.J.: Erlbaum.

Cairns, R. B. 1979b. *Social development: The origins and plasticity of interactions.* San Francisco: Freeman.

Cairns, R. B., & Green, J. A. 1979. How to assess personality and social patterns: Observations or ratings? In R. B. Cairns (Ed.), *The analysis of social interactions: Methods, issues, and illustrations.* Hillsdale, N.J.: Erlbaum.

Cottrell, L. S. 1942. The analysis of situational fields in social psychology. *American Sociological Review, 7,* 370–382.

Cottrell, L. S. 1969. Interpersonal interaction and the development of the self. In D. A. Goslin (Ed.), *Handbook of socialization theory and research.* Chicago: Rand McNally.

Darwin, C. 1872. *The expression of the emotions in man and animals.* London: John Murray.

de Beer, G. 1958. *Embryos and ancestors* (3rd ed.). London: Oxford University Press.

Eckerman, C. O. 1979. The human infant in social interaction. In R. B. Cairns (Ed.), *The analysis of social interactions: Methods, issues, and illustrations.* Hillsdale, N.J.: Erlbaum.

Fuller, J. L. 1966. Transitory effects of experiential deprivation upon reversal learning in dogs. *Psychonomic Science, 4,* 273–274.

Gesell, A., & Thompson, H. 1934. *Infant behavior: Its genesis and growth.* New York: McGraw-Hill.

Gewirtz, J. L. 1961. A learning analysis of the effects of normal stimulation, privation, and deprivation on the acquisition of social motivation and attachment. In B. M. Foss (Ed.), *Determinants of infant behavior.* London: Methuen.

Gewirtz, J. L., & Baer, D. M. 1958. Deprivation and satiation of social reinforcers as drive conditions. *Journal of Abnormal and Social Psychology, 57,* 165–172.

Gottlieb, G. 1970. Conceptions of prenatal behavior. In L. R. Aronson, E. Tobach, D. S. Lehrman, & J. S. Rosenblatt (Eds.), *Development and evolution of behavior.* San Francisco: Freeman.

Gottlieb, G. 1971. *Development of species identification in birds: An inquiry into the prenatal determinants of perception.* Chicago: University of Chicago Press.

Gottlieb, G. 1976a. The roles of experience in the development of behavior and the nervous system. In G. Gottlieb (Ed.), *Neural and behavioral specificity.* New York: Academic Press.

Gottlieb, G. 1976b. Conceptions of prenatal development. *Psychological Review, 83,* 215–234.

Gottlieb, G. (Ed.). 1976c. *Neural behavior and specificity.* New York: Academic Press.

Gould, S. J. 1977. *Ontogeny and phylogeny.* Cambridge, Mass.: Belknap Press of Harvard University Press.

Green, J. A., Gustafson, G. E., & West, M. J. 1979. The effects of infant development on mother-infant interactions. *Infant Behavior and Development, 2,* 301–308.

Gustafson, G. E., Green, J. A., & West, M. J. 1979. The infant's changing role in mother-infant games: The growth of social skills. *Child Development,* in press.

Hall, W. M. 1973. *Observational and interactive determinants of aggressive behavior in boys.* Unpublished doctoral dissertation, Indiana University.

Hinde, R. A., & Stevenson-Hinde, J. (Eds.). 1973. *Constraints on learning: Limitations and predispositions.* New York: Academic Press.

Holmberg, M. C. 1977. *The development of social interchange patterns from 12 to 42 months: Cross-sectional and short-term longitudinal analysis.* Unpublished doctoral dissertation, University of North Carolina at Chapel Hill.

Kagan, J., & Moss, H. A. 1963. *Birth to maturity: A study in psychological development.* New York: Wiley.

Kaye, K. 1977. Toward the origins of dialogue. In H. R. Schaffer (Ed.), *Studies in mother-infant interaction.* London: Academic Press.

King, A. P., & West, M. J. 1977. Species identification in the North American cowbird: Appropriate responses to abnormal song. *Science, 195,* 1002–1004.

King, M., & Wilson, A. C. 1975. Evolution at two levels in humans and chimpanzees. *Science, 188,* 107–116.

Kohlberg, L. 1969. Stage and sequence: The cognitive-developmental approach to socialization. In D. A. Goslin (Ed.), *Handbook of socialization theory and research.* Chicago: Rand McNally.

Kuo, Z. Y. 1967. *The dynamics of behavior development: An epigenetic view.* New York: Random House.

Lehrman, D. S. 1961. Hormonal regulation of parental behavior in birds and infrahuman animals. In W. C. Young (Ed.), *Sex and internal secretions* (3rd ed.). Baltimore: Williams and Wilkins.

Lewin, K. 1935. *A dynamic theory of personality.* New York: McGraw-Hill.

MacCombie, D. J. 1978. *The development of reciprocity in children's social interchanges.* Unpublished doctoral dissertation, University of North Carolina at Chapel Hill.

Mason, W. A. 1968. Scope and potential of primate research. In J. H. Masserman (Ed.), *Science and psychoanalysis (Vol. 12): Animal and man.* New York: Grune and Stratton.

Mason, W. A. in press. Social ontogeny. In P. Marler & J. C. Vandenbergh (Eds.), *Social behavior and communication.* New York: Plenum.

McGraw, M. B. 1939. Swimming behavior of the human infant. *Journal of Pediatrics, 15,* 485–490.

Mead, G. H. 1934. *Mind, self, and society.* Chicago: University of Chicago Press.

Michel, G. F., & Moore, C. L. 1978. *Biological perspectives in developmental psychology.* Monterey, Calif.: Brooks/Cole.

Mills, W. 1899. The nature of animal intelligence and the methods of investigating it. *Psychological Review, 6,* 262–274.

Mischel, W. 1973. Toward a cognitive social learning reconceptualization of personality. *Psychological Review, 80,* 252–283.

Mueller, E., & Lucas, T. 1975. A developmental analysis of peer interaction among toddlers. In M. L. Lewis & L. A. Rosenblum (Eds.), *Friendship and peer relations.* New York: Wiley.

Novak, M. A., & Harlow, H. F. 1975. Social recovery of monkeys isolated for the first year of life: I. Rehabilitation and therapy. *Developmental Psychology, 11,* 453–465.

Nowlis, V. 1952. The search for significant concepts in a study of parent-child relationships. *American Journal of Orthopsychiatry, 22,* 286–299.

Patterson, G. R. 1979. A performance theory for coercive behavior in family interaction. In R. B. Cairns (Ed.), *The analysis of social interactions: Methods, issues, and illustrations.* Hillsdale, N. J.: Erlbaum.

Piaget, J. 1978. *Behavior and evolution.* (Translated by Donald Nicholson-Smith.) New York: Random House.

Preyer, W. 1888. *The mind of the child* (2 Vols.). New York: Appleton.

Raush, H. L. 1965. Interactive sequences. *Journal of Personality and Social Psychology, 2,* 487–499.

Rosenblatt, J. S. 1972. Learning in newborn kittens. *Scientific American, 227,* 18–25.

Ross, H. S., & Goldman, B. D. 1977. Establishing new social relations in infancy. In T. Alloway, P. Pliner, & L. Krames (Eds.), *Attachment behavior.* New York: Plenum.

Sackett, G. P. (Ed.). 1978. *Observing behavior, Vol. 2: Data collection and analysis methods.* Baltimore: University Park Press.

Sameroff, A. J. 1975. Early influences on development: Fact or fancy? *Merrill-Palmer Quarterly, 21,* 267–294.

Schaffer, H. R. (Ed.). 1977a. *Studies in mother-infant interaction.* New York: Academic Press.

Schaffer, H. R. 1977b. *Mothering.* New York: Harvard University Press.

Schaffer, H. R. 1979. Acquiring the concept of the dialogue. In M. M. Bornstein & W. Kessen (Eds.), *Psychological development from infancy.* New York: Erlbaum.

Schneirla, T. C. 1966. Behavioral development and comparative psychology. *Quarterly Review of Biology, 41,* 283–302.

Scott, J. P. 1976. Genetic variation and the evolution of communication. In M. E. Hahn & E. C. Simmel (Eds.), *Communicative behavior and evolution.* New York: Academic Press.

Sears, R. R. 1951. A theoretical framework for personality and social behavior. *American Psychologist, 6,* 476–483.

Seligman, M. E., & Hager, V. L. (Eds.). 1972. *Biological boundaries of learning.* Englewood Cliffs, N.J.: Prentice-Hall.

Shirley, M. M. 1933. *The first two years: A study of twenty-five babies.* Minneapolis: University of Minnesota Press.

Stone, L. J., Smith, H. T., & Murphy, L. B. (Eds.). 1973. *The competent infant.* New York: Basic Books.

Thoman, E. C., Barnett, C. R., & Leiderman, P. H. 1971. Feeding behaviors of newborn infants as a function of parity of mother. *Child Development, 42,* 1471–1483.

Thomas, A., Chess, S., & Birch, H. G. 1968. *Temperament and behavior disorders in children.* New York: New York University Press.

Tinbergen, N. 1972. *The animal in its world: Explorations of an ethologist.* London: Allen & Unwin.

Waddington, C. H. 1968. The theory of evolution today. In A. Koestler & J. R. Smythies (Eds.), *Beyond reductionism.* New York: Macmillan.

Wilson, E. O. 1975. *Sociobiology: The new synthesis.* Cambridge, Mass.: Harvard University Press.

Wilson, R. S. 1978. Synchronies in mental development: An epigenetic perspective. *Science, 202,* 939–947.

Yarrow, M. R., Campbell, J. D., & Burton, R. V. 1968. *Child rearing: An inquiry into research and methods.* San Francisco: Jossey–Bass.

Young, W. C. (Ed.). 1961. *Sex and internal secretions* (3rd ed.). Baltimore: Williams and Wilkins.

PART II

EARLY BEHAVIOR AND
SOCIAL DEVELOPMENT:
CASE STUDIES

CHAPTER 5

Parent–Neonate Interaction and Its Long-Term Effects[1]

PETER de CHATEAU

ORIGINS AND BACKGROUND

A group of new mothers in our maternity ward were discussing with each other their experiences of pregnancy, delivery, and the hours and days following. Each expressed her individuality in her use of language, her behavior, and her approach to her own particular experience. However, all these mothers had one thing in common: the unique start with what was their very special baby and the sudden realization of a developing relationship with a brand new and enormously intriguing infant. Their hopes that this relationship would be a sound and happy one were very obvious. Overhearing these and similar conversations aroused our interest and was the starting point of our research projects.

The studies referred to in this chapter began, therefore, during practical day-to-day routine work on the delivery floor and in the maternity and neonatal wards. Another reason for our research was that mothers with sick newborn infants very often expressed feelings about numerous problems and difficulties connected with childbirth and the perinatal period. Many of

[1] This research was supported by funds from the Swedish Save the Children Foundation and from the Swedish Medical Research Council (grant number B79-19X-05443-01).

109

these were nonphysical problems and had to do with existing routines and practices in the hospital and in child rearing. The general attitudes of the hospital staff seemed of special importance to the situation of the mother–infant dyad. The facilities for fathers to participate were obviously very poor, as is confirmed by a study of the relevant literature. Hospital personnel have concentrated on providing a high quality of physical care of both the mother and her infant, but unfortunately, little attention has been paid to the importance of the neonatal period to the development of the unique mother–father–infant relationship. In planning hospital buildings, the big and well equipped centers have often served as a model for smaller county hospitals. Costs have become enormous, and in future planning, new forms must be tried. The individual and personal touch has gradually disappeared. Moreover, many routines in our maternity and neonatal wards, such as separation (Barnett, Leiderman, Grobstein, & Klaus, 1970; Klaus & Kennell, 1970), were introduced to prevent infections and to improve treatment of the newborn. Whereas the adverse influences on the parent–infant relationship have been recognized (Leiderman, Leifer, Seashore, Barnett, & Grobstein, 1973; Leifer, Leiderman, Barnett, & Williams, 1972), many mothers are still not allowed to touch, hold, and care for their newborn premature or sick infants. Even facilities for mothers with normal, healthy, and full-term infants continue to differ very much from one place to another. If the period immediately following delivery is a particularly special and sensitive one (Kennell, Trause, & Klaus, 1975), many changes in our day-to-day care and hospital practices need to be made to ensure that parents and infants remain together during this period.

Early Post-Partum Contact

In recent years the scope of research programs dealing with the perinatal period and its impact on future psychosocial development within families has been increasing. New methods and a different approach to this important field of interest have come forward, and our knowledge is growing fast. An important part of this new interest is certainly a general trend in our societies toward a more natural way of living, which is not confined to the medical field. Several studies of caregiving procedures around the time of delivery have emerged from this new attitude toward the process of childbirth. The early hours, days, weeks, and months after birth are of special importance to the development of the infant toward a state of stability, adaptation, and functional affection in relation to the mother. To be exposed at an early stage to certain modalities such as skin and suckling contact, and also to experiences such as hunger, pain, and distress, may perhaps be absolutely necessary to enable an integration in one's personality and a subsequent capacity to relate to other individuals. Other maternal or adult behavior, such as holding, carrying, touching, talking, and showing different objects, may be equally elementary as a means of meeting the psychogenic needs of the neonate (Langmeyer & Matejcek, 1975). A sound relationship between parent and infant has to start immediately after birth if the early period is to be used adequately and effectively. The alertness of the newborn is highly significant and complements maternal receptivity very well, thus preparing for a synchronous development of their interrelationship. In fact, the early mother–infant interaction will itself largely determine the amount and quality of sensory stimuli received by the newborn. In a number of studies, Klaus and Kennell have questioned whether present hospital practices may affect later maternal behavior; they have given evidence that the immediate post-partum period is a particularly sensitive one in the development of the mother–infant relationship. Twelve mothers with healthy full-term infants were filmed during their first contact, and an orderly progression of tactile contact was observed in all mothers (Klaus, Kennell, Plumb, & Zuehlke, 1970). The mothers started with explorative fingertip touch of the infant's extremities, followed by palm contact on the trunk, encompassing of the infant, and eye-to-eye contact. Mothers of normal premature infants followed a similar sequence of behavior, but at a much slower rate. In another study, 14 mothers (control group) had the usual routine contact with their healthy full-term infants after delivery, and 14 mothers (extended contact) were given their naked babies for 1 hour within the first 3 hours after birth and for 5 extra hours of contact each afternoon of the 3 days after delivery. In follow-up studies 1 month, 1 year (Klaus, Jerauld, Kreger, McAlpine, Steffa, & Kennell, 1972), and 2 years after delivery, differences were found in maternal attachment behavior and linguistic behavior between the extended contact group and the control group (Kennell, Jerauld, Wolfe, Chesler, Kreger, McAlpine, Steffa, & Klaus, 1974; Ringler, Kennell, Jarvelle, Navojosky, & Klaus, 1975). In a very large current study, O'Conner (1977) is investigating low-income primiparous mothers, assigned randomly to either extra contact or hospital routine care. So far over 300 families have been followed for a period of 1–2 years. Abuse, neglect, abandonment, and failure to thrive have been observed more commonly in routine care infants (O'Conner, Vietze, Hopkins, & Altmeier, 1977). These observations have been confirmed in an Italian study (Kropf, Negroni, and Nordio, 1976), albeit in a slightly different form, 1 month after delivery, emphasizing that perinatal medicine should be considered an important part of maternal and child health.

In a series of our own observations, a change in maternal behavior was seen even when the extra contact was limited to 20 minutes during the first post-partum hour. Twenty-two healthy primiparous mothers, with normal pregnancies and deliveries, were given an extra skin-to-skin and suckling contact with their infants after delivery (extra contact). A control group of 20 primiparous mothers and infants was given routine care, as was a second control group of 20 multiparous mothers and infants. The subjects were assigned randomly to either the early-contact or the control group. At 36 hours maternal and infant behavior were observed during breast feeding. At this stage primiparae with extra contact showed behavior much more like the behavior of multiparae with routine care. Infants of primiparae with routine care cried most frequently (de Chateau & Wiberg, 1977a). At 3 months a follow-up study of the two groups of primiparae and their infants was made by observing mother–infant free play and personally interviewing the mothers. Background data concerning pregnancy, delivery, neonatal period, and the first 3 months at home were comparable in the two groups. Mothers in the extra-contact group spent more time kissing and looking en face at their infants, and the infants smiled more often and cried less frequently (de Chateau & Wiberg, 1977b). One year after delivery, the primiparous mothers with extra contact showed more close body contact with their infants during observation of a routine physical examination (de Chateau & Wiberg, in press). More detailed information is given later in this chapter.

Infant Ability

It is accepted generally that influences from the immediate surroundings during the early postnatal period have an impact on subsequent development of behavior. At birth the brain is not completely developed. Schapiro and Vukovisch (1970) have shown that in rats the number of synapses in pyramid-cell dendrites is correlated with the amount of sensory stimulation during the first weeks of life. Conel (1970) states that the main growth period of brain cells and dendrites between cells in the human infant is during fetal life and up to 3 months of age. The myelinization and isolation of axons starts in the second trimester of pregnancy and is complete by the age of 2 years (Dobbing, 1970). Malnutrition during this period may result in impaired neuronal growth and may result subsequently in relative brain damage. The sensitivity of the brain seems especially great during the early period in human and animal life and, therefore, is also an important factor in the development of behavior and relationships with other individuals.

The individual reactive capacity of the newborn baby and his influence on the environment can be illustrated in a number of ways. Immediately after delivery most infants in the alert state (Prechtl, 1974) are able to see and to follow, albeit primitively and in an uncoordinated fashion, slow movements of bright objects, provided that the mother has given birth with a very limited analgesia and without anesthesia. They are also able to turn their heads toward sound, especially the human voice (Brazelton, 1973; Condon & Sander, 1974). Bowlby (1958, 1969) states that infant smiling, crying, clinging, suckling, and following are activities that may release and facilitate feelings of attachment and a caring response from the mother. Although Richards (1971) is critical of Bowlby's explanation —that all five infant behaviors bring about the proximity of mother and child, resulting in their mutual attachment—he agrees that smiling plays a role in the growing mother–infant relationship. The infant's cry may have various causes and may be seen as a way of communicating with the adult. Wasz-Höckert et al. (Valanné, Vuorenkoski, Partanen, Lind, & Wasz-Höckert, 1967; Wasz-Höckert, Lind, Vuorenkoski, Partanen, & Valanné, 1968) were able to identify in a spectrographic study four types of infant cry during the neonatal period: the birth cry, the hunger cry, the pain cry, and the pleasure cry. These different types of cry may be specific signals to the mother and may be able to trigger her response. In lactating primiparous mothers, the hunger cry caused an increase in temperature over the breasts (Lind, Vuorenkoski, & Wasz-Höckert, 1972). Experience seemed to influence the degree of this reaction; mothers who had listened to their own infant's cry more often had higher skin temperature (Wasz-Höckert, Seitamo, Vuorenkoski, Partanen, & Lind, 1972). Some mothers reacted weakly and others strongly to their infant's cry.

Blauvelt and McKenna (1962) studied infants' special capacity for responding to the environment that their mothers provided. Tactile stimulation of the infant's face from the ears to the lips resulted in the infant turning his face toward the mother. This head turning and orienting to the mother's face might release maternal response behavior. Turkewitz, Moreau, and Birch (1968) noted that normal infants were more responsive to stimulation of the right side of the perioral region than of the left side. The capacity of a neonate to fix, follow, and be alert to a visual stimulus appears to be good evidence of an intact central nervous system (Brazelton, Scholl, & Robey, 1966; Emde, Swedberg, & Suzuki, 1975). Fantz (Fantz, 1963; Fantz & Miranda, 1975) demonstrated the presence of discriminatory ability in neonates in selecting different patterns when vision was tested. Miranda (1970) showed that, when presented with two identical pictures, newborn infants more often looked at the one on the right than they did at the one on the left. In about 80% of cases, mothers have been reported to hold their infants to the left side of the body (de Chateau, 1976a; de Chateau, 1977; de Chateau, Holmberg, & Winberg, 1978; Salk, 1960; Salk, 1962; Salk, 1970; Weiland, 1964; Weiland & Sperber, 1970). The infant's preference for turning to the right and looking to the right may be a species-specific adaptation to maternal holding to the left (i.e., when looking and turning to the right the baby can see his mother). The infant's preference for right-side looking and turning could also be a signal to the mother to favor holding on the left.

At 5 days of age, clinically normal babies spent significantly more time turning toward their own mother's breast pad than they did toward a clean breast pad. This difference was not found at 2 days. It may be that, after birth, the infant gradually becomes aware of his mother; this awareness may become more specific as the infant is exposed to her longer (MacFarlane, 1975). The symptoms of distress exhibited by a variety of caregivers during feeding, as observed by Burns, Sanders, Stechler, and Julia (1972), may be partly explained by MacFarlane's (1975) observations. Infants of 14 months of age with sleep problems had already been more irritable during the neonatal period and had fussed more at a neurological examination and during a suckling test than had infants without sleep problems (Bernal, 1972, 1973). This illustrates the individuality of the newborn infant and shows how careful we must be in assuming that the parents' handling of the infant is always the source of developing problems within a given family. Korner and Thoman (1972) found that some newborn infants could be soothed more easily than could others. Vestibular–proprioceptive stimulation, as a part of mother–infant body contact, had a highly potent soothing effect. Soothing can be a very important mode of stimulating an infant. When a crying infant is picked up and put over the shoulder during the first weeks of life, it usually stops crying and becomes bright-eyed, thus being able to scan its visual surroundings and provide itself with a great deal of visual stimulation (Korner & Grobstein, 1966; Korner & Thoman, 1970). Crying infants may therefore need to be picked up more than do infants capable of providing visual experiences for themselves. Maternal neglect of a crying infant may thus provide the infant with less visual stimulation and influence psychomotor and even affective development (Korner, 1971). Birns, Blank, and Bridger (1966) also reported individuality in soothing; a neonate who is easily soothed by one stimulus (e.g., rocking) tends to be easily soothed by others (e.g., a dummy), and vice versa. In another study, Birns (1968) reported that individual differences in responsiveness to stimulation were found over time, and that stability in the individual reactions was evident. Bell (1974) illustrated the social interaction between the neonate and his caregiver. The infant's cry can bring the caregiver into the vicinity and thus start an interaction, although large individual differences have been found and the tolerance of caregivers probably shows a great range of response. During the first year of the infant's life, a number of maternal behavior types take place in response to crying, such as picking up, talking, feeding, and touching, as reported by Bell and Ainsworth (1972). This illustrates that the individual ways of response found during the neonatal period also continue later on. The early maternal responses to infant signals may therefore influence later social interaction (Thoman, 1975).

Early Infant Stimulation

In recent years increased attention has been given to the effects of early stimulation on the human infant. Wachs and Cucinotta (1972) provided 13 normal newborn infants with 140 minutes of supplementary handling, audio–visual stimulation, and rocking every day for the first 3 days after birth. At 4 days of age these stimulated infants showed better conditioned head turning and at 30 days their visual attentiveness was greater than it was in control infants. By 10 months, however, no difference in development was found between the two groups. The authors suggest that permanence of effects may not have been achieved in their study because the optimal amount of critical stimulation may not have been reached. Another explanation might be that the extra stimulation was not given by the infants' own mothers or was not given at the appropriate time. If a particularly sensitive period for the developing mother–infant relationship exists, stimulation by the infant's own mother might be found to produce more lasting advantages. Ourth and Brown (1961) found significantly less crying in infants who were given 5 hours of extra handling daily by their own mothers during the first $4\frac{1}{2}$ days of life, as compared with control infants without this extra handling (mild, firm support and rhythmical body stimulation at feeding time). Distress during feeding expressed by infants looked after by more than one person has been pointed out by Burns et al. (1972). Enrichment of the infant's hospital environment by means of single-caregiver practices could reduce this distress. In another study (White & Castle, 1964), infants given extra handling during the first 5 weeks of life showed significantly more visual interest in their environment than did nonhandled controls. No differences were found in weight gain, development, or general health. In infants of low birth weight, early stimulation might be of extra importance, especially if they are born to mothers of low socioeconomic level or with other disadvantages. An experimental group of low birth weight infants was given visual, tactile, and kinesthetic stimulation during 6 weeks in the neonatal ward (Scarr-Salopatek & Williams, 1973). Weekly home visits were also made to improve maternal care during the first year of life. Tests at 4 weeks and 1 year indicated greater developmental progress in these infants than was indicated in controls without extra stimulation and without weekly home visits.

In the foregoing, many different aspects of the importance and potency of the neonatal period have been discussed. The facts and observations presented should have implications for this special period, as well as for child-rearing practices later on. However, infants differ greatly from each other from the start. Their families have different and distinctive backgrounds and individual capacities. Flexibility to the individual requirements of each family is needed. Certain child-rearing practices and certain forms of early stimulation and soothing are generally considered to be universally beneficial, regardless of the individual needs of a particular infant or child. The interpretation of interactive patterns is still tentative, and much more needs to be known before we can fully understand their meaning and importance. In the following sections of this chapter some aspects of methodology and of early mother–infant interaction and its long-term effects will be discussed. The chapter concludes by speculating on future trends in the study of these problems.

PROBLEMS OF METHODOLOGY

Problems of methodology in the study of the parent–infant relationship and its development are many and are far from solved today. Many different investigative methods have been used without any one being completely successful. Combinations of methods have been employed to try to overcome the disadvantages of each used alone, but looking at the subject from a variety of angles has not always reduced the inaccuracies. In the following section, examples of the methods used in our own group and the findings obtained from them will be presented and discussed.

Direct Observation of Behavior

Direct observation is a highly suitable method of studying mother–infant relations in young children and infants (Moss, 1965; Rheingold, 1960). The most obvious advantage of observation is that one can see what is happening without having to rely on poorly established techniques. Direct observation may therefore be preferred to filming and videotape recording, techniques that are a less natural form of observation. Moreover, the camera lens covers a restricted area (Cooper, Costella, Douglas, Ingleby, & Turner, 1974), and analysis becomes excessively time consuming and expensive. During direct observation, on the other hand, one has to be selective about what is to be observed and recorded. There is always the risk that valuable information will be missed. It is obviously an advantage if a limited number of behavioral items to be observed can be chosen from the start. Clear-cut definitions of these behavioral items have to be made in advance, and agreement must be reached on their occurrence. It may be very important for mothers to remain unaware of what is being recorded in their behavior, especially when only a few items are registered (de Chateau, 1976a; de Chateau, Holmberg, & Winberg, 1978). The presence of an observer may be disconcerting (Lewis, 1972) and is certainly felt differently by different subjects. The setting of the observation is also of great importance. During their stay in the maternity ward, mothers are used to contact with the hospital staff (e.g., for lectures on infant care) and very seldom show any signs of discomfort during the observation (de Chateau, 1976a). For the newborn infant and his mother the maternity ward is, in our culture, a natural environment.

As an example of the use of direct observational methods and the problems inherent in them, consider one of our first studies of maternal behavior. This study dealt with the preference for holding newborn infants to a point on the left side of the body midline. The original observation of this phenomenon was made by Salk (1960). In his observations he was sitting opposite the mother and handed the baby to her. He was therefore part of what was happening, and his way of handing over the infant (and possibly whether he was right- or left-handed) might have influenced the mother's side preference. To avoid this potential bias, a subsequent study dealing with the same behavior was somewhat differently designed (de Chateau, 1976a; de Chateau, Holmberg, & Winberg, 1978). The infant was presented to the mother in another way, not using any of the observers to initiate maternal behavior. Before entering the observation room, furnished as shown in Figure 5-1, the mother was told what to do by the experimenter, who then followed her in. The mother's own infant was placed on the table with his

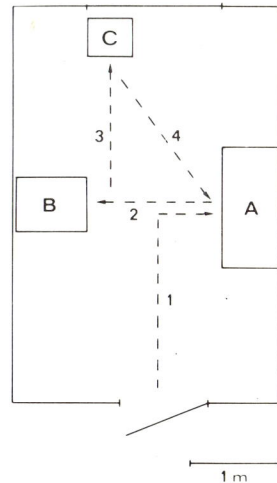

Figure 5-1. The room in which the observations of maternal holding and carrying of newborn infant were made. A = nursing table; B = crib; C = chair. (From de Chateau, 1976a.)

feet toward her so that the mother was able to make her own choice of which side she would place the baby (Figure 5-2). The mother entered the room as indicated by Arrow 1 and her route through the room is shown by Arrows 2–4 (Figure 5-1).

The mother was asked to take her infant from the table (A) and carry him to the crib (B) and put him down there. Notes were taken of whether the mother carried the infant in her hands or arms and, in the latter instance, the side of her body on which she carried him and whether she supported the infant's head when putting him into the crib. The mother was then asked to pick up her infant again, walk over to the chair (C), and sit down with the infant. When the mother was sitting on the chair, a note was made of the side of her body on which she held her infant and whether she held him close against her body or away from it. The observer was standing nearby in front of the mother. This rather complex way of letting the mother move through the room lessened the risk that the activity of the observer would influence the behavior of the mother. The same behavior was observed at different points in the course of the mother's progress through the room, and correlations of the stability of behavior over time could be obtained. An illustration of the different ways of holding and carrying is given in Figure

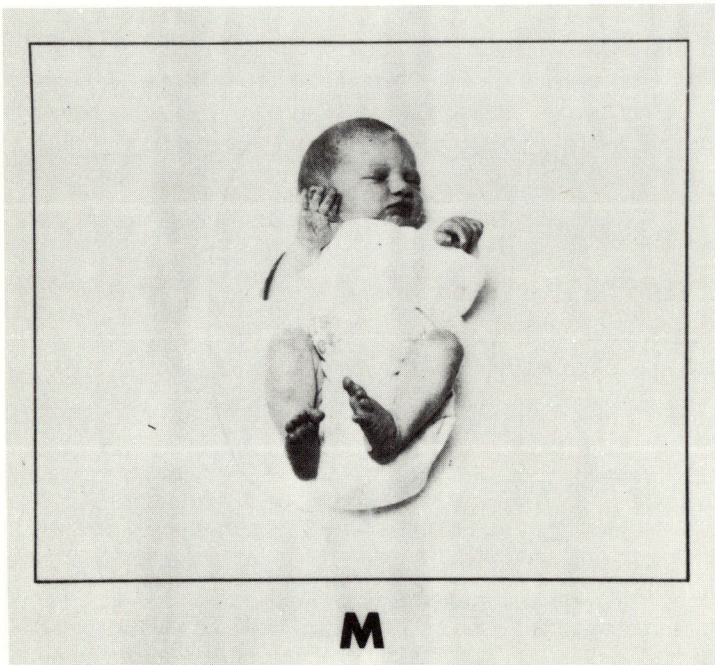

M

Figure 5-2. The position of the infant on the table and the position of the mother (M) at the beginning of the observation. (From de Chateau, 1976a.)

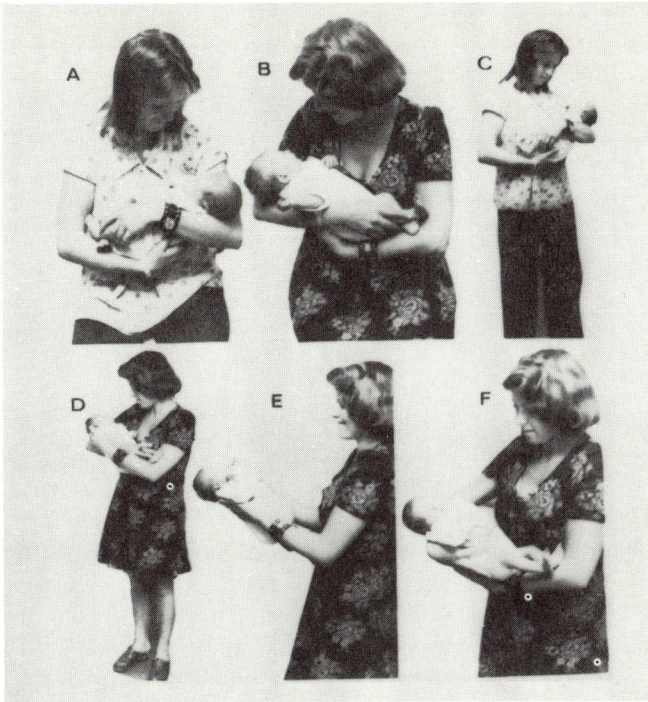

Figure 5-3. A, A mother sitting holding her infant to the left. B, A mother sitting holding her infant to the right. C, A mother carrying her infant to the left. D, A mother carrying her infant to the right. E, A mother carrying her infant "in her hands." F, A mother holding her infant away from her body, as opposed to A and B. (From de Chateau, 1976a.)

5-3, and definitions are given in Appendix A. In exploring the development of side preference during childhood, a slightly modified and altered method of observation was used (de Chateau & Andersson, 1976). Children aged from 2 to 16 years and of both sexes participated in these studies. The children entered the room through the door and were asked to take a doll from the bed (B) and pretend it was a newborn baby (Figure 5-4).

The size and weight of the doll varied with the age of the children. After picking up the doll, the children were asked to sit down in the chair (A) and hold the doll. A note was made of which side of the body they held the doll against. Then they were asked to go to the observer and hand over the doll. During this walk, the observer watched how the children carried the doll (left arm, right arm, or in hands). The different positions are illustrated in Figure 5-5. During the observations it was noted that 2-year-old boys and girls had great difficulty following the instructions given to them by the experimenter prior to the observation, whereas the 4-year-olds could generally do so. The older children were all able to understand the instructions in

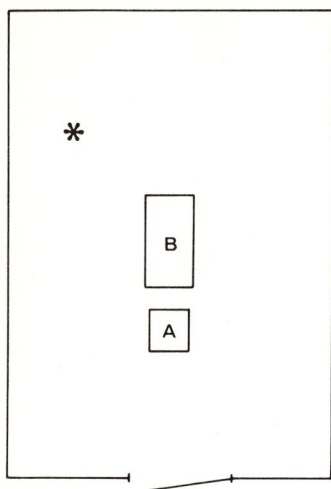

Figure 5-4. The room used for observation of the children holding and carrying a doll. A = chair; B = doll's bed; * = approximate position of observer. (From de Chateau & Anderson, 1976.)

the observation setting. This illustrates the need for age-appropriate methods in the study of child behavior. By studying both holding and carrying, the stability of side preference could be demonstrated, with only 6% of a total of 305 children holding on one side and carrying on the other.

Maternal and Infant Behavior in Extra-Contact Studies

Since the main topic of this chapter is early parent–neonate interactions and their long-term effects, a fairly detailed report of the methods used in our

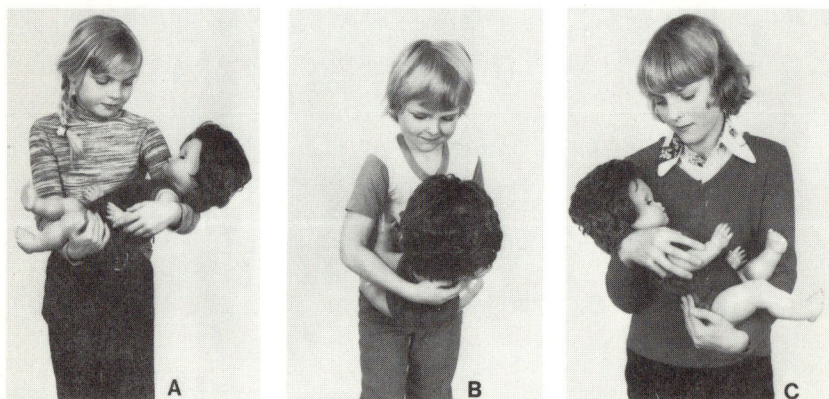

Figure 5-5. A, A 6-year-old girl carrying a doll to the left. B, A 4-year-old boy carrying "in the hands." C, A 13-year-old boy carrying to the right. (From de Chateau, 1976a.)

research on this topic will be given here. The longitudinal study started in December 1974 and aimed to examine the effect that extra contact (limited to 15–20 minutes) immediately following delivery might have on the behavior of mother and infant, and on the development of their mutual relationship (de Chateau, 1976a, b; de Chateau & Wiberg, 1977a, b; de Chateau, Holmberg, Jakobson, & Winberg, 1977; de Chateau, Cajander, Engström, & Lundberg, 1978). The study included 62 mother–infant pairs divided into three groups:

1. P+ group: Primiparous women (N = 22), given extra contact with their newborn infants followed by routine care.
2. P group: Primiparous women (N = 20), given routine care with their newborn infants.
3. M group: Multiparous women (N = 20), given routine care with their newborn infants.

The basic conditions for participation in the study were that mothers and infants should be healthy and live in the Umeå area, and that pregnancy and delivery should have been normal. Background data on the subjects are shown in Table 5-1.

Other criteria that all mother–infant pairs had to meet were: no history of previous abortions or miscarriages, no use of drugs except iron medication and vitamins during pregnancy, normal weight gain (Pitkin, Kaminetzky, Newton, & Pritchard, 1972), normal blood-pressure and Hb-percentage, and no protein–uria (Pasamanick, Rogers, & Lilienfeld, 1956). The mother must have come into labor spontaneously at full-term. All infants must have been born in vertex presentation and must have had no signs of intra- or extrauterine asphyxia. There must have been no signs or symptoms of cogenital malformation or disease at physical examination 1 day and 6 days post partum. Many of these criteria are described by Prechtl (1968) as optimal obstetrical conditions, and others have been used by Thoman, Leiderman, and Olson (1972). Midwives made a preliminary selection of the subjects when the mothers arrived at the hospital for delivery. At this point, mothers and midwives were not familiar with each other. This preliminary selection was thus based solely on existing data concerning previous obstetric history, present pregnancy, and residence within the Umeå area. By this preliminary procedure, 74 mother–infant pairs were selected for the study. After delivery the primiparous mothers were randomly assigned to either the P or the P+ group. Twelve mother–infant pairs who did not fulfill the established criteria concerning residence, delivery, infant, and neonatal period were excluded (see Table 5-2). The final study groups thus comprised 62 mother–infant pairs.

TABLE 5-1
Data on Mother–Infant Pairs in Three Observational Groups

	P+ ($N = 22$)	P ($N = 20$)	M ($N = 20$)
Mother—years	25.0	25.5	28.3
Father—years	25.6	26.3	29.4
Social categories I/II/III[a]	5/7/10	3/9/8	2/9/9
"Married"[b]/total	20/22	19/20	20/20
Mean number of visits to antenatal clinics	13	13	13
Mean of mother weight gain (in percentage of weight at delivery)	17.3	16.5	17.4
Father present at delivery	19/22	17/20	17/20
Duration of delivery	7 hr 43 min	7 hr 40 min	4 hr 28 min
Analgesia			
N$_2$O	20/21	19/19	17/18
Pethidin Chloride	11/21	12/19	2/18
Pethidin in milligrams (mean)	90	85	90
Time before delivery (range)	2–12 hr	2–8 hr	2–5 hr
Diazepam (Valium)	5/21	5/19	0/18
Time before delivery (range)	3.5–12	2–8 hours	————
Pudental block (carbocain–adrenalin)	19/21	19/20	14/19
Time before delivery (range)	15 min–2 hr	15 min–3 hr	7 min–30 min
Gestational age (weeks)	40.05	40.40	39.95
Males/females	12/10	13/7	10/10
Birth weight (in kilograms)	3.532	3.386	3.607
Apgar score at 1 and 10 minutes	9/9	9/9	9/9
Number of previous breast-feedings	4.73	4.55	4.65
Time of observation post partum (hours)	36.27	35.70	36.20

[a] Social categories: I = highest; II = middle; III = lowest.
[b] "Married" = includes married and steadily living together.

Routine Care Immediately Following Delivery (P and M Groups). After delivery the baby lies on the delivery table, between the legs of the mother. Mouth and upper airways are rinsed and the stomach is emptied. Face, trunk, and legs are wiped dry with a towel. The infant is then shown to the mother for a brief glance, but usually she does not touch him. A numbered bracelet is put around the wrist of both mother and infant. After cord clamping, 2–6 minutes post partum, the baby is taken to another part of the delivery room for weighing, bathing, physical examination, Credé prophylaxis, and dressing. This takes approximately 30 minutes. Meanwhile the mother is helped to deliver the placenta, and is washed and cleaned. The baby, with clothes on, is put in a crib and covered with a blanket. The crib is placed beside the mother's bed so that she can watch her baby and touch the face. In some instances the baby, dressed and wrapped in a blanket, is placed in the mother's bed. The mother, the infant, and the father, who has

TABLE 5-2
Mother–Infant Pairs (N = 12) Excluded from the Study after Preliminary Selection in the Delivery Ward

Group	Number	Reason for exclusion
P+	4	1. Ablatio placentae 2. Hyperbilirubinaemia neonatorum 3. Not living in Umeå district 4. Wrong observation time
P	4	1. Bleeding post partum 2. Hyperbilirubinaemia neonatorum 3. Not living in Umeå district 4. Wrong observation time
M	4	1. Dysmaturity, induced labor 2. Hypotonia 3. Erythema toxicum 4. Unsatisfactory Moro reflex

often attended the delivery of the infant, stay together in the delivery room until approximately 2 hours after the actual time of birth, when the mother and the infant are transferred to the maternity ward.

Extra Contact Immediately Following Delivery (P+ Group). The mouth and upper airways are rinsed, the stomach is emptied, the body dried with a towel, and a numbered bracelet fastened around the wrists of infant and mother as in routine care. The midwife puts the naked baby onto the mother's abdomen after clamping the cord. This skin to skin contact begins approximately 10 minutes post partum. About 5 minutes later the midwife moves the baby upwards onto the mother's chest and helps him to suckle from his mother's breast, that is, approximately 15 minutes post partum (Figure 5-6). This extra contact lasts for about 10 to 15 minutes. After this period, when the baby is about 24–30 minutes old, the normal routine procedure as described above is continued. A schedule of the post-partum care in the three groups is given in Table 5-3.

Routine Care at the Maternity Ward from about Two Hours after Delivery until Discharge from Hospital Six to Eight Days Later (P+, P, and M Groups). During the first 3 days, the mother sees and nurses her infant every 4 hours during the day. During the night and most of the day, the infant stays in a separate baby room. During the second half of the post-partum week, the infant stays in his mother's room during the day. The mother takes a more active part in the care for her infant, giving him a bath, changing diapers and clothes, and so on. Most rooms hold four mothers and their infants.

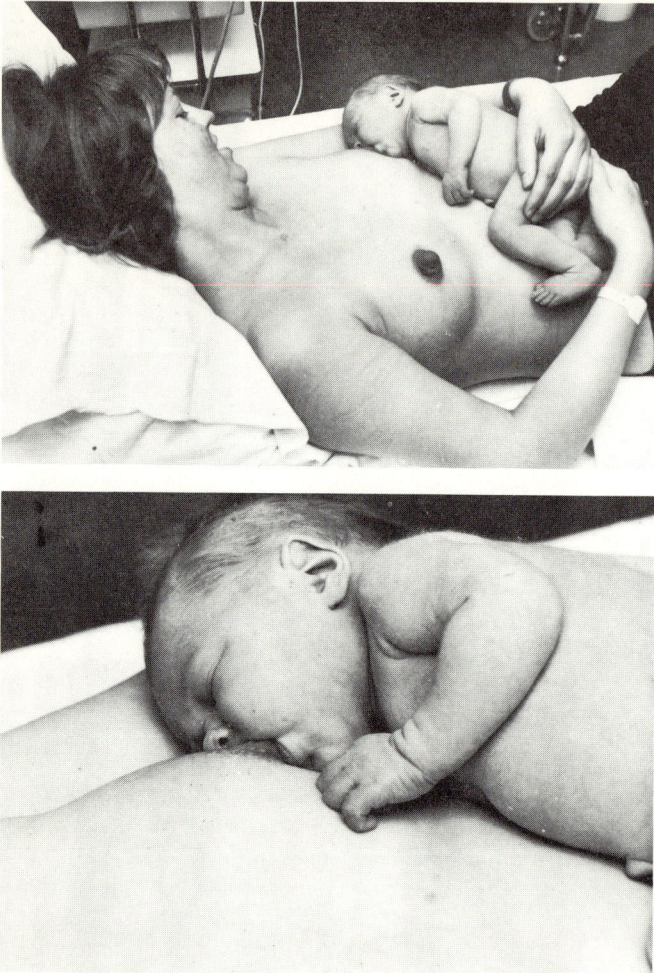

Figure 5-6. The extra skin-to-skin and suckling contact after delivery (group P+ only).

Observation of Mother–Infant Behavior at Thirty-Six Hours. Before leaving the delivery floor, the mothers were asked to participate with their infants in an ongoing study and told that observation was going to take place later in the maternity ward. None of the mothers refused, probably because the approach was via the midwives, who by that time were well known to and trusted by the mothers. Observation of all subjects was made about 36 hours after delivery (range 32–40 hours) in the mother's own room during breast feeding. Two observers participated in the study, and the subjects were assigned randomly to one of them. The observers did not know to which

TABLE 5-3
Schedule of Post-Partum Care of Infant

	Time post partum		
Group[a]	0–30 minutes	Next 15–30 minutes	45–120 minutes
P (N = 20) and M (N = 20)	Weighing, bathing, Credé- prophylaxis, dressing, etc.	Resting dressed in crib or mother's bed	Resting dressed in crib or mother's bed
P+ (N = 22)	15–20 minutes of skin-to-skin and suckling contact with mother	Weighing, bathing, Credé-prophylaxis, dressing, etc.	Resting dressed in crib or mother's bed

[a] P = primiparous mothers with routine care; M = multiparous mothers with routine care; P+ = primiparous mothers with extra contact.

group the mother–infant pairs belonged. Only one observer was present at each observation. All mothers were in a four-bed room. During the observation the other mothers in the room were nursing their own babies as usual. The positions of the mother, her infant, and the observer are shown in Figure 5-7. The observer was present in the room for a few minutes before the infant was brought in, so as to be less obtrusive. After the infant's crib was brought into the mother's room, observation started immediately with notes of how the mother picked up the baby from the crib and carried him to her bed or chair for breast feeding. No conversation between mother and observer was allowed during the observation. Thirty-five different behavioral items were scored and noted on a check sheet. Most of the observational items are self-explanatory; for full details see Appendix B. The observation period was 15 minutes, divided into 20 periods of 15 seconds spent actually observing and 20 periods of 30 seconds spent writing down on the check sheet all that had happened during the previous 15-second period. A small tape recorder provided signals through an earphone to indicate the observation and writing periods. The use of this apparatus was explained to the mothers before the actual observation was started. Each time a behavior occurred during the observation, it was scored as 1. At the end of the observation the score for every behavior item was added up, and the total was used as a measure of frequency of the particular behavior during the observation. The maximum score for any item was therefore 20. Behavior not included in our observation sheet did sometimes occur, and although it was noted, none of these behaviors could be used in the final data analysis.

Interobserver Reliability. The reliability of the two observers was tested before and after the study. Each of these reliability studies comprised eight

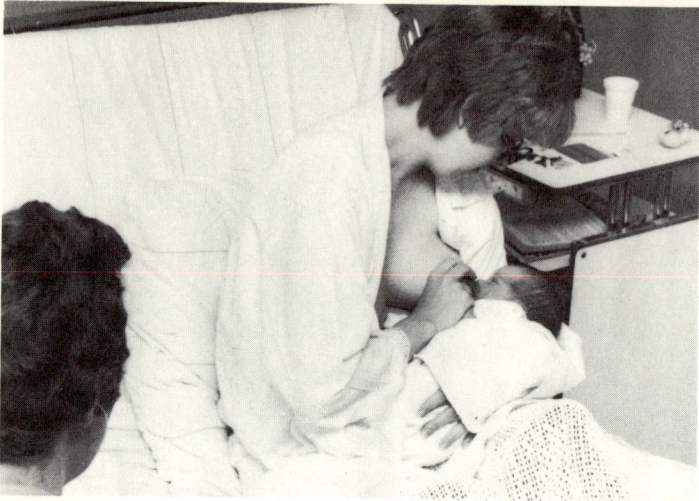

Figure 5-7. The position of the mother, the infant, and the observer during the observation at 36 hours post partum. (From de Chateau, 1976a.)

mother–infant pairs. The observation was performed during an ordinary breast-feeding period, as in the study. These mothers and infants did not meet any specific criteria other than that pregnancy, delivery, and the first post-partum days had been normal. The mothers had agreed to the presence of two observers. The correlation coefficient (r) was above .90 for all of the 35 behavioral items both before and after the study proper.

Statistical Methods. For every item observed, the mean frequency for each of the three observation groups (P+, P, and M) was calculated. The t test was used in analyzing these results, and the p values given were obtained by this method; $p < .05$ is regarded as significant.

Observation of Mother–Infant Behavior at Three Months

After completing the observation at 36 hours in the maternity ward, the observer talked to the mother and answered her questions. During this conversation we asked if we could contact her again for a follow-up study when the infant was 3 months old. This follow-up study was restricted to the two groups of primiparous mothers and infants only, both for practical reasons and because it was assumed that the effect of extra contact could best be studied in such groups, and that at least one factor (parity) was controlled in an adequate and undisputable way. All mothers agreed to this follow-up. The same two observers participated in this study. The appointment for the home visit was made by a secretary. The mother–infant pairs were thereafter assigned randomly to one of the two observers. Neither of the observers was aware of the group (P+ and P) to which the mother–infant pairs belonged. The follow-up study was done during a home visit and included a mother–infant free-play observation. An unstructured personal interview was also held with the mothers. This interview covered the mother's perception of pregnancy, the delivery, the neonatal week, and the first 3 months at home (see Table 5-4). All home visits were made at 1 P.M., at which time most infants were asleep. After an initial interview, mother–infant free play, approximately $2-2\frac{1}{2}$ hours after the last feeding, was observed. This is a good time for observation (Beintema & Prechtl, 1968), since the infant is usually alert and cooperative. The mother and infant were placed on a carpet on the floor. The observer also sat on the floor approximately 1 meter away from them (Figure 5-8). Before the observation started the mother was told by the observer that we wanted to watch her and her infant during 10 minutes of free play. The mother was given a bell, a dangling ring, and a rattle bag similar to those used in Gesell's Developmental Test (Gesell & Armatruda, 1962). The mother could use the toys in

TABLE 5-4
Selected Background Data on All Subjects at Three Months

	P+ (N = 21)	P (N = 19)
A. Maternal		
Mean maternal age (years)	25.3	25.8
Married and steadily living together	19/21	18/19
Socioeconomic group I/II/III	4/7/10	3/8/8
Mean number of days in maternity ward	7	7
Mean number of days rooming-in	3	3
B. Infant		
Sex of infant (males/females)	11/10	12/7
Mean infant weight loss (in percentage of birth weight) during neonatal period	8.9	9.3
Mean infant age (days)	97	96
Range (days)	91–104	92–103
Postnatal growth and psychomotor development	within normal range	within normal range
C. Child Health Center		
Mean number of contacts:		
1. Total	7.4	7.4
2. Visiting doctor	2.1	2.0
3. Visiting nurse	2.2	3.3
4. Telephone contact	1.4	0.3
5. Nurse home visits	1.7	1.8

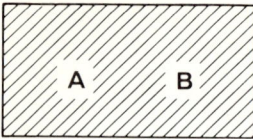

Figure 5-8. The approximate placement of mother (A) and infant (B) on the carpet (shaded area) and observer (C) during observations of free play at 3 months. (From de Chateau, 1976a.)

whatever way and sequence she liked. Sixty-one different behavioral items, most of which were very descriptive of what was observed, were scored and noted on a check sheet (see Appendix C).

Duration and Technique of Observation.   During a pilot study we discovered that infants very soon got tired during observation. The frequency of crying in observation of eight infants was .25 during the first 5 minutes and 1.40 during the second 5-minute period. Similarly, the mothers used toys more frequently during the second half of the observation time than they did during the first half. The observation periods were therefore kept as short as 10 minutes, and cooperation was obtained from all mother–infant pairs studied. This observation period of 10 minutes was divided into 10 periods of 15 seconds spent actually observing and 10 periods of 45 seconds spent writing down all that had happened during the previous 15-second period. The number of items observed made it necessary to have a longer writing period than at 36 hours. Each time a behavior occurred, it was scored as 1. At the end of the observation the score for each behavior item was added up, and the total was used as a measure of the frequency of that particular behavior during the observation. The maximum score for any item was therefore 10. As on the previous occasion, behavior not included on our observation sheet sometimes occurred, but as before, although it was noted, none could be used for data analysis. A tape recorder provided signals through an earphone to indicate the observation and writing periods. The use of this apparatus was known to the mothers from our first observation at the maternity ward and, if necessary, reexplained to the mothers before the observation started.

Interobserver Reliability.   For reliability purposes a study was made of 11 mother–infant pairs during a routine 3-month check-up at the Child Health Center in our hospital before the study proper started. These mothers and infants did not meet any specific criteria other than that pregnancy, delivery, the first postnatal week at the maternity ward, and the first 3 months at home had been normal; they also agreed to participate in the reliability study and to the presence of two observers. The correlation coefficient (r) was not lower than .92 for any of the 61 items used during the observation. The statistical methods used in the evaluation of the results were the same as those after the 36-hour observation (see the preceding).

Observation of Mother–Infant Behavior at One Year

When the children had reached the age of 1 year, a new follow-up study was made, this time in the out-patient clinic of our department. The mothers were contacted by a secretary and two new observers were engaged. This procedure was chosen in order to prevent any kind of bias due to the previous observers knowing the group (P or P+) to which some of the couples studied belonged. Again, observation of maternal and infant behavior followed a standard pattern. The subjects were randomly assigned to one of the new observers. Only one observer was present at each observation. All the observations took place in the same examination room of the policlinic during a routine physical examination of the infant by a pediatrician. The approximate position of mother, infant, doctor, and observer and the placement of the furniture is shown in Figure 5-9. The same doctor conducted all the examinations.

The observer was present when mother, infant, and doctor entered the room. Observation started after an initial talk and undressing the infant. This observation was divided into two parts: one of 3 minutes, 45 seconds while the infant was seated in his mother's lap on chair C (Figure 5-9) and a second part of the same duration while the infant was lying on the examination table D. In both parts of the observation a routine and standardized physical examination was made by a doctor; the placements of the doctor were at E for the first part and at F for the second part of the observation period. No conversation between the observer and the other persons in the room was

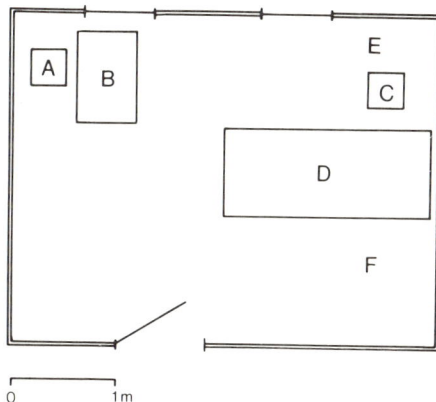

Figure 5-9. The approximate placement of the mother (at C) and infant (at C or D), the doctor (at E or F), and observer (at A) during observations of a physical examination of the infant at 1 year. A = chair; B = table, C = chair; D = examination table; E and F = doctor's placements.

allowed during the actual observation. Of course, mother, infant, and doctor could communicate freely among themselves during the whole period. Twenty-six different behavioral items were scored and noted on a check sheet. Most of these items are self-explanatory; for full details and definitions see Appendix D of this chapter. The total observation period was two times 3 minutes, 45 seconds; each observation was divided into five periods of 30 seconds spent actually observing and five periods of 15 seconds spent writing down on the check sheet all that had happened during the foregoing 30-second observation period. As in the earlier studies, a small portable tape recorder with an earphone was used to indicate the different periods. Each time a behavior occurred during the observation time, it was scored as 1. At the end of the observation the score for every item of behavior was added up, and the total was used as a measure of the frequency of that particular behavior during the observation. The maximum score for any item during one of the two periods was therefore 5, for the total period 10. The infant behavior varied a great deal, however, probably due to the age of the children, and was difficult to score. Moreover, some behavior not included in our observation sheet occurred. For example, a child might leave his mother's lap or the examination table during observation and thus make a standardized observation impossible. However, it was easy to observe and score maternal behavior. As before, interobserver reliability was checked in a pilot study and found to be high with respect to maternal behavior. The same statistical methods were used as at 36 hours and 3 months.

The choice of what behavioral items to study is difficult, but some help can be obtained from the literature (Brazelton, Tronick, Adamson, Als, & Weise, 1975; Klaus & Kennell, 1970; Lewis, 1972; Richards, 1971; Thoman, Turner, Leiderman, & Barnett, 1970). Some of our own methods have already been presented, but these methods have their limitations. For the study of sequences or interactions of behavior, filming or videotape recording is probably superior, although a camera lens only covers a restricted area (Cooper et al., 1974). The use of a one-way screen has the disadvantage of the laboratory environment; the more natural circumstances of the maternity ward or the home are lost.

Other Methods

Indirect procedures for studying the mother–infant relationship, such as interviews and questionnaires, have certain limitations (Moss, 1965; Yarrow, 1963). Mothers may have a limited memory of things that have happened in the past, and the use of retrospective reports should therefore be avoided. Moreover, mothers may give a distorted report of their relationship with their children, being influenced by what they believe is expected culturally. An example of this may be cited from one of our studies (de

Chateau, 1976a). Three years after observation, left-holding and right-holding mothers were interviewed. No significant differences were found between the two groups when they were asked about child-rearing practices. From our Child Health Centers we knew, however, that during this 3-year period certain differences had, in fact, existed between these groups. The fact that we could not demonstrate these differences retrospectively in the interview could be due to the limited number (70) of mother–infant pairs investigated, but it might also illustrate the limitations of a retrospective interview, which almost certainly minimizes the true differences that exist (Yarrow, 1963). Because mothers often have difficulty in recalling details exactly from the recent and more distant past, concerning both themselves and their children, other ways of collecting information may be used (de Chateau, 1976a; de Chateau, Holmberg, Jakobson, & Winberg, 1977). To obtain more reliable data on the duration of breast feeding, the children's health records were consulted and the duration of lactation calculated. In Sweden over 95% of all mothers visit their local Child Health Center. Many data on feeding, development, vaccinations, and so forth are registered on these records, and the staff are very careful to fill in these details in a standard way. These notes are of great value for following up children who have taken part in various studies. In another study (de Chateau, Cajander, Engström, & Lundberg, 1978) the number of contacts with, and the number of home visits by, the nurses from the Child Health Centers were taken directly from the health records. Data concerning the mother's pregnancy, delivery, and earlier obstetrical history were collected from her records in antenatal clinics and the maternity ward (de Chateau, 1976a). In order to evaluate the postnatal adaptation and state of health during the neonatal period, objective criteria such as birth weight, laboratory investigations, and duration of hospital stay were taken from records at the maternity ward. By using objective data from existing records, made by persons not aware of our interest in particular facts, circumstances, or measurements, some of the disadvantages of interviews and questionnaires may have been avoided. The value of these methods of investigation is greater, however, if they can be combined with other methods of study.

EARLY POSTNATAL CONTACT AND MOTHER–INFANT INTERACTION DURING BREAST FEEDING THIRTY-SIX HOURS AFTER DELIVERY

Results

Extended contact between mother and infant during the first post-partum days may influence the development of mother–infant interaction and attachment. Klaus Jerauld, Kreger, McAlpine, Steffa, and Kennell (1972) gave 14 mothers 1 hour of close physical contact with their nude full-term infants within the first 3 hours after delivery and another 15 extra hours of contact in the first 3 days post partum (extended contact); a control group of mothers was given routine contact with their newborn babies. In follow-up studies 1 month, 1 year (Kennell, Jerauld, Wolfe, Chester, Kreger, McAlpine, Steffa, & Klaus, 1974), and 2 years (Ringer, Kennell, Jarvelle, Navojosky, & Klaus, 1975) after delivery, differences between the extended contact and the control group were found with regard to maternal attachment behavior and linguistic behavior. Maternal and infant behavior is controlled by many factors other than early physical contact. Prenatal influences such as the mother's relationship with her own mother (Nilsson, 1970) and the infant's father, her cultural background, planning, and preparations for pregnancy, delivery, and so on may be of great importance. They must therefore be checked when studies of the impact of changes in the immediate post-partum period on maternal and infant behavior are presented.

In our studies we have examined the effect that extra contact limited to 15 minutes immediately following delivery might have on mother and infant behavior. Three groups of mother–infant pairs were studied: 22 primiparae (P+) and their infants with extra skin-to-skin and suckling contact during the first hour after delivery; 20 primiparae (P) and their infants with the usual routine care after delivery; and 20 multiparae (M) and infants with routine care. At 36 hours, observation was made of maternal and infant behavior during breast feeding. The two groups of primiparae and their infants have also been followed at 3 months and 1 year. (For details of the material and methods see the previous section and Appendixes B, C, and D of this chapter.)

The difference in experimental conditions between Klaus et al. (1972), Kennell et al. (1974), and Ringler et al. (1975), and our study is that they studied the impact on maternal behavior of early and extended contact, whereas we studied only the impact of extra contact immediately following delivery (early contact). On the other hand, we also looked at infant be-havior, at child-rearing practices, and at the children's development.

A comparison of maternal behavior between the three groups (P+, P, and M) revealed a number of interesting differences, some highly significant, others less distinctive, but all pointing in the same direction: Extra contact seems to favor a maternal behavior that is more synchronized with the infant. Primiparous mothers with extra contact differed in a highly significant way from those with routine care in 3 of the 35 items observed, 2 of which were mutually exclusive. Multiparous women with routine care differed in only 1 instance from primiparous women with extra contact, but differed in 5 from primiparae mothers with routine care (Table 5-5).

TABLE 5-5

Maternal and Infant Behavior during Breast Feeding on the Second Day of Life (Figures Denote Mean Frequency of Behavior during the Twenty Fifteen-Second Observation Periods)

Observation	Mean frequencies[a]			p values		
	P+ (N = 22)	P (N = 20)	M (N = 20)	P+/P	P+/M	P/M
1. Mother absent	0	0	0	—	—	—
2. Mother other	0	1.4	2.1	—	0.1	—
3. Mother in bed	20.0	18.6	17.9	—	0.1	—
4. Mother lying down	8.1	9.2	3.2	—	0.04	0.02
5. Mother leaning on elbow	2.4	7.9	3.5	0.02	—	0.08
6. Mother sitting up	10.1	3.3	13.6	0.009	0.2	0.0003
7. Mother asleep	0	0	0	—	—	—
8. Mother drowsy	0.4	0	0	0.2	0.2	—
9. Mother awake	19.7	20.0	20.0	0.2	0.2	—
10. Infant own bed far from mother	0	0	0	—	—	—
11. Infant own bed near mother	0	0	0	—	—	—
12. Infant in mother's bed	20.0	19.9	19.9	—	—	—
13. Infant quiet	5.5	6.5	7.9	—	0.1	—
14. Infant active	13.9	12.5	12.7	—	—	—
15. Infant crying	1.0	2.4	0.5	0.2	—	0.03
16. Bottle feeding	0	0	0	—	—	—
17. Mother nurses	10.9	10.3	10.9	—	—	—
18. Burps	0.6	0.2	1.1	0.1	—	0.1
19. Diapers	0	0	0	—	—	—
20. Uncovers/undresses	0.9	1.5	1.2	0.2	—	—
21. Infant on knees	0.5	0.2	0.8	0.2	—	0.2
22. Holds infant	10.9	2.9	11.7	0.001	—	0.0005
23. Encompassing	9.3	5.3	10.9	0.1	—	0.03
24. A.T.L.	17.1	15.9	15.7	—	—	—
25. Close contact	16.6	14.0	16.7	0.1	—	0.2
26. Looks at infant	19.6	19.9	20.0	—	0.2	—
27. En face	2.6	1.6	2.0	0.2	—	—
28. Talks to infant	6.4	6.9	7.7	—	—	—
29. Smiles at infant	2.9	2.6	3.3	—	—	—
30. Kisses infant	0.4	0.3	0.4	—	—	—
31. Mother occupied with breast	0.1	0.3	0.2	—	—	—
32. Talks to adult	2.5	3.4	3.8	—	0.1	—
33. Listens to radio/TV	5.5	8.0	9.0	—	0.2	—
34. Others present	20.0	18.1	18.0	0.1	0.1	—
35. Nurse aid helps	0.2	0.3	1.3	—	0.09	0.1

[a] P+ = primiparae with extra contact; P = primiparae with routine care; M = multiparae with routine care.

The mother's position during observation differed greatly between the three groups. P+ and M mothers were more frequently sitting up, whereas P mothers were more often lying down or leaning on one elbow. The meaning of these differences of maternal position during breast feeding is not quite clear. The differences were, however, highly significant statistically, and they were not due to there being more episiotomies in the control group. Being bothered by the irritation of an episiotomy that was still healing might otherwise have been an explanation for the preference of position shown by mothers with different postnatal care. P+ and M mothers held their infants more often than did P mothers. Encompassing, which could occur both when mothers were sitting and when they were lying down, was observed twice as often in P+ as in P mothers, although this difference was not significant. Similarly, M mothers encompassed their infants significantly more than P mothers. Infants of P mothers cried significantly more frequently than did infants in the M group and twice as often as did P+ infants.

When mother–infant behavior within each of the three groups, P+, P, and M (Table 5-6), was compared by sex of infant, the most marked differences were found within the P+ group. Mothers of males in this group held their infants significantly more often, made more attempts to burp them, showed more encompassing, and smiled more frequently at them than did mothers of female infants. Mothers of female infants in the P+ group talked to their infants more often. The differences by sex of infant were much less pronounced in the P group, being significant only for infant on knees and encompassing, which were more common in mothers with females. Within the M group no prominent differences were seen in maternal or infant behavior when mothers with males and mothers with females were compared.

Within each sex, mother–infant behavior also differed between the different care and parity groups. The complete details of these analyses are given in Tables 5-7 and 5-8. P+ mothers sat up, held, and encompassed their boys with close body contact significantly more often than did P mothers. The P+ mothers also made more frequent attempts to let their boys burp. P+ infants were significantly less quiet than M infants. Like the P+ mothers with male infants, M mothers sat up significantly more often than did P mothers; male infants in the P group cried more frequently than did infants in the P+ and M groups. No significant differences were found between P+ and P mothers and their female infants. P+ mothers with girls lay down significantly more often and talked less frequently to others than did M mothers with girls. No significant differences were seen in maternal and infant behavior when comparison was made between P and M groups with female infants.

Before the actual observation during breast feeding, notes were made of

TABLE 5-6
Behavior Differences by Sex of Infant within the Three Groups (P+, P, and M) [a]

Observation	P+ group (12 ♂–10 ♀) p value	P group (12 ♂–7 ♀) p value	M group (10 ♂–10 ♀) p value
1. Mother absent	—	—	—
2. Mother other	—	—	—
3. Mother in bed	—	—	—
4. Mother lying down	0.1	—	0.2
5. Mother leaning on elbow	—	—	0.08
6. Mother sitting up	0.09	0.2	—
7. Mother asleep	—	—	—
8. Mother drowsy	0.2	—	—
9. Mother awake	0.2	—	—
10. Infant own bed far from mother	—	—	—
11. Infant own bed near mother	—	—	—
12. Infant on mother's bed	—	—	—
13. Infant quiet	—	0.2	0.2
14. Infant active	—	0.1	0.2
15. Infant crying	—	—	—
16. Bottle feeding	—	—	—
17. Mother nurses	—	—	—
18. Burps	0.04	0.2	—
19. Diapers	—	—	—
20. Uncovers/undresses	—	0.1	0.1
21. Infant on knees	—	0.05	—
22. Holds	0.02	0.08	—
23. Encompassing	0.07	0.01	—
24. A.T.L.	—	—	—
25. Close contact	—	—	—
26. Looks at infant	—	—	—
27. En face	0.04	0.07	—
28. Talks to infant	0.01	0.08	—
29. Smiles at infant	0.02	0.2	—
30. Kisses infant	—	—	0.09
31. Mother occupied with breast	—	—	—
32. Talks to adult	—	0.2	0.09
33. Listens to radio/TV	—	—	—
34. Others present	—	—	—
35. Nurse aid	0.2	—	0.2

[a] P+ = primiparae with extra contact; P = primiparae with routine care; M = multiparae with routine care.

how the mother picked up her baby from the crib and carried him to her bed (Figure 5-10). The observation setting did not allow a study of the holding behavior, and not all mothers participated in this part (see the section entitled "Problems of Methodology"). The distribution of ways of carrying in the P+ and P group is given in Table 5-9, and the differences are statistically

TABLE 5-7

Behavior Mean Frequencies and Differences by Care and Parity within the Infants of Male Sex

Observation	Mean frequencies[a]			p values		
	P+ (N = 12)	P (N = 13)	M (N = 10)	P+ versus P	P+ versus M	P versus M
1. Mother absent	0	0	0	—	—	—
2. Mother other	0	1.5	2.2	—	0.2	—
3. Mother in bed	20.0	18.5	17.9	—	0.2	—
4. Mother lying down	5.8	9.0	4.9	—	—	0.2
5. Mother leaning	1.8	9.4	1.0	0.01	—	0.01
6. Mother sitting up	13.1	1.9	14.1	0.0009	—	0.0009
7. Mother asleep	0	0	0	—	—	—
8. Mother drowsy	0.8	0	0	0.1	0.1	—
9. Mother awake	19.4	20.0	20.0	0.1	0.2	—
10. Infant own bed far from mother	0	0	0	—	—	—
11. Infant own bed near mother	0	0	0	—	—	—
12. Infant mother's bed	0	19.9	20.0	—	—	—
13. Infant quiet	4.7	7.5	9.5	0.1	0.04	—
14. Infant active	14.6	11.3	11.2	0.1	0.1	—

	P+	P	M			
15. Infant crying	0.9	2.9	0.2	0.1	—	0.03
16. Bottle feeding	0	0	0	—	—	—
17. Mother nurses	10.1	10.9	9.8	0.04	—	—
18. Burps	0.9	0.1	1.4	—	—	0.2
19. Diapers	0	0	0	—	—	—
20. Uncovers	1.0	0.8	1.1	—	—	0.1
21. Infant on knees	0.3	0	1.2	—	—	0.1
22. Holds	14.7	0.5	13.3	0.0001	—	0.001
23. Encompassing	12.1	2.2	10.7	0.001	—	0.01
24. A.T.L.	17.1	15.5	16.7	—	—	—
25. Close contact	18.1	13.0	17.5	0.04	—	0.07
26. Looks at infant	19.1	19.9	20.0	0.2	—	—
27. En face	2.2	0.9	1.5	0.08	0.2	—
28. Talks to infant	4.3	5.0	7.1	—	—	—
29. Smiles at infant	4.1	1.9	3.0	0.08	—	—
30. Kisses infant	0.5	0.3	0	—	0.2	—
31. Mother occupied with breast	0.1	0.5	0.1	—	—	—
32. Talks to adult	2.9	3.9	2.5	—	—	—
33. Listens to radio/TV	5.0	7.7	8.0	—	—	—
34. Others present	20.0	18.6	18.0	—	0.2	—
35. Nurse aid	0.4	0.3	0.5	—	—	—

[a] P+ = primiparae with extra contact; P = primiparae with routine care; M = multiparae with routine care.

137

TABLE 5-8

Behavior Mean Frequencies and Differences by Care and Parity within the Infants of Female Sex

Observation	Mean frequencies[a]			p values		
	P+ (N = 10)	P (N = 7)	M (N = 10)	P+ versus P	P+ versus M	P versus M
1. Mother absent	0	0	0	—	—	—
2. Mother other	0	1.1	2.0	—	—	—
3. Mother in bed	20.0	18.9	18.0	0.2	—	—
4. Mother lying down	11.0	9.6	1.4	—	0.006	0.07
5. Mother leaning	3.2	5.0	6.0	—	—	—
6. Mother sitting up	6.6	5.7	13.0	—	0.1	0.1
7. Mother asleep	0	0	0	—	—	—
8. Mother drowsy	0	0	0	—	—	—
9. Mother awake	20.0	20.0	20.0	—	—	—
10. Infant own bed far from mother	0	0	0	—	—	—
11. Infant own bed near mother	0	0	0	—	—	—
12. Infant in mother's bed	20.0	20.0	19.7	—	—	—
13. Infant quiet	6.4	4.4	6.2	—	—	—
14. Infant active	13.0	14.7	14.1	—	—	—
15. Infant crying	1.1	1.6	0.8	—	—	—

16. Bottle feeding	0	0	0	—	—	—
17. Mother nurses	12.0	9.1	11.9	0.2	—	—
18. Burps	0.1	0.3	0.7	—	0.2	—
19. Diapers	0	0	0	—	—	—
20. Uncovers	0.7	2.9	0.8	0.1	—	0.2
21. Infant on knees	0.6	0.4	0.4	—	—	—
22. Holds	6.3	7.3	10.0	0.2	0.2	—
23. Encompassing	5.9	10.8	11.1	—	—	—
24. A.T.L.	17.1	16.7	14.7	—	—	—
25. Close contact	14.9	15.9	15.9	—	—	—
26. Looks at infant	20.0	20.0	20.0	—	—	—
27. *En face*	3.0	3.0	2.4	—	—	—
28. Talks to infant	8.9	10.6	8.2	0.2	—	—
29. Smiles at infant	1.6	3.7	3.6	—	0.2	—
30. Kisses infant	0.2	0.3	0.7	—	0.2	—
31. Mother occupied with breast	0.2	0	0.2	—	—	—
32. Talks to adult	1.9	2.3	5.0	—	0.03	0.09
33. Listens to radio/TV	6.0	8.6	10.0	—	—	—
34. Others present	20.0	17.1	18.0	0.2	—	—
35. Nurse aid	0	0.1	2.1	—	0.07	0.2

a P+ = primiparae with extra contact; P = primiparae with routine care; M = multiparae with routine care.

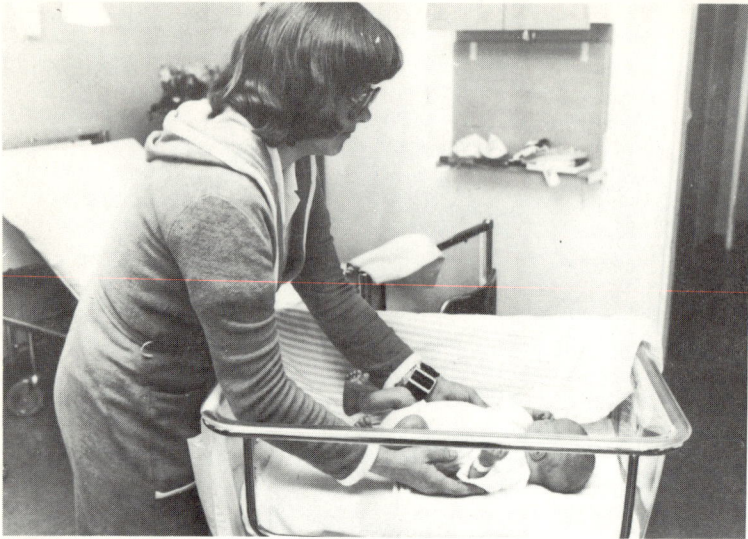

Figure 5-10. The mother takes her baby from the crib at the start of the observation.

significant ($p < .05$); the proportions for the P group are fully consistent with the results in a larger sample of primiparae with routine care (de Chateau, Holmberg, & Winberg, 1978). In the P+ group more mothers carried to the left; carrying in the hands (see Appendix A of this chapter) had disappeared completely. The sex of the infant had no clear-cut influence on either holding or carrying (de Chateau, 1976a; de Chateau, Holmberg, & Winberg, 1978).

TABLE 5-9
Distribution of Ways of Carrying Infants in Two Groups of Mothers[a]

	P+ (N = 21)	P (N = 15)
Carrying to the left	18	7
Carrying in the hands	0	5
Carrying to the right	3	3

[a] P+ = primiparae with extra contact; P = primiparae with routine care.

Summary and Discussion

The results of observation during breast feeding indicate that mothers with boys behave differently from mothers with girls, although there has been the same immediate post-partum care; that at 36 hours post partum, differences in behavior occur between a group of mothers and infants who have had 15–20 minutes extra skin-to-skin and suckling contact immediately following delivery (P+) and a group of mothers and infants with routine care (P); and that the influence of post-partum care is greater on the behavior of boys and their mothers than it is on that of girls and their mothers. Differences in behavior between primiparous (primis) and multiparous (multips) mothers and their infants were also found, the differences being most pronounced between primis and multips with routine care, and very small between primis with extra contact and multips with routine care. In an interview with the mothers, no differences were found between P+ and P mothers with regard to their relationship with their own mothers, their husbands, planning of pregnancy, preparations for pregnancy, delivery, and baby, nor to their perception of pregnancy, delivery, and the first postpartum week. Thus it is not very probable that background factors such as these could account for the observed differences in behavior. An interview has many limitations, however, and it may be that many important issues are never taken up, simply because their significance is unknown. The findings in P+ and P groups are similar to those reported by Klaus, Kennell, Plumb, and Zuehlke (1970) in a study of 14 mother–infant pairs with and without extended contact. The main difference between the two studies is that Klaus et al. gave their babies 1 hour of naked contact following birth and, in addition, 5 extra hours with their mothers each afternoon of the 3 days after delivery, whereas in the present study only 15–20 minutes of naked extra contact separated the two groups (P+ and P). The fact that this brought about the same effect lends support to the opinion that the very first hours after delivery may be of the greatest importance. If this is true, humans will fit into a pattern similar to that of other mammals that have been studied during the neonatal period in an attempt to identify specific maternal caretaking behavior. Studies of variations in neonatal care and their possible impact upon the development of the offspring and their behavior as adults have given further evidence of the special importance of the early postpartum period. A short separation of goat mothers and their young can lead to deviant maternal behavior (Klopfer, 1971), whereas a 5-minute contact between the goat mother and her own or alien young immediately after birth results in the normal accepting and caretaking behavior of the mother. Herscher et al. (Herscher, Moore, & Richmond, 1958; Herscher, Richmond, & Moore, 1963) demonstrated in goats and in sheep that separation reduces the mother's feeding and caretaking ability in about 50% of the animals studied. In rats a short separation of mother and infant in the neonatal period has been shown to alter maternal caretaking upon reunion of mother and litter (Rosenblatt, 1965). The quality and quantity of sensory stimulation during the neonatal period seems to be of special importance to the normal development of the infant and to maternal behavior. Harlow, Harlow, and Hansen (1963) have shown that, after 2 weeks of tactile deprivation of their infants, rhesus-monkey mothers who were allowed to see and hear, but not to touch, their infants spent less time viewing these infants. Harlow and Zimmerman (1959) and Harlow and Harlow (1965) also demonstrated that contact clinging is the primary variable that binds the mother to her infant and the infant to his mother. Infant monkeys were placed together with wire and with cloth mother-substitutes, both equivalent as providers of milk, but not equivalent as providers of tactile or psychological stimulation. The infant monkeys spent significantly more time with the cloth mother-substitutes and clung to the cloth mother-substitutes more often in a frightening or strange situation. These infant monkeys, deprived of tactile contact with their own mothers, failed when grown up to rear their own young normally.

According to Denenberg (1969) the way of handling the infant rat during infancy has wide and profound effects upon its behavior and physiology in adulthood. Likewise Levine (1956, 1960) has pointed out that handled rats show more adaptive responses to stress than do nonhandled ones, and that stimulated rats grow more rapidly, given the same amount of food as controls; using conditioned avoidance as a criterion of learning ability, they learn more quickly. The consequences of handling (gentle cutaneous stimulation in early infancy) seem to be more important where emotional factors are concerned than they are in matters of cognitive function (Levine, 1960).

The fallacies in the methods used in studies of the development of parent–infant relations are still incompletely explored. Therefore some points will be discussed here. Using 35 observational items as in our studies, one can expect some differences on the 5% level to occur by chance, although some items logically excluded others. More differences than could be expected by chance were found. By combining several behavioral items into groups (attachment behavior, for example), one can obtain significant differences between care groups (Klaus et al., 1970). It is difficult to know exactly what is the real meaning of the different components, however, and the interpretation of combinations of them is even more hazardous. Therefore we felt it was more appropriate to demonstrate significant differences only for individual behavioral items, feeling that, in a way, this can be regarded as extending our knowledge. Differences in maternal behavior during breast feeding depending upon parity have been reported (Thoman, Barnett, & Leiderman, 1971; Thoman, Leiderman, & Olson, 1972), with primiparae spending more time in nonfeeding activities and changing activities. In our study, pronounced differences in maternal and infant behavior were found between multiparae (M) and primiparae (P); primiparae with extra contact (P+) and multiparae (M) and their infants, however, were very much alike. This may give further support to the opinion that extra contact influences maternal and infant behavior.

Studying visual alertness in certain neonates, Korner and Thoman (1970) found no differences between male and female infants, but Leiderman, Leifer, Seashore, Barnett, and Grobstein (1973) found differences in maternal behavior depending on the sex of the infant. Moss (1967) demonstrated pronounced differences in both maternal and infant behavior at 3 weeks; boys slept less and cried more and thereby initiated more extensive and stimulating interaction with the mother. When the state of the infants was controlled, most of these sex differences became weaker, however. Thus the sex differences observed in our investigation have some support in earlier studies, but our data extend these by showing that early contact had far more profound effects on boy–mother pairs than on girl–mother pairs. In the P+ group, mothers of boys held, smiled (Bowlby, 1969), and made attempts to burp them more often, whereas mothers of girls talked to them more frequently. Within the P group the differences that were correlated with the sex of the infant were much smaller, mothers with girls more often having them on their knees and encompassing them. Within the M group no significant differences were found.

SYNCHRONY IN THE DEVELOPMENT OF PARENT–INFANT INTERACTION FOLLOWING EARLY POST-PARTUM CONTACT

The two primiparous mother–infant groups (P+ and P), those with and without extra contact, have been followed up using different modes of investigation at 3 months and at 1 year after delivery. A 3-year follow-up is currently being carried out. A summary of the methods used in these follow-up studies is given in Table 5-10. The aim of these studies has been to investigate whether immediate post-partum contact has a long-term effect on the infant–parent relationship. Details of the material and a description of the methods of observation have been given earlier and are shown in Appendixes B, C, and D (pp. 165–173). A brief description of other methods used will be given with the discussion of the results.

Observation of Maternal and Infant Behavior during Free Play at Home

One mother–infant pair in each group was lost in the 3-month follow-up. One family was on holiday at the time of follow-up, and one had left the

TABLE 5-10
Schedule of Follow-Up Studies of Extra Contact Post Partum

1. At 3 months during a home visit:
   a. Mother–infant free play observation
   b. Interview with mother
   c. Duration of breast feeding

2. At 12 months in the out-patient clinic:
   a. Mother–infant behavior during a physical examination of infant
   b. Gesell Development Test
   c. Interview
   d. Vineland Test
   e. C.M.P.S. Test
   f. Mother's diary on infant sleeping and feeding habits
   g. Duration of breast feeding

3. At 36 months in the hospital:
   In planning and preparation

country for an extended stay abroad. Some selected background data on the 40 participating families were given earlier, in Table 5-4. The results of observations during the mother–infant free play at 3 months are given in Tables 5-11–5-15. Table 5-11 is a comparison between the groups with different post-partum care as a grand total, that is, without reference to the sex of the infant. A comparison by sex of infant is made within groups with the same type of care (Tables 5-12 and 5-13). We present the results for different kinds of care and compare for each sex separately (Tables 5-14 and 5-15). Only those items of behavior with p values in the t test of .10 or less in any of the above-mentioned comparisons are given in the tables.

A comparison of both groups (Table 5-11) reveals a number of significant differences in maternal behavior: Mothers in the extra-contact group spent more time looking *en face* ($p = .008$) and kissing their infants ($p = .009$), whereas they cleaned them less frequently ($p = .05$). Holding the infant was equally frequent in both groups, but mothers with extra contact more frequently encompassed their infants, although this difference was not significant. Infant crying was more frequently observed for non-extra-contact infants ($p = .02$) and covaried with mother rocking more frequently, but the difference did not reach a significant level. Infant smiling and or laughing appeared significantly more often in the extra-contact infants ($p = .02$).

Within the routine-care group (P), a comparison of behavior with regard to sex of infant showed that male infants had their eyes open during the entire observation period, whereas female infants had their eyes closed during a part of the time observed ($p = .05$). Consequently, male infants were more alert and played with one of the three toys used (bell, rattle,

TABLE 5-11
All Subjects Comparison P+ and P during Home Visit at Three Months (Mean Frequency and p Values)

	Mean frequency		
Observation	P+ (N = 21)	P (N = 19)	p value P+/P
Infant behavior			
Eyes closed	0	1.1	0.1
Eyes open	10	8.9	0.1
Crying	0.2	1.2	0.02
Smiling/laughing	2.7	1.4	0.02
Looks at mother	7.5	7.3	0.7
Plays with hands	0.6	0.8	0.7
Plays with toy	3.9	4.7	0.4
Holds mother's hand	1.1	0.8	0.5
Maternal behavior			
Leaning on elbow	0.3	1.1	0.3
Looks en face	3.1	0.8	0.008
Smiles	5.5	4.5	0.2
Laughs	0.9	0.5	0.5
Kisses	1.1	0.3	0.009
Cleans	0.1	0.5	0.05
Gives toy	4.6	4.0	0.5
Rocking infant	0.1	0.5	0.1
Others present	3.6	2.5	0.5

dangling ring) during a greater proportion of the observation time ($p = .05$); mothers more often gave toys to boys to play with ($p = .08$). Girls cried somewhat more frequently and mothers cleaned them significantly more often ($p = .02$) than they did boys (Table 5-12). Table 5-13, which gives the data on differences in behavior within the extra-contact group (P+) with regard to sex of infant, shows that, although boys and girls were alert with open eyes during the entire observation period, male infants played with their hands more frequently ($p = .04$). Mothers in both groups looked at their infants during the entire observation period, mothers of boys spending a significantly longer proportion of their time in the en face position ($p = .04$).

Primiparous mothers with extra contact (P+) spent more time looking en face ($p = .01$) and kissed their boys significantly more often ($p = .01$); they smiled somewhat more frequently at their boys ($p = .07$), and other persons (father, visitor) were slightly more often present during our observation ($p = .08$). Boys with extra contact smiled significantly more frequently at their

TABLE 5-12
**Routine-Care Group (P) during Home Visit at Three Months: Boys Compared to Girls
(Mean Frequencies and *p* Values)**

	Mean frequency		
Observation	Boys ($N = 12$)	Girls ($N = 7$)	*p* value Boys/Girls
Infant behavior			
Eyes closed	0	3.1	0.05
Eyes open	10	6.9	0.02
Crying	0.8	2.0	0.1
Smiling/laughing	1.3	1.6	0.7
Looks at mother	7.2	7.4	0.8
Plays with hands	1.0	0	0.3
Plays with toys	5.7	3.1	0.05
Holds mother's hand	0.9	0.6	0.6
Maternal behavior			
Leaning on elbow	1.2	1.8	0.9
Looks *en face*	0.8	0.7	0.8
Smiles	3.7	5.9	0.1
Laughs	0.3	1.0	0.4
Kisses	0.3	0.3	0.9
Cleans	0.1	1.1	0.02
Gives toy	4.8	2.7	0.08
Rocking infant	0.2	1.0	0.2
Others present	1.5	4.3	0.2

mothers ($p = .03$), although no differences were found in alertness (Table 5-14).

Finally, when mothers and girls with and without extra contact were compared (Table 5-15), it was found that maternal behavior differed significantly in only one respect: Mothers without extra contact cleaned, with a napkin or a piece of cleaning tissue, their girls more often ($p = .02$). Girls in the extra-contact groups had their eyes open during the entire period of observation, whereas girls in the noncontact group had eyes closed ($p = .08$) for some part of the observation period. The P girls also cried slightly more frequently ($p = .09$).

These observations of maternal and infant behavior 3 months after delivery have shown that maternal behavior with boys and girls within groups with the same type of immediate postnatal care differs in a number of ways, and that different kinds of neonatal care influence both maternal and infant behavior. In the extra-contact group (P+), mothers spent more time looking *en face* and kissing, and their infants laughed or smiled more frequently. In the control group (P), mothers spent more time cleaning their infants, who

TABLE 5-13
Extra Contact Group (P+) during Home Visit at Three Months: Boys Compared to Girls (Mean Frequencies and p Values)

Observation	Mean frequencies		p value Boys/Girls
	Boys (N = 11)	Girls (N = 10)	
Infant behavior			
Eyes closed	0	0	—
Eyes open	10	10	—
Crying	0.2	0.3	0.6
Smiling/laughing	3.0	2.4	0.5
Looks at mother	8.5	6.5	0.1
Plays with hands	1.5	0.1	0.04
Plays with toy	3.8	3.9	0.9
Holds mother's hand	1.9	0.5	0.07
Maternal behavior			
Leaning on elbow	0.8	0	0.2
Looks *en face*	4.6	1.5	0.04
Smiles	5.9	5.1	0.6
Laughs	1.0	0.7	0.7
Kisses	1.2	0.9	0.6
Cleans	0.1	0.1	—
Gives toy	5.2	4.0	0.3
Rocking infant	0.2	0.3	0.7
Others present	4.7	2.3	0.3

cried significantly more often. The effects of the extra contact during the first hour after delivery were more pronounced for boys and their mothers than they were for girls and their mothers. For example, mothers in the extra-contact group (P+) kissed and smiled at their boys more frequently, and boys in the extra-contact group (P+) smiled more often at their mothers than did boys in the P group. No such differences between P+ and P were found for girls and their mothers. Background factors concerning pregnancy, delivery, neonatal period, and the first 3 months at home were comparable in the two groups, thus reinforcing the reality of the observed differences in behavior. The methodology in this field is so far explored incompletely. Advantages and disadvantages of the methods used here were discussed earlier in this paper, and it was concluded that reliable results can be obtained.

Klaus *et al.* (1970) have shown more systematically than have others that neonatal care influences maternal behavior both in the neonatal period and later on. The present study extends their observations in three respects. First, it suggests that 15–20 minutes extra naked contact was associated with changes in maternal behavior similar to those accompanying the considera-

TABLE 5-14
Mother and Boys at Three Months with (P+) and without Extra Contact (P) (Mean Frequencies and *p* Values)

Observation	Mean frequency		*p* value P+/P
	P+ (N = 11)	P (N = 12)	
Infant behavior			
Eyes closed	0	0	—
Eyes open	10	10	—
Crying	0.2	0.8	0.2
Smiling/laughing	3.0	1.3	0.03
Looks at mother	8.5	7.2	0.2
Plays with hands	1.5	1.0	0.6
Plays with toy	3.8	5.7	0.2
Holds mother's hand	1.9	0.9	0.3
Maternal behavior			
Leaning on elbow	0.8	1.2	0.7
Looks *en face*	4.6	0.8	0.01
Smiles	5.9	3.7	0.07
Laughs	1.0	0.3	0.1
Kisses	1.2	0.3	0.01
Cleans	0.1	0.1	—
Gives toy	5.2	4.8	0.8
Rocking infant	0.1	0.2	0.9
Others present	4.8	1.5	0.08

bly longer extra contact used by Klaus *et al.* (i.e., 1 hour immediately after delivery and an additional 5 extra hours each afternoon during the next 3 days). Second, Klaus found differences between the treatment groups only when he lumped together several behavioral items that he called "maternal attachment behaviour." In this study we found differences in separate behavioral items. In addition to maternal behavior that can be involved in the development of attachment, such as kissing, looking *en face*, smiling, and crying (Bowlby, 1969), we also found differences in other behavior, such as cleaning of the infant and rocking. Third, we found differences in infant behavior that have not been studied by others. In our view, many of the differences we observed have an emotional background and are of value in the relationship between mother and infant. Behavior that can be expected to have a positive influence and value was found to occur more frequently in the extra-contact group (P+). One of the marked differences in infant behavior between the two groups concerned crying and smiling, the former occurring more frequently in the routine-care group, the latter more fre-

TABLE 5-15
Mothers and Girls at Three Months with (P+) and without Extra Contact (P) (Mean Frequencies and *p* Values)

Observation	Mean frequency P+ (N = 10)	Mean frequency P (N = 7)	*p* value P+/P
Infant behavior			
Eyes closed	0	2.9	0.08
Eyes open	10.0	7.1	0.04
Crying	0.3	2.0	0.09
Smiling	2.4	1.6	0.4
Looks at mother	6.5	7.4	0.5
Plays with hands	0.1	0	0.4
Plays with toy	3.9	3.1	0.5
Holds mother's hand	0.3	0.6	0.4
Maternal behavior			
Leaning on elbow	0	1.0	0.1
Looks *en face*	1.5	0.7	0.3
Smiles	5.1	5.9	0.6
Laughs	0.7	1.0	0.7
Kisses	0.9	0.3	0.2
Cleans	0.1	1.1	0.02
Gives toy	4.0	2.7	0.1
Rocking infant	1.0	0.1	0.1
Others present	2.3	4.3	0.4

quently in the extra-contact group. Infant crying could be a sign of less well developed mother–infant synchrony. It elicited cleaning and rocking more often in control-group mothers. Cleaning, as well as rocking (Bowlby, 1958), may be interpreted as a kind of maternal soothing behavior. Since such behavior was more frequent in mothers giving routine care, it could have been the effect caused by infants in this group crying more frequently. Infant smiling and laughing, on the other hand, was more frequent in the extra-contact group, possibly acting as a release for positive maternal behavior (i.e., kissing and looking *en face*) more frequently shown by mothers in the extra-contact group. These findings receive support from Lewis (1972), who during observation of mothers and 3-month-old infants found a positive correlation between mother's smiling and infant's smiling. I will not try to evaluate the impact of different behavior on later development, but only mention that Bowlby (1958, 1969) and Richards (1971) agree that smiling plays a role in the growing mother–infant relationship.

In studies of monkeys, Mitchell (1968) found that frequency and form of mother–infant contact depends on the behavior of the mother and on the age and sex of infant. In 1-year-old children, Feldman and Ingham (1975) demonstrated more distress caused by separation from the mother in boys than in girls. Other similar results have been shown in studies by Maccoby and Jacklin (1973); Lewis, Weinraub, and Ban (1972); and Brooks and Lewis (1974) in opposite sex twins at the age of 13 months. In our study we found differences in maternal and infant behavior within groups with the same care, depending on the infant's sex. For example in the P+ group, mothers with boys looked en face more frequently; in the P groups, mothers cleaned girls more often. Such sex differences might be acquired—caused by a difference in maternal attitudes associated with a difference in their expectations of boys and girls. Obviously they might also have a biological background. The fact that sex differences were already present at 36 hours might speak in favor of a genetic cause, or at least a prenatal molding. A most interesting and unexpected finding was that a change in care routine influenced boys and their mothers more than it did girls and their mothers. For example, infant smiling was seen more frequently in the P+ group among both girls and boys, but the influence was greatest among boys. Not only did infants behave differently according to their sex, but mothers did also (i.e., in kissing). Whether this was due to acquired difference in attitude, to maternal responsivity (Lewis, 1972), or to a biological mechanism, such as differences in the signals given by boys and girls, must await further studies. Moss (1967) found differences between the behavior of mothers with boys and mothers with girls reared under similar circumstances. The change in post-partum care seems to reinforce this pre-existing difference between the two sexes.

Personal Interview with Mothers at Three Months

The main results of the interview with the mothers during the home visit 3 months after delivery are given in Table 5-16. The groups were comparable in planning of the pregnancy and whether it was welcome, perception of physical well-being during the first 4 months and the second part of pregnancy, participation in antenatal clinic programs, preparations for and perception of delivery, husband's visiting patterns at the maternity ward, and mother's perception of the first week at home.

The infants in both groups slept for equal lengths of time at 3 months, and an equal number had suffered from colic and received medication for it. Although the mothers reported the same frequency of waking at night, and infants in the extra-contact group were given night feedings twice as long as were infants in the control group, mothers in the control group reported more problems with night feeding. Mothers in the control group had help in the household during a longer period after discharge from the maternity ward and felt that adaptation to their infants was somewhat more difficult.

TABLE 5-16
The Personal Interview with All Mothers

	P+ (N = 21)	P (N = 19)
Pregnancy		
Planned and welcome	12	12
Unplanned and welcome	8	5
Unplanned and not welcome	1	2
Participation in antenatal program	17	12
Preparations for delivery		
Little	11	8
Moderate	2	6
Many	8	5
Perception of delivery		
Hard	4	1
Normal	3	3
Easy	14	15
Husband visits in maternity ward		
Frequently	16	16
Not frequently	4	2
First week at home		
Difficult	19	15
Easy	2	3
Adaptation to child		
Easy	13	3
As expected	7	14
Difficult	1	2
Problems with night feeding		
Yes	1	6
No	17	10
Mean time of night feeding (in days)	42	24
Mean number of days the mother had help at home	7.6	19.5
Percentages of mothers still breast feeding	58	26

More mothers in the extra-contact group were still breast feeding their infants at 3 months than were mothers in the control group. The sex differences were not as clear-cut as in the behavioral studies, except for the duration of breast feeding, which will be discussed below.

Observation of Maternal and Infant Behavior at One Year

One year after delivery the primiparous mothers and their infants were invited to participate in a follow-up study at the out-patient clinic of our department. Details of methods were given earlier in Table 5-10 and Figure 5-9 and can also be found in Appendix D. Unfortunately, five mother–infant pairs did not come to this follow-up. This may have been partly due to our approach. Only one telephone contact was made with the families, and no active efforts were made after an initial rejection to persuade them to reconsider their decision. Our 3-year follow-up is somewhat differently designed, and it is hoped that this will result in a decrease in the frequency of drop-outs. Maternal behavior in the two groups studied showed some marked differences. As shown in Figure 5-11, mothers in the P+ group were holding their infants with close body contact for a larger proportion of the total observation time, both on the examination table and in the mother's lap. Of course, the situation was unusual and maybe even frightening for the children, and the P+ mothers were obviously able to comfort their children more easily. Touching and caressing not related to caregiving was seen more frequently among extra-contact mothers. An attempt was made to measure the content of what mothers said to their children during the observation period. Control mothers used more direct commands and more often told the children to behave properly—for example, not to cry, scream, or fuss. Extra-contact mothers, on the other hand, were more inclined to comfort their children with words, saying things such as "this does not hurt," "it will

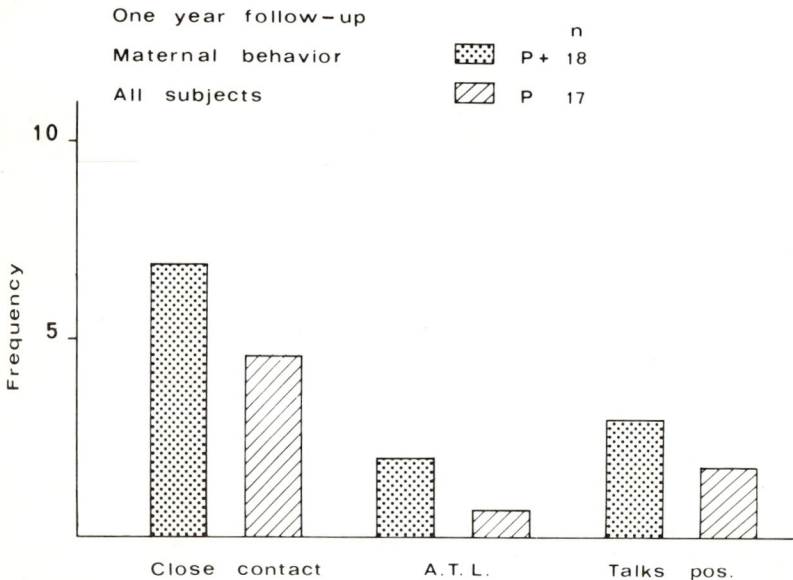

Figure 5-11. Maternal behavior 1 year after delivery during a physical examination in the out-patient clinic.

soon be over," and "mother is staying with you." There seemed to be greater warmth in what P+ mothers said to their children.

Other differences between the two groups were also found that, although not statistically significant, pointed in the same direction, such as P+ mothers spending slightly more time kissing and smiling at their children. Infant behavior showed some differences between the two groups, but as mentioned above, the observation may not have been fully reliable and therefore will not be presented in detail. Differences in maternal behavior that correlated to the sex of the child were also found. The differences were again greater for boy–mother dyads than they were for girl–mother dyads. The observations at 1 year seem to confirm the differences in behavior demonstrated at 36 hours and 3 months.

Psychomotor Development at One Year

It was felt strongly that the infants' development could have been influenced by early experiences. If the development of the relationship between parents and infants is synchronous, the children seem more likely to develop satisfactorily. Many different tests can be used at the age of 1 year. In our department a large body of experience with the Gesell Developmental Test and the Denver Test is available. This is the main reason why those tests are used in our studies, since in our opinion it is of great importance to use methods that are well known to the experimenters from routine practical work with children. The Gesell Developmental Test was given to all children and consists of five major parts: gross-motor, fine-motor, adaptive, linguistic, and social development (Gesell & Armatruda, 1962). The results are shown in Table 5-17.

In all five parts of the test, children with extra contact after delivery (P+) are ahead of the children in the control group (P). The main differences are found in gross-motor, fine-motor, and social development. The value of these different parts is difficult to estimate. Could the observed effect be the result of more training or of more time spent together? The difference in linguistic behavior is perhaps most interesting when compared with the results obtained by Ringler et al. (1975), who studied maternal language after extended post-partum contact. She found that extended-contact mothers asked twice as many questions and used more words per preposition, fewer content words, more adjectives, and fewer commands than did control mothers. Another comparison at 5 years of age was that made in the Cleveland study between extended-contact and control children. In two language tests, children of extended-contact mothers had more advanced scores (Ringler, Trause, & Klaus, 1976). This is also consistent with our observations of maternal behavior and the warmth of the language used and

TABLE 5-17
Results of the Gesell Developmental Test at One Year

	Study group (P+) (weeks)[a]	Control group (P) (weeks)[a]
Gross motor	+5.6	+2.3
Fine motor	+2.8	+1.3
Adaptive	+0.7	+0.3
Linguistic	−0.1	−0.8
Social	−1.1	−2.5

[a] Weeks +(−) = mean number of weeks ahead (behind) in development in relationship to biological age.

emphasizes the importance of following the language development of the children in our study.

The Interview with Mothers at One Year

A short, semistructured interview covering socioeconomic and occupational circumstances, health, some child-rearing practices, and the fathers' participation in the daily care of the children was made at the beginning of the 1-year follow-up. This interview contained a total of 15 questions. The answers to 4 of these questions revealed statistically significant differences between extra-contact and control families. Table 5-18 gives a summary of these results. Mothers with extra contact immediately postpartum had returned to their employment outside the home to a lesser extent than had control mothers. There were no actual differences between the two groups in occupational distribution or other socioeconomic circumstances. An equal proportion of mothers in both groups were in a position to resume work if they wished. Therefore the results illustrate that P+ mothers preferred and consciously chose to stay at home with their children for a longer period of time than did P mothers. Somewhat to our surprise, a relatively large number of mothers had started bladder training their children by the age of 1 year. This was more common among control mothers, possibly indicating a greater need for firm rules and training when maternal self-confidence is low or the interaction with the infant is not always smooth. A greater proportion of extra-contact children were reported by their mothers to sleep in a room of their own. In both groups an equal number of rooms was available to to each family. Around the age of 1 year the process of normal separation–individuation has started for many children (Freud, 1965; Gaddini & Gaddini, 1970; Piaget, 1951). The physical presence or absence of the parents during the night and the going-to-sleep pattern that children gradually develop together with their parents play an important role

TABLE 5-18
Summary of Results of Interview with All Mothers at One Year[a]

		P+	P
Mother returned to professional work			
	Yes	10	14
	No	8	3
Started bladder training of infant			
	Yes	5	10
	No	13	7
Infant sleeps in own room			
	Yes	9	4
	No	9	13
Father engaged in daily care of infant			
	Yes	10	14
	No	8	9

[a] P+ = primiparous mothers with extra contact following delivery; P = primiparous mothers with routine care after delivery.

in this process (Gaddini, 1971). It seems rather obvious in the light of these observations and those of Winnicott (1971) that the families in our study with extra contact probably had advanced further in the development of the separation–individuation process. Unfortunately, the frequency of a transitional object in the two groups of infants was not investigated at 1 year, but this will be studied in the next follow-up study at 3 years. The father's role in the early development of the mother–infant relationship seems, when relevant literature is studied (Howells, 1969; Nash, 1965), to have been rather poorly investigated. According to the mothers, fathers in the P+ group participated to a lesser extent in the daily care of infants (for instance, feeding, changing diapers, playing, and putting children to bed) than did fathers in the control group. It is, of course, hazardous to give a definite explanation. First, this is the account of the situation through the eyes of the mothers; second, some fathers might quite simply have more opportunities to participate in infant care than do others. Judging by their occupations, however, the fathers should have had equal chances to be with their children in both groups. As shown earlier, the maternal and infant behavior during our different observations seems to have developed in a more synchronous way in the P+ group. This may also have led to, or be correlated with, certain child-rearing practices or opinions on such practices. Mothers in the routine-care group may feel less reluctance to let the father take care of the infant, and mothers with extra contact may see greater difficulty in doing so. Whether there is a certain optimum level of participation by the father in the day-to-day care of children is still not known; flexibility to the individual needs and requirements of each family is probably the ideal in this respect.

The Vineland Scale at One Year

The Vineland Social Maturity Scale was developed by Doll (1936) at the Vineland Training School. The scale is meant to measure social development and maturity in children. A Swedish version has been used since 1960. The greatest value and strength of the method is its indirect approach to the subjects; the experimenter interviews a third person (the mother) who is closely related to the subject. The scale gives quite a clear picture of the social environment and social behavior of the child. In our study no significant differences between the two groups (P and P+) were found. Both P+ and P mothers rated their children somewhat more highly than was to be expected from their actual age. No obvious sex-linked differences have so far been found. More detailed information about this and possibly about other parts of the study will be given elsewhere (de Chateau & Wiberg, in press).

The Cesarec–Marke Personality Scale at One Year

The samples of extra contact in our studies were randomized, and a large number of relevant and accessible background factors were comparable in both groups. Nevertheless, an unknown bias could have slipped into these investigations. The validity and value of the results and also those of other studies has quite fairly been questioned. In order to meet these criticisms and to enable us to be more confident of our results, a check on the psychological needs of the mothers was made 1 year after delivery. For this we used the Cesarec–Marke Personality Scale (C.M.P.S.) (Cesarec & Marke, 1968) based on Murray's personality theory (Murray, 1938). This scale has been shown to be stable over time when used on the same subjects and was one with which we were familiar.

The C.M.P.S. is considered to be one of the most useful and accessible of the multidimensional questionnaires that have been standardized for Swedish conditions (Perris & Strandman, in press). Figure 5-12 shows the mean scores, in stanine-points, for the two groups of mothers investigated and the normal range of these scores for women in the same age group. The scale consists of 12 requirement factors (A to L, Figure 5-12), which are intended to measure achievement, affiliation, aggression, defense of status, guilt feelings, dominance, exhibition, autonomy, nurturance, order, succorance, and acquiescence. No significant differences between P+ and P groups were found in any of the 12 items, nor did the results of *either* of the

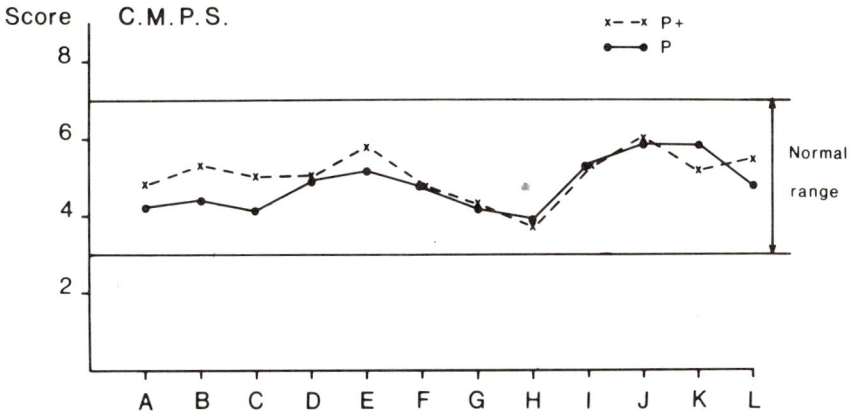

Figure 5-12. Profile of the results of mothers' C.M.P.S. at 1 year. A–L = 12 factors forming the C.M.P.S.; 0–9 = Stanine score.

groups deviate in any way from the normal range. As the C.M.P.S. has been shown to be stable over time (Strandman, 1977), the conclusion from this part of our studies must be that at the time of delivery the two groups were fully comparable in psychological needs such as nurturance, succorance, autonomy, and so forth.

Mother's Diary at One Year

During the week before the follow-up at the hospital 1 year after delivery, all mothers were asked to keep a diary of infant sleeping and feeding habits. Most mothers kept these diaries conscientously. No statistically significant differences between the two groups caused by type of neonatal care or sex of the infant were present. Even a detailed survey of different types of food consumed did not reveal any major differences. The total number of hours, during the night and the day, that the children were asleep is shown in Figure 5-13. The number of sleep periods was also quite similar in both groups, although the dispersion in the control group was perhaps somewhat greater (Figure 5-14). Sleeping patterns in children around 1 year of age seem to be individual and correlated to very early infant behavior during the first 10 days of life (Bernal, 1973). These sleeping patterns have been found to be only very slightly influenced by parental handling or care routines. According to the evidence of the mothers' diaries, this was also true of the infants we studied. Where infants slept, whether in their parents' room or in their own room, had no influence on their sleeping habits, nor were correlations with the sex of the infant found.

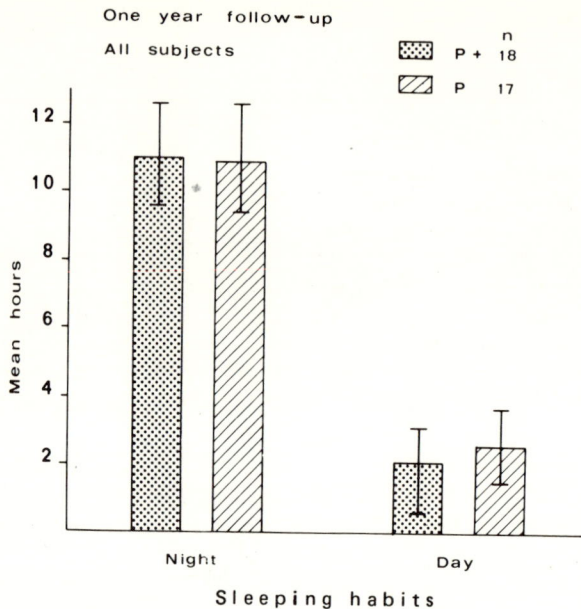

One year follow-up

All subjects

Figure 5-13. The mean number of hours the children are asleep at 1 year.

Duration of Breast Feeding

It is by now generally accepted that breast feeding has considerable medical advantages over artificial feeding. The low frequency of infection in breast-fed babies is due not only to less contamination, but also to the antiinfectious properties of breast milk itself. Protection against allergy, malabsorption, and constipation are examples of other important properties; recent reviews summarize our present knowledge (Mata & Urrutia, 1971; Hansson & Winberg, 1972; Goldman & Smith, 1973; Taylor, Norman, Orgel, Stokes, Turner, & Soothill, 1973; Gerrard, 1974; Gothefors & Winberg, 1975; MacKeith & Wood, 1977; Jelliffe & Jelliffe, 1978). The socio-psychological advantages of breast milk are not as easy to determine as are the medical ones. As part of a series of investigations of factors promoting and inhibiting lactation, the mothers in the extra-contact study were followed up until the children were 1 year old in order to ascertain their success in breast feeding (de Chateau, 1976a; de Chateau et al., 1977). The data were collected during the interview with the mothers at 3 months and at 1 year and checked through scrutiny of the Child Health Center records. The mean duration for the mothers in the P+ group was 175 days, compared with 108 days for mothers in the P group. The mean duration of breast feeding is in full concordance with data collected from a larger sample

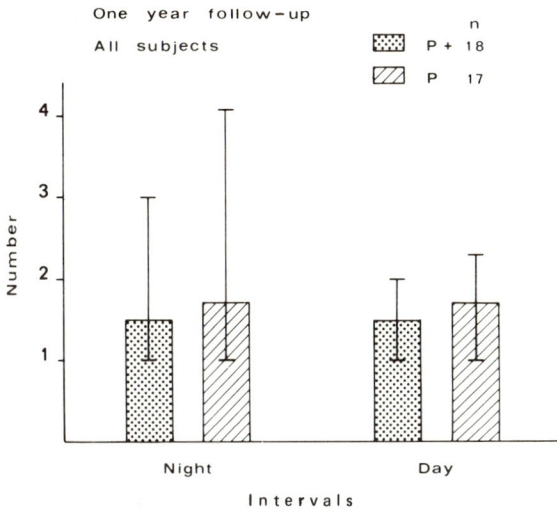

Figure 5-14. The mean number of periods of sleep at 1 year.

during the same period and in the same area (de Chateau et al., 1977). However, the range of the duration (P+: 21–365 days; P: 10–240 days) was very wide. The median values are given in Table 5-19, and the percentages of mothers totally breast feeding, without supplementary feeding, is shown in Table 5-16. There was a considerable sex difference in the duration of breast feeding, boys being fed longer than girls in both the routine-care and the extra-contact groups. The effect of extra contact seems to be very powerful, especially in mother–boy pairs. The mean lactation period was $2\frac{1}{2}$ months longer in the extra-contact group than it was among controls. However, the influence of early contact cannot rule out all other factors. Whereas the available data indicate that the $2\frac{1}{2}$ months prolongation of breast feeding is a consequence of the early skin-to-skin and suckling contact, it is obvious that this early contact does not always promote breast feeding; hence the wide range in the observed nursing periods. However, the present study suggests that early contact may be a relatively simple way of promoting breast feeding for some mother–infant pairs cared for in the

TABLE 5-19
Duration of Breast Feeding at One Year (Median Number of Days)

	P+	P
Whole group	180 (N = 21)	90 (N = 20)
Boys	270 (N = 11)	105 (N = 12)
Girls	75 (N = 10)	60 (N = 8)

highly technical and "unnatural" environments of today's delivery and maternity units. Johnson (1976) compared mothers under an existing maternity-ward routine, who nursed their infants for the first time 16 hours after delivery, with a group of mothers who nursed their infants during the very first hour post partum. When the infants were 8 weeks old, mothers with the early suckling experience seemed to be more likely to breast feed. In other populations, too, such as those of Brazil and Guatemala, significant differences have been found in the duration of breast feeding: In three out of four populations studied, mothers who had early access to their infants were more likely to leave the maternity ward breast feeding and were likely to breast feed for a longer period of time (Sousa, Barros, Gazelle, Begeres, Pinheiro, Menezes, & Arruda, 1974; Sosa, Kennell, Klaus, & Urrutia, 1976). A decisive factor may be that extra contact during the first hours and days following delivery does influence the mother–infant relationship. Emotional reactions and psychological factors have been shown to influence the "let-down reflex" (Newton, 1971a, b) or "milk ejection reflex" (Jelliffe & Jelliffe, 1974), which may be the main key to success or failure in lactation. This might also be illustrated by the fact that, although the mothers in the early-contact group gave night feeding for almost twice as long as did the control group, they considered these feedings to be less of a problem than did the control mothers (Table 5-16). This might indicate that the early contact had influenced mother–infant cooperation in feeding. Breast feeding is an act of cooperation between mother and infant, and if extra contact during the early postnatal period does promote mother–infant relations, it should also be associated with more successful breast feeding. Any measure that increases self-confidence and diminishes anxiety would also increase success in breast feeding (Jelliffe & Jelliffe, 1971, 1974). Mothers who have extra contact during the first hour after delivery probably also experience the advantage of an early sucking reflex, which stimulates the secretion of prolactin, a trigger for secretion in the breasts, and releases oxytocin, which produces the "let-down reflex." A study comparing prolactin and oxytocin levels in mothers who have and mothers who have not had extra skin-to-skin and/or suckling contact with their newborn infants immediately following delivery is currently being carried out in our unit. In this respect the differences in the duration of breast feeding connected with the infant's sex are also of great interest.

DISCUSSION AND SPECULATIONS

I have already commented on our results at the end of each individual section, but provide the following comments here by way of conclusion. The interpretation of studies of early stimulation is still very hazardous and should be approached with great caution. However, it is noticeable that results of different studies, both of humans and of animals, tend to fit into a similar pattern. Among mothers and infants, a large number may have special needs. For example, mothers with an unwanted pregnancy might not be capable of accepting and benefiting from early extra contact with their infants. In fact, we have found that during the period following our first studies, some mothers have refused the extra contact offered to them. Therefore, one must be very cautious in offering all mothers this contact immediately after delivery. The offer should be made in a tentative way, permitting the mother to make her own choice and decision, preferably together with the baby's father. Since one possible negative side effect of early contact between mother and infant has been reported, concerning the father's involvement in the day-to-day care of the child at 1 year, more research needs to be done and more clear evidence needs to be gathered on the long-term effects of such early contact on the development of intrafamily relations.

In our view the relatively short period of "extra contact" during the first hour following delivery is hardly sufficient by itself to explain the differences in maternal and infant behavior later on. Mothers and infants might have an opportunity during this early contact to exchange signals that may be important to the establishment of mother–infant synchrony. Consequently, the development of the mother–infant relationship may proceed more smoothly. Other variables, such as parity of the mother, family, social background, parents' age, and health, may be of equally great importance. The same is true of the mothers' relationship with their husbands and their own parents, the planning and course of pregnancy, the mode of delivery, and so on. From a biological point of view, caring for a newborn infant is an extremely delicate task. The optimal physical condition of the newborn child is characterized by rather narrow boundaries. For example, this applies to temperature regulation, caloric requirements, need for oxygen, regulation of water and salt metabolism, and so on. These boundaries have not been known to parents, and in fact, science has only recently revealed their importance. The newborn infant should be protected against great departures from these needs.

During the sensitive early postdelivery phase of development, these needs are probably best served by a pattern of maternal behavior that for the most part is genetically determined. It is still very common, however, for people other than the infant's own parents (nurses, midwives, nurses aides, etc.) to have full access to him after delivery. Certain check-ups must then be carried out that may be important but not absolutely vital from a medical point of view. The possible permanent psychological damage done to the development of the subsequent parent–infant relationship is still incompletely known, although the results of recent research strongly suggest that there is some damage.

The importance of the first hour after delivery should not be overemphasized. Mothers and infants have a great range of individual patterns of behavior and interaction. The ability to care for the child can be learned, and differences between primiparae and multiparae in this respect are well known. Primiparae with extra contact showed a behavior during breast feeding much like the behavior of the more trained and more experienced multiparae with routine care after delivery (de Chateau & Wiberg, 1977a). This extra contact might have put the primiparae in a favored position that, in a way, could be compared to the position of the multiparae with more training and experience. The extra contact might have had other physiological advantages as well. Through a close skin-to-skin contact, the infant is perhaps kept warm so that his unstable temperature regulation immediately after delivery is protected and not disturbed by our routines, such as bathing, weighing, and so forth. We usually cover the baby's back with a blanket; a heat panel is not used. No instances of low body temperature have been reported in the extra-contact groups. The regulation of body temperature may have had an economical start through this extra contact. Extra contact may be particularly valuable to vulnerable mother–infant pairs with negative traits in their personal, family, or social environment. A mother who refuses an extra contact offered to her may need support and help during her stay in the maternity ward. The mere knowledge of the importance and possible positive effects of extra contact shortly after delivery may help to minimize the deleterious influence of necessary separation in cases of prematurity, asphyxia, malformation, and the like. The hospital staff should be well informed of the results of recent research in this field; this is especially desirable now that separation of the sick newborn infant from the mother and father during observation and treatment in neonatal wards has become routine procedure in many situations. In view of the unique character of the immediate post-partum period, our routine for caring for sick infants and infants at risk deserves increased attention. Examples of measures that can be taken to prevent the subsequent development of problems in family relations are no restriction of visiting by parents, transport of infant together with mother from one referring hospital to another where the intensive-care unit is located, and a decrease in the admittance of some babies, for instance those of diabetic mothers (Lithner, de Chateau, Wickman, & Wiklund, 1977). The benefit of intensive observation in the neonatal ward should be carefully weighed against the possible harmful effects of the separation.

In our 1-year follow-up of extra contact, the differences in the behavior of groups with differing types of postnatal care, which were also demonstrated at 36 hours and at 3 months, seem to be correlated with other developmental characteristics. Many of these results, for instance better psychomotor development and longer duration of breast feeding, may be regarded as desirable. The sex of the infant seems to be an important determinant of both maternal and infant behavior. The extra contact obviously influences boys and their mothers more than it does girls and their mothers. Categorical conclusions from these results should be avoided, however. Families have a great range of individual needs, backgrounds, and capacities. Therefore, flexibility to the individual requirements and needs of each family is needed.

It is regrettable that the trend in our society is in exactly the opposite direction: Certain child-care practices and certain forms of early stimulation and soothing are considered universally beneficial regardless of a given child's particular needs. We should also be very cautious about labeling some interactive patterns as "good" or "bad" (Hofer, 1975), since evidence for these judgments is still lacking. What might be "good" for one infant–parent dyad could be "bad" for another one. The impact of behavioral interaction during the early period on the growing parent–infant relationship is still unknown.

The methodological problems are also far from solved. In our studies mean frequencies of defined behavior are measured by a time-sampling technique. So far we have not studied sequences of behavior and real interactions. This is obviously a consequence of the method of direct observation. At present, however, we are transforming our data in such a way that sequences and interactions can also be studied. One of the key questions still to be answered is whether the mother or the infant initiates the interaction pattern, and how the partner reacts. The changing pattern of behavior over time is another complication in these studies (Hinde, 1975). An even more interesting study is that of certain types of early behavior and their possible correlation with later opinions on child-rearing matters. This question is also currently being investigated in our unit.

Perhaps the most powerful and drastic effect of extra contact has been on the duration of breast feeding. Mothers with early skin-to-skin and suckling contact breast fed their infants for $2\frac{1}{2}$ months longer on an average than did control mothers. Three out of 21 mothers with extra contact were still partly breast feeding their infants at 1 year, as opposed to none of the 19 control mothers. Preliminary results from our 3-year follow-up, currently in the course of preparation, show that one of these three mothers still has her child, now 3 years old, suckle daily from her breasts. This extraordinarily long period of breast feeding is highly unusual in our culture and is perhaps the most remarkable result of our studies. As the impact on the duration of breast feeding seems to be marked, a correlation with the presence of certain hormones might be found in future studies, and we have recently started to explore this area further.

As has been mentioned, the children in our early extra-contact studies are now at the age of about 3 years, and a brief outline of the design of the 3-year follow-up study will be presented as an end to this chapter. This 3-year follow-up study takes place at the outpatient clinic of the Department of Child Psychiatry of our hospital, where three rooms are available and three independent experimenters carry out the program. The design of this program is given in Table 5-20.

The participating families are invited by letter, and a telephone appointment is made for the whole day. Upon arrival at the clinic at approximately 9:30 A.M., a short introduction is given to the family by Observers 1 and 2. After this introduction the parents and the child are separated; the parents follow Observer 1 to an interview and answer a questionnaire; the child goes with Observer 2 for a structured and standardized observation of play in accordance with Lowenfeld's "World Test"-method (Danielsson, 1962; Lowenfeld, 1948, 1950). While the parents are still with Observer 1, the child is brought by Observer 2 to the next activity, a Denver Test carried out by Observer 3. At noon the family gathers again to have luncheon in a private room at the clinic; some time is also scheduled for rest. At around 1 P.M., mother and child are invited to play with dolls and a dolls' house, and a videotape recording of this session is made. In the meantime the father is asked to wait outside. As soon as the recording has been completed, the whole family is asked to watch a playback with Observer 1. At the end of the day child play is again observed (Observer 2), while the parents have the opportunity to have a closing discussion (Observer 1). During this day a

TABLE 5-20
Design of the Three-Year Follow-Up Study of Families with Extra Contact and with Routine Care after Parturition

Time	Method–examination	Participant(s)[a]
9:30 A.M.	Arrival of family (1, 2)	M, F, and C
10:00 A.M.	Observation (2)	C
	Interview (1)	M and F
11:00 A.M.	Denver Test (3)	C
	Interview continued (1)	M and F
12:00 A.M.	Luncheon	M, F, and C
1:00 P.M.	Videotape recording (1)	M and C
2:00 P.M.	Observation (2)	C
3:30 P.M.	End of follow-up	

[a] M = Mother; F = Father; C = Child. (1), (2), and (3) = Experimenter 1, 2, and 3.

large body of information on all the families studied will be obtained. So far almost 30 of 42 families have agreed to come to the follow-up, and we expect to assemble approximately 40 families altogether. More detailed reports on the material, methods, and results will be given in forthcoming publications. Parts of this follow-up will be evaluated in cooperation with the University of Stockholm, Departments of Experimental Psychology and Language Development. Our present and future research must build on interdisciplinary cooperation between medicine, physiology, psychology, sociology, anthropology, and so forth (de Chateau, 1979). Only then can we gain a better understanding of the process involved in the growth of the parent–infant relationship.

APPENDIX A

Definitions of different ways of holding and carrying newborn infants

Holding to the left (right): Mother holding infant in her arms, the infant's head pointing to the left (right) side of the mother's body.

Carrying to the left (right): Mother walking with her infant in her arms, the infant's head pointing to the left (right) side of the mother's body.

Carrying in the hands: Mother walking with infant in her hands, not in her arms, without body contact and regardless of side of the mother's body to which the infant's head is pointing.

Body contact: At least half of the infant's body in direct contact with mother's body.

APPENDIX B

Definitions of behavior and observation sheet (p. 167) used during the study 36 hours after delivery[1]

1. *Mother absent:* Mother is not present in observation room.
2. *Mother in bed:* Mother in her own bed.
3. *Mother other:* Mother in room where observations taking place, but not in bed. May be standing or sitting in chair.
4. *Mother lying down:* Mother recumbent.
5. *Mother leaning on elbow:* Mother lying down in bed with upper part of body and head supported by elbow.
6. *Mother sitting up:* Upper part of body raised from bed, may be leaning back for support.

[1] Definitions prepared in cooperation with Mary Anne Trause and based mainly on experience gained in studies performed at the Department of Pediatrics, Case Western Reserve University, Cleveland, Ohio (Head, Marshall H. Klaus).

7. *Mother asleep:* Mother usually in bed although may be in chair, has eyes closed and breathes regularly for at least a few minutes without moving.

8. *Mother drowsy:* Mother's eyes closed with increasing frequency over a short period of time, respirations become more regular and pronounced than when awake.

9. *Mother awake:* Mother's eyes open and she is relatively alert. May be in any position.

10. *Infant in own bed far from mother:* Infant in own crib, which is located farther than arm's length from mother.

11. *Infant in own bed near mother:* Infant in own crib within arm's length of mother.

12. *Infant on mother's bed or chair:* Infant is in mother's bed or with mother in chair.

13. *Infant quiet:* Infant making no sounds, no major movements of arms, legs, or hands, eyes usually closed, infant may be sucking.

14. *Infant active:* Infant moving arms, legs, or head or vocalizing or looking around in wide-eyed alert state.

15. *Infant crying:* Infant crying hard or fussing continuously.

16. *Mother bottle feeds:* Mother gives infant bottle.

17. *Mother nurses:* Mother has infant at breast. May be suckling or not.

18. *Mother burps:* Mother makes attempts to let the baby burp.

19. *Mother diapers:* Mother changing diaper.

20. *Mother uncovers or undresses:* Definite moves by mother to expose infant's skin.

21. *Mother infant on knees:* Mother sitting up in bed with infant on her knees.

22. *Mother holds infant:* Mother has infant in her arms or resting on her torso.

23. *Encompassing:* Mother's upper arm, lower arm, and hand around the infant's body.

24. *A.T.L. = Affectionate Touch Love:* Any extra touching of infant or infant's clothes by mother's fingers.

25. *Close contact:* At least half of the infant's body touching mother's trunk.

26. *Mother looks at infant:* Mother's open eyes on infant, for a short glance or longer period.

27. *Looks en face:* Mother's face parallel to infant's in same vertical plane of rotation with mother's eyes directed toward infant's eyes.

28. *Mother talks to infant:* Mother vocalizes to infant, including nonspeech noises.

29. *Mother smiles at infant:* Definite widening of mouth and heightening of eyebrows by mother directed towards infant. Positive effect shown on mother's face.

30. *Mother kisses infant:* Mother's lips touching infant's body.

31. *Occupied with breast:* Mother manually expelling milk from breast, putting cream on breast or on nursing pads.

32. *Mother talks to adult:* Mother talks to any adult present in the room.

33. *Mother listens radio/TV:* Radio/TV set on, mother listens to sound.

34. *Others present:* Other adults present in room, excluding observer.

35. *Nurse aid:* Nurse helping mother with infant, either spontaneously or at mother's request.

Name:

Date:

Maternal behavior with her infant on the second day of life

Time:

Time:

	1	2	3	4	5	6	7	8	9	10	11	12	13	14	15	16	17	18	19	20
1 Location mother: absent																				
2 other																				
3 in bed																				
4 Mother lying down																				
5 Mother leaning on elbow																				
6 Mother sitting up																				
7 State of mother: asleep																				
8 drowsy																				
9 awake																				
10 Loc. inf.: own bed far from mo																				
11 own bed near mo																				
12 mo's bed or chair																				
13 State of infant: quiet																				
14 active																				
15 crying																				
16 Mother bottle feeds																				
17 Mother nurses																				
18 Mother burps																				
19 Mother diapers																				
20 Mother uncovers or undresses																				
21 Mother infant on knees																				
22 Mother holds infant																				
23 Encompassing																				
24 A.T.L.																				
25 Close contact																				
26 Mother looks at infant																				
27 Looks en face																				
28 Mother talks to infant																				
29 Mother smiles at infant																				
30 Mother kisses infant																				
31 Occupied with breast																				
32 Mother talks to adult																				
33 Mother listens radio/TV																				
34 Others present																				
35 Nurse aid																				

167

APPENDIX C

Definitions of behavior and observation sheet (pp. 169–170) used at 3 months during home visit

Infant behavior:
1. *Absent:* Not present in observation room.
2. *Other:* Present in room, not on carpet.
3. *On carpet:* On carpet, where observation of behavior is made.
4. *Supine:* Lying down on back, face upwards.
5. *Prone:* Lying down on front, face downwards or upwards.
6. *Side:* Lying on one side of the body, face sideways directed.
7. *Standing:* Standing up with mother's help.
8. *Sitting:* Sitting up with mother's help.
9. *Eyes closed:* Eyelids definitely closed, no movements.
10. *Eyes open:* Eyelids open or moving.
11. *Movement:* Any active movements of the infant's arms, legs, trunk, and head.
12. *Vocalization:* Makes sounds, mouthing movements, not including crying or laughing.
13. *Crying:* Active bawling, crying hard or continuously, single bouts not included.
14. *Smiles/laughs loudly:* Definite smiling or laughing with positive effect shown on face.
15. *Looks at mother:* Eyes on mother, may be a shorter glance or longer period.
16. *Looks at feet:* Eyes on own feet.
17. *Looks at hands:* Eyes on own hands.
18. *Plays with hands:* Plays with own hands actively, eyes directed at hands, no toys involved.
19. *Touches clothes:* Touches own clothes with one or both hands.
20. *Looks at toy:* Eyes open and on toy.
21. *Holds toy:* Holds toy in one or both hands.
22. *Plays with toy:* Touches toy or moves toy with hands actively and eyes directed at toy.
23. *Toy in mouth:* Has toy in mouth, may move toy in and out of mouth and/or suck toy.
24. *Thumb in mouth:* Has thumb in mouth, may move thumb in and out of mouth and/or suck thumb.
25. *Dummy in mouth:* Has dummy in mouth, may move dummy in and out of mouth and/or suck dummy.
26. *Holds mo's hand:* Holds mother's finger(s) or hand with firm grip.
27. *Drinks bottle:* Attached to bottle, may suckle or not.
28. *Burps:* Burping.

Maternal behavior:
29. *Absent:* Not present in observation room.
30. *Other:* Present in room, not on carpet.
31. *On carpet:* On carpet, where observation of behavior is made.
32. *Lying down:* Mother recumbent.
33. *Leaning on elbow:* Mother reclining with upper part of body and head supported by elbow.

Maternal and infant behavior during free play three months after delivery

		1	2	3	4	5	6	7	8	9	10
1	Infant: absent										
2	other										
3	on carpet										
4	supine										
5	prone										
6	side										
7	standing										
8	sitting										
9	eyes closed										
10	eyes open										
11	movement--act										
12	vocalization										
13	crying										
14	smiles/laughs loudly										
15	looks at mother										
16	looks at feet										
17	looks at hands										
18	plays with hands										
19	touches clothes										
20	looks at toy										
21	holds act toy										
22	plays act toy/touches toy										
23	toy in mouth										
24	thumb in mouth										
25	dummy in mouth										
26	holds mother's hand										
27	drinks bottle										
28	burps										

		1	2	3	4	5	6	7	8	9	10
29	Mother: absent										
30	other										
31	on carpet										
32	lying down										
33	leaning on elbow										
34	sitting up--crossed legs										
35	sitting up--on heels										
36	sitting up--on knees										
37	drowsy										
38	awake										
39	A.T.L.										
40	holding infant										
41	infant on knees										
42	encompassing										
43	rocks										
44	close contact										
45	looks at infant										
46	looks en face										
47	smiles at infant										
48	laughs										
49	kisses infant										
50	voc-talks to infant										
51	uncovers infant										
52	cleans infant										
53	gives toy										
54	holds toy										
55	gives dummy										
56	changes diaper										
57	gives bottle										
58	talks to adult										
59	listens radio/TV										
60	reading										
61	others present										

170

34. *Sitting up—crossed legs:* Upper part of body raised from surface, legs tailor fashion.
35. *Sitting up—on heels:* While body raised from surface, only contact with feet, knees, and hips bent and kept close together.
36. *Sitting up—on knees:* Sitting on knees.
37. *Drowsy:* Mother's eyes closed with increasing frequency over a short period of time, respirations become more regular and pronounced than when awake.
38. *Awake:* Mother's eyes open and she is relatively alert. May be in any position.
39. *A.T.L.:* Any extra touching of infant or infant's clothes by mother's fingers.
40. *Holding infant:* Mother has infant in her arms or resting on her torso.
41. *Infant on knees:* Mother sitting up in bed with infant on her knees.
42. *Encompassing:* Mother's upper arm, lower arm around the infant's body.
43. *Rocks:* Rocking infant.
44. *Close contact:* At least half of the infant's body touching mother's trunk.
45. *Looks at infant:* Mother's open eyes on infant, for a short glance or longer period.
46. *Looks en face:* Mother's face parallel to infant's in same vertical plane of rotation with mother's eyes directed toward infant's eyes.
47. *Smiles at infant:* Definite widening of mouth and heightening of eyebrows by mother directed towards infant. Positive effect shown on mother's face.
48. *Laughs:* Active laughing with positive effect shown on face, including single bouts of laughter.
49. *Kisses infant:* Mother's lips touching infant's body.
50. *Voc–talks to infant:* Mother vocalizes to infant, including nonspeech noises.
51. *Uncovers infant:* Definite moves by mother to expose infant's skin.
52. *Cleans infant:* Mother removes dirt, saliva, food, etc.
53. *Gives toy:* Mother actively gives toy to infant.
54. *Holds toy:* Mother holds toy, not including active giving of toy.
55. *Gives dummy:* Mother actively gives dummy to infant, puts in infant's hand or mouth.
56. *Changes diaper:* Mother changing diaper.
57. *Gives bottle:* Mother gives infant bottle.
58. *Talks to adult:* Mother talks to any adult present in the room.
59. *Listens to radio/TV:* Radio/TV set on, mother listens to sound.
60. *Reading:* Mother looks at or reads magazine, book, etc.
61. *Others present:* Other adults present in room, excluding observer.

APPENDIX D

Definitions of behavior and observation sheet (p. 172) used during the 1-year follow-up

Maternal behavior:
1. *Holds infant positively:* Mother holds infant with positive empathy.
2. *Holds infant negatively:* Mother holds infant, no positive empathy expressed by body posture.

Mother and infant behavior during physical

examination of infant at one year

Maternal behavior	1	2	3	4	5
1 Holds infant positively					
2 Holds infant negatively					
3 Close contact					
4 No body contact					
5 Face toward infant					
6 Face away					
7 Holds right					
8 Holds left					
9 Holds in front					
10 Looks at infant					
11 Looks at doctor					
12 Looks around					
13 Plays with infant					
14 A.T.L.					
15 Kisses					
16 Smiles					
17 Talks positively					
18 Talks negatively					
19 Talks to doctor					
Infant behavior 20 Plays					
21 Moves					
22 Sitting					
23 Crying					
24 Smiles/laughs					
25 Vocalizes					
26 Quiet					

3. *Close contact:* At least half of the infant's body touching mother's trunk.
4. *No body contact:* Less than half of the infant's body in direct contact with mother's body.
5. *Face towards infant:* Mother's face directed towards infant.
6. *Face away:* Mother's face away from infant.
7. *Holds right:* Mother holds infant in her lap, infant's body at a point to the right side of the mother's body.
8. *Holds left:* Mother holds infant in her lap, infant's body at a point to the left side of the mother's body.
9. *Holds infant:* Mother holds infant in her lap, no clear decision can be made whether the infant is held to the left or the right.
10. *Looks at infant:* Mother's open eyes on infant, for a short glance or longer period.
11. *Looks at doctor:* As 10, doctor instead of infant.
12. *Looks around:* Mother does not look at infant or doctor.
13. *Plays with infant:* Plays actively with infant, with or without toy.
14. *A.T.L.:* Any extra touching of infant or infant's clothes by mother's fingers.
15. *Kisses:* Mother kisses infant.
16. *Smiles:* Mother smiles at infant.
17. *Talks positively:* Talks directly to infant, giving support, encouragement, and comfort with her language.
18. *Talks negatively:* Talks directly to infant, giving orders, urgings, and prohibitions.
19. *Talks to doctor:* Mother talks to doctor during the physical examination of the infant.

Infant behavior:
20. *Plays:* Infant plays with toys or own body actively.
21. *Moves:* Infant moves with any part of body.
22. *Sitting:* Infant sitting on mother's lap without gross body movements.
23. *Crying:* Infant crying hard or fussing continuously.
24. *Smiles/laughs:* Definite smiling or laughing with positive effect shown on face.
25. *Vocalizes:* Makes sound, mouthing movements, not including crying or laughing.
26. *Quiet:* Infant making no sounds, no major movements of arms, legs, or hands, eyes usually closed, infant may be sucking.

REFERENCES

Barnett, C. R., Leiderman, P. H., Grobstein, R., & Klaus, M. H. 1970. Neonatal separation, the maternal side of interactional deprivation. *Pediatrics, 45,* 197–205.
Beintema, D. J., & Prechtl, H. F. R. 1968. *A neurological study of newborn infants.* London: Spastic International Society Publications. Pp. 24, 30.
Bell, R. Q. 1974. Contributions of human infants of caregiving and social interaction. In M. Lewis & L. A. Rosenblum (Eds.), *The effect of the infant on its caregiver.* New York: Wiley. Pp. 1–19.

Bell, S. M., & Ainsworth, M. D. S. 1972. Infant crying and maternal responsiveness. *Child Development, 43,* 1171–1190.

Bernal, J. F. 1972. Crying during the first 10 days of life and maternal responses. *Developmental Medicine and Child Neurology, 14,* 362–372.

Bernal, J. F. 1973. Night waking in the first 14 months. *Developmental Medicine and Child Neurology, 15,* 760–769.

Birns, B. 1968. Individual differences in human neonates' responses to stimulation. *Child Development, 36,* 249–256.

Birns, B., Blank, M., & Bridger, W. H. 1966. The effectiveness of various soothing techniques on human neonates. *Psychosomatic Medicine, 28,* 316–321.

Blauvelt, H., & McKenna, J. 1962. Mother–neonate interaction: Capacity of the human newborn for orientation. In B. Foss (Ed.), *Determinants of infant behavior.* New York: Wiley. Pp. 3–25.

Bowlby, J. 1958. The nature of the child's tie to his mother. *International Journal of Psychoanalysis, 39,* 350–373.

Bowlby, J. 1969. *Attachment and Loss—Vol. I.* London: Hogarth Press.

Brazelton, T. B. 1962. Observations of the neonate. *American Journal of Psychiatry, 1,* 38–57.

Brazelton, T. B. 1973. Neonatal behavioural assessment scale. *Clinics in Developmental Medicine No. 50.* London: Spastics International Medical Publications, Heineman.

Brazelton, T. B., Scholl, M. L., & Robey, J. S. 1966. Visual responses in the newborn. *Pediatrics, 37,* 284–290.

Brazelton, T. B., Tronick, E., Adamson, L., Als, K., & Weise, S. 1975. Early mother–infant reciprocity. In *Parent–infant interaction.* Ciba Foundation Symposium 33, Amsterdam, Elsevier. Pp. 137–149.

Brooks, J., & Lewis, M. 1974. Attachment behaviour in thirteen-month-old, opposite-sex twins. *Child Development, 45,* 243–247.

Burns, P., Sander, L. W., Stechler, G., & Julia, H. 1972. Short-term effects of caretaker environment of the first 10 days. *Journal of the American Academy of Child Psychiatry, 11,* 427–439.

Cesarec, Z., & Marke, S. 1968. *C.M.P.S. Manual.* Stockholm: Skandinaviska Testförlaget AB.

Conel, J. L. 1970. Life as revealed by the microscope. In F. Vester (Ed.), *Denken, Lernen, Vergessen.* Stuttgart: Deutsche Verlag Anstalt.

Condon, W. S., & Sander, L. B. 1974. Neonate movement is synchronized with adult speech: International participation and language acquisition. *Science, 183,* 99–101.

Cooper, E. S., Costella, A. J., Douglas, J. W. B., Ingleby, J. D., & Turner, R. K. 1974. Direct observations. *Bulletin of the British Psychological Society, 27,* 3–7.

Danielsson, A. 1962. Sandlådeobservationer enligt Erica-metoden. *Nordisk Medicin, 68,* 1197–1202.

de Chateau, P. 1976a. *Neonatal Care Routines: Influences on maternal and infant behaviour and on breast feeding.* Umeå, Sweden: Umeå University Medical Dissertations, New Series: 20.

de Chateau, P. 1976b. The influence of early contact on maternal and infant behaviour in primiparae. *Birth and Family Journal, 3,* 149–155.

de Chateau, P. 1977. Left-side preference in holding and carrying newborn infants. *Journal of Maternal Child Health, 2,* 418–421.

de Chateau, P. 1979. Effects of hospital practices on synchrony in the development of the infant-parent relationship. *Seminars in perinatology, 3*(1), 45–60.

de Chateau, P., & Andersson, Y. 1976. Left-side preference for holding and carrying newborn infants. II. Doll-holding and carrying from 2 to 16 years. *Developmental Medicine and Child Neurology, 18,* 738–744.

de Chateau, P., Cajander, K., Engström, A. C., & Lundberg, A. 1978. Long-term effect of early post partum contact: One year follow-up. *Proceedings Vth International Congress of Psychosomatic Obstetrics and Gynecology.* New York: Academic Press.

de Chateau, P., Holmberg, H., Jakobson, K., & Winberg, J. 1977. A study of factors promoting and inhibiting lactation. *Developmental Medicine and Child Neurology, 19,* 575–584.

de Chateau, P., Holmberg, H., & Winberg, J. 1978. Left-side preference in holding and carrying newborn infants. I. Mothers holding during the first week of life. *Acta Paediatrica Scandinavica, 67,* 169–175.

de Chateau, P., & Wiberg, B. 1977a. Long-term effect on mother–infant behaviour of extra contact during the first hour post partum. I. First observations at 36 hours. *Acta Paediatrica Scandinavica, 66,* 137–144.

de Chateau, P., & Wiberg, B. 1977b. Long-term effect on mother–infant behaviour of extra contact during the first hour post partum. II. A follow-up at three months. *Acta Paediatrica Scandinavica, 66,* 145–151.

de Chateau, P., & Wiberg, B. In press. Long-term effect on mother–infant behaviour of extra contact during the first hour post partum. III. One year follow-up. *Developmemtal Medicine and Child Neurology.*

Denenberg, V. H. 1969. The effects of early experience. In E. S. E. Hafex (Ed.), *The behaviour of domestic animals* (2nd ed.). London: Bailliere, Tindall, and Cox.

Dobbing, J. 1970. Undernutrition and the developing brain. *American Journal of Diseases of Children, 120,* 411–416.

Doll, E. A. 1936. *The Vineland Social Maturity Scale.* Vineland, N. J.: Revised, condensed publication of the Training School at Vineland, Department of Research No. 3.

Emde, R. N., Swedberg, J., & Suzuki, B. 1975. Human wakefulness and biological rhythms after birth. *Archives of General Psychiatry, 32,* 780–786.

Fantz, R. L. 1963. Pattern vision in newborn infants. *Science, 140,* 296–297.

Fantz, R. L., & Miranda, S. B. 1975. Newborn infant attention to form and contour. *Child Development, 46,* 224–228.

Feldman, S. S., & Ingham, M. E. 1975. Attachment behavior: A validation study in two age groups. *Child Development, 46,* 319–330.

Freud, A. 1965. *Normality and pathology in childhood.* New York: International University Press.

Gaddini, R. 1971. Re-union symbolisation in infancy: A contribution on child development. *Proceedings XIIth International Congress of Pediatrics,* Vienna. Pp. 199–208.

Gaddini, R., & Gaddini, E. 1970. Transitional objects and the process of individuation: A study of three different social groups. *Journal of the American Academy of Child Psychiatry, 9,2* 347–365.

Gerrard, J. W. 1974. Breast feeding: Second thoughts. *Pediatrics, 54,* 757–764.

Gesell, A., & Armatruda, C. S. 1962. *Developmental diagnosis* (2nd ed.). New York: Paul Hoeber.

Goldman, A. S., & Smith, C. W. 1973. Host resistance factors in human milk. *Journal of Pediatrics, 82,* 1082–1090.

Gothefors, L., & Winberg, J. 1975. Host resistance factors. *Environmental Child Health, 21,* 260–263.

Hansson, L. Å., & Winberg, J. 1972. Breast milk and defence against infection in the newborn. *Archives of Disease in Childhood, 47,* 845–848.

Harlow, H. F., & Harlow, M. K. 1965. The affectional systems. In A. M. Schrier, H. F. Harlow, & F. Stollnitz (Eds.), *Behavior of non-human primates.* New York: Academic Press.

Harlow, H. F., Harlow, M. K., & Hansen, E. W. 1963. The maternal affectional system of rhesus monkeys. In H. L. Rheingold (Ed.), *Maternal behavior in mammals.* New York: Wiley.

Harlow, H. F., & Zimmerman, R. R. 1959. Affectional responses in the infant monkey. *Science, 130*, 421–432.

Herscher, L., Moore, A. U., & Richmond, J. B. 1958. Effect of post partum separation of mother and kid on maternal care in the domestic goat. *Science, 128*, 1342–1343.

Herscher, L., Richmond, J. B., & Moore, A. U. 1963. Maternal behaviour in sheep and goats. In H. L. Rheingold (Ed.), *Maternal behavior in mammals.* New York: Wiley.

Hinde, R. A. 1975. Mothers' and infants' roles: Distinguishing the questions to be asked. In *Parent–infant interaction.* Ciba Foundation Symposium 33, Amsterdam, Elsevier. Pp. 5–12.

Hofer, M. A. 1975. Summing up. In *Parent–infant interaction.* Ciba Foundation Symposium 33, Amsterdam, Elsevier. Pp. 309–314.

Howells, J. 1969. Fathering. In J. Howells (Ed.), *Modern perspectives in international child psychiatry.* Edinburgh: Oliver and Boyd, pp. 125–156.

Jelliffe, D. B., & Jelliffe, E. F. P. 1971. The uniqueness of human milk. *American Journal of Clinical Nutrition, 24*, 968–969.

Jelliffe, D. B., & Jelliffe, E. F. P. 1974. Doulas, confidence, and the science of lactation. *Journal of Pediatrics, 84*, 462–464.

Jelliffe, D. B., & Jelliffe, E. F. P. 1978. *Human milk in the modern world.* Oxford: Oxford University Press.

Johnson, N. W. 1976. Breast feeding at one hour of age. *American Journal of Maternal and Child Nursing, 1*, 12–16.

Kennell, J. H., Jerauld, R., Wolfe, H., Chesler, D., Kreger, N., McAlpine, W., Steffa, M., & Klaus, M. H. 1974. Maternal behavior one year after early and extended post partum contact. *Developmental Medicine and Child Neurology, 16*, 172–179.

Kennell, J. H., Trause, M. A., & Klaus, M. H. 1975. Evidence for a sensitive period in the human mother. In *Parent–infant interaction.* Ciba Foundation Symposium 33, Amsterdam, Elsevier. Pp. 87–101.

Klaus, M. H., Jerauld, R., Kreger, N., McAlpine, W., Steffa, M., & Kennell, J. H. 1972. Maternal attachment—importance of the first post partum days. *New England Journal of Medicine, 286*, 460–463.

Klaus, M. H., & Kennell, J. H. 1970. Mothers separated from their newborn infants. *Pediatric Clinics of North America, 17*, 1015–1035.

Klaus, M. H., Kennell, J. H., Plumb, N., & Zuehlke, S. 1970. Human maternal behaviour at the first contact with her young. *Pediatrics, 46*, 187–192.

Klopfer, P. 1971. Mother love: What turns it on? *American Scientist, 59*, 404–407.

Korner, A. F. 1971. Individual differences at birth: Implications for early experience and later development. *American Journal of Orthopsychiatry, 41*, 608–619.

Korner, A. F., & Grobstein, R. 1966. Visual alertness as related to soothing in neonates: Implications for maternal stimulation and early deprivation. *Child Development, 37*, 867–876.

Korner, A. F., & Thoman, E. B. 1970. Visual alertness in neonates as evoked by maternal care. *Journal of Experimental Child Psychology, 10*, 67–78.

Korner, A. F., & Thoman, E. B. 1972. The relative efficacy of contact and vestibular–proprioceptive stimulation in soothing neonates. *Child Development, 43*, 443–453.

Kropf, V., Negroni, G., & Nordio, S. 1976. Influenza della separazione madre–bambino nel periodo neonatale sullo sviluppo di atteggiamenti materni. *Rivista Italiana di Pediatria, 2*, 199–305.

Langmeyer, J., & Matejcek. 1975. *Psychological deprivation in childhood.* St. Lucia, Queensland: University of Queensland Press.

Leiderman, P. H., Leifer, A., Seashore, M., Barnett, C., & Grobstein, R. 1973. Mother–infant interaction: Effects of early deprivation, prior experience, and sex of infant. *Early Development, 51,* 154–175.

Leifer, A., Leiderman, P. H., Barnett, C., & Williams, J. 1972. Effects of mother–infant separation on maternal attachment behaviour. *Child Development, 43,* 1203–1218.

Levine, S. 1956. A further study of infantile handling and adult avoidance learning. *Journal of Personality, 27,* 70–80.

Levine, S. 1960. Stimulation in infancy. *Scientific American, 202,* 81–86.

Lewis, M. 1972. State as an infant–environment interaction: An analysis of mother–infant interaction as a function of sex. *Merrill-Palmer Quarterly, 18,* 95–121.

Lewis, M., Weinraub, M., & Ban, P. 1972. Mothers and fathers, girls and boys: Attachment behaviour in the first two years of life. *Research Bulletin,* 60–72.

Lind, J., Vuorenkoski, V., & Wasz-Höckert, O. 1972. The effect of cry stimulus on the temperature of the lactating breast of the primipara. *Psychosomatic medicine in obstetrics and gynaecology.* Basel, Switzerland: Karger. Pp. 293–295.

Lithner, F., de Chateau, P., Wickman, M., & Wiklund, D-E. 1977. Treatment of pregnant diabetics in a scarcely populated region of northern Sweden. *Opuscula Medica, 22,* 119–122.

Lowenfeld, M. 1948. *On the psychotherapy of children.* London: Tavistock.

Lowenfeld, M. 1950. The nature and use of the Lowenfeld World Technique in work with children and adults. *Journal of Psychology, 30,* 325–331.

Maccoby, E. E., & Jacklin, C. N. 1973. Stress, activity, and proximity seeking: Sex differences in the year-old child. *Child Development, 44,* 34–42.

MacFarlane, A. 1975. Olfaction in the development of social preferences in the human neonate. In *Parent–infant interaction.* Ciba Foundatiom Symposium 33, Amsterdam, Elsevier. Pp. 103–117.

MacKeith, R., & Wood, C. 1977. *Infant feeding and feeding difficulties* (5th ed.). Edinburgh and London: Churchill Livingstone.

Mata, L. J., & Urrutia, J. J. 1971. Intestinal colonization of breast fed children in a rural area of low socio-economic level. *Annals of the New York Academy of Science, 176,* 93–109.

Miranda, S. B. 1970. Visual abilities and pattern preferences of premature infants and full-term neonates. *Journal of Experimental Child Psychology, 10,* 189–205.

Mitchell, G. D. 1968. Attachment differences in male and female infant monkeys. *Child Development, 39,* 611–616.

Moss, H. A. 1965. Methodological issues in studying mother–infant interaction. *American Journal of Orthopsychiatry, 35,* 482–486.

Moss, H. A. 1967. Sex, age, and state as determinants of mother–infant interaction. *Merrill-Palmer Quarterly, 3,* 19–36.

Murray, H. A. 1938. *Explorations in personality.* New York: Oxford University Press.

Nash, J. 1965. The father in contemporary culture and current psychological literature. *Child Development, 36,* 261–297.

Newton, N. 1971a. Mammary effects. *American Journal of Clinical Nutrition, 24,* 987–990.

Newton, N. 1971b. Psychological differences between breast and bottle feeding. *American Journal of Clinical Nutrition, 24,* 933–1004.

Nilsson, Å. 1970. Paranatal emotional adjustment. *Acta Psychiatrica Scandinavica,* Suppl. 220.

O'Connor, S. M., Vietze, P. M., Hopkins, J. B., & Altmeier, W. A. 1977. Post partum extended maternal–infant contact: Subsequent mothering and child health. San Francisco: Society for Pediatric Research Abstracts.

Ourth, L., & Brown, B. 1961. Inadequate mothering and disturbance in the neonatal period. *Child Development, 32,* 287–295.

Pasamanick, B., Rogers, M. E., & Lilienfeld, A. M. 1956. Pregnancy experience and the development of behaviour disorder in children. *American Journal of Psychiatry, 112,* 613–618.

Perris, C., & Strandman, E. In press. Psychogenic needs in depression. *Psychological Medicine.*

Piaget, J. 1951. *Play, dreams, and imitation in childhood.* New York: Dutton.

Pitkin, R. M., Kaminetzky, H. A., Newton, M., & Pritchard, J. A. 1972. Maternal nutrition: A selective review of clinical topics. *Obstetrics and Gynecology, 40,* 773–785.

Prechtl, H. F. R. 1968. Neurological findings in newborn infants after pre- and postnatal complications. In J. Jonxis (Ed.), *Nutricia Symposium: Aspects of praematurity and dysmaturity.* Leiden, Netherlands: Stenfert Kroese. P. 303.

Prechtl, H. F. R. 1974. The behavioral states of the newborn infant. *Brain Research, 76,* 185–189.

Rheingold, H. L. 1960. The measurement of maternal care. *Child Development, 31,* 565–575.

Richards, M. P. M. 1971. Social interaction in the first weeks of human life. *Psychiatria Neurologia Neurochirurgia, 74,* 35–42.

Ringler, N. M., Kennell, J. H., Jarvelle, R., Navojosky, B. J., & Klaus, M. H. 1975. Mother to child speech at two years—effect of early postnatal contact. *Journal of Pediatrics, 86,* 141–144.

Ringler, N. M., Trause, M. A., & Klaus, M. H. 1976. Mother's speech to her two-year-old, its effect on speech and language comprehension at 5 years. *Pediatric Research, 10,* 307–312.

Rosenblatt, J. S. 1965. The basis of synchrony in the behavioural interaction between the mother and her offspring in the laboratory rat. In B. M. Foss (Ed.), *Determinants of infant behaviour* (Vol. 3). London: Methuen. Pp. 17–32.

Salk, L. 1960. The effects of the normal heartbeat sound on the behaviour of the newborn infant: Implications for mental health. *World Mental Health, 12,* 168–175.

Salk, L. 1962. Mothers heartbeat as an imprinting stimulus. *Transactions of the New York Academy of Sciences, 7,* 753–763.

Salk, L. 1970. The critical nature of the post partum period in the human for the establishment of the mother–infant bond: A controlled study. *Diseases of the Nervous System,* Suppl. 11, 110–116.

Scarr-Salapatek, S., & Williams, M. L. 1973. The effects of early stimulation in Low-Birth-Weight Infants. *Child Development, 44,* 94–101.

Schapiro, S., & Vukovisch, K. R. 1970. Early experience effects upon dendrites. *Science, 167,* 292–294.

Sosa, R., Kennell, J. H., Klaus, M. H., & Urrutia, J. J. 1976. The effect of early mother–infant contact on breast feeding, infection, and growth. In *Breast feeding and the mother.* Ciba Foundation Symposium 45 (new series), Amsterdam, Elsevier. Pp. 179–193.

Sousa, P. L. R., Barros, F. C., Gazalle, R. V., Begeres, R. M., Pinheiro, G. N., Menezes, S. T., & Arruda, L. A. 1974. Attachment and lactation. Paper presented at the Fourteenth International Congress of Pediatrics, Buenos Aires, Argentina.

Strandman, E. 1977. Depressive disorders: Genetic, clinical, and diagnostic concepts. Umeå, Sweden: Umeå University Medical Dissertations, New Series: 29.

Taylor, B., Norman, A. P., Orgel, H. A., Stokes, C. R., Turner, M. W., & Soothill, J. 1973. Transient IgA deficiency and pathogenesis of infantile atopy. *Lancet, 2,* 111–113.

Thoman, E. B. 1975. Development of synchrony in mother–infant interaction in feeding and other situations. *Federation Proceedings, 34,* 1587–1592.

Thoman, E. B., Barnett, C. R., & Leiderman, P. H. 1971. Feeding behavior of newborn infants as a function of parity of the mother. *Child Development, 42,* 1471–1483.

Thoman, E. B., Leiderman, P. H., & Olson, J. P. 1972. Neonate–mother interaction during breast feeding. *Developmental Psychology, 6,* 110–118.

Thoman, E. B., Turner, A. M., Leiderman, P. H., & Barnett, C. R. 1970. Neonate mother interaction: Effects of parity on feeding behaviour. *Child Development, 41,* 1103–1111.

Turkeqitz, G., Moreau, T., & Birch, H. G. 1968. Relation between birth condition and neuro-behavioural organization in the neonate. *Pediatric Research, 2,* 243–249.

Valanné, E., Vuorenkoski, V., Partanen, T., Lind, J., & Wasz-Höckert, O. 1967. The ability of human mothers to identify the hunger cry signals of their own newborn infants during the lying-in period. *Experientia, 23,* 768–769.

Wachs, T. D., & Cucinotta, P. 1972. The effect of enriched neonatal experiences upon later cognitive functioning. In T. Williams (Ed.), *Infant care: Abstracts of the literature.* Washington: Consortium on Early Childbearing and Childrearing. Pp. 10–22.

Wasz-Höckert, O., Lind, J., Vuorenkoski, V., Partanen, T., & Valanné, E. 1968. *The infant cry: A spectrografic and auditory analysis.* Clinics in Developmental Medicine No. 29, London: Heineman.

Wasz-Höckert, O., Seitamo, L., Vuorenkoski, V., Partanen, T., & Lind, J. 1972. Emotional attitudes towards the child and child rearing and the effect of cry stimulus on the skin temperature of the lactating breasts in primiparous. *Psychosomatic medicine in obstetrics and gynaecology.* Basel, Switzerland: Karger. Pp. 284–286.

Weiland, J. H. 1964. Heartbeat rhythm and maternal behaviour. *Journal of American Academy of Psychiatry, 3,* 161–164.

Weiland, J. H., & Sperber, Z. 1970. Patterns of mother–infant contact, the significance of lateral preference. *The Journal of Genetic Psychology, 117,* 157–165.

White, B. L., & Castle, P. W. 1964. Visual exploratory behavior following postnatal handling of human infants. *Perceptual Motor Skills, 18,* 497–502.

Winnicott, D. W. 1971. *Playing and reality.* London: Tavistock.

Yarrow, M. R. 1963. Problems of methods in parent–child research. *Child Development, 34,* 215–226.

Early Development of Exploratory Behavior and Dominance in Three Litters of German Shepherds[1]

JOHN C. WRIGHT

TWO KINDS OF DOMINANCE

There has been some recent attention focused on the problems involved in defining *dominance* in canids, specifically in wolves and coyotes (Fox, 1972; Lockwood, 1975; Zimen, 1975; Bekoff, 1977, 1978). Yet few attempts have been made to investigate the formation of dominance behaviors throughout the primary socialization period (Wright, in press) and to clarify the different kinds of dominance that exist in domestic dog litters. The following is a description of data I collected on individuals from three litters of German shepherds, concerning the ontogeny of two kinds of dominance and exploratory behavior. Attention is also given to the immediate effects of hand- versus litter-rearing on the development of dominance and exploratory behaviors.

By describing each individual's performance through the use of tests and log reports, some consistencies as well as changes in the development of dominance and exploratory behaviors are identified for German shepherd litters. Particular attention is given to describing some effects of hand-rearing, in comparison with litter-rearing, on the development of exploratory behaviors of two of the litters.

[1] This work was supported in part by a grant from Berea College.

181

The bone-in-pen test has been used extensively as a test of competitive dominance, where the dominant individual is identified as the one which possesses a bone, placed between two pups, for the greatest amount of time. Breed comparisons of relative "aggressiveness" have been determined through the use of this test (James, 1949, 1951; Scott & Fuller, 1965; Fox, 1971a), as well as sex differences within a particular breed (Fuller, 1970). Scott and Marston (1950) reported the first appearance of dominance behavior in six breeds of dogs during the fourth week of life, and conducted a bone-in-pen test at 5 weeks of age. They found that, at this age, 31% of the puppies' relationships could be called "dominance," and that one puppy could be recognized as dominant over another in 95% of all relationships by 11 weeks of age.

Fox (1971a) described the development of behavior patterns in beagles and mongrels in either isolated, hand-reared, or "normal" conditions, through 17 weeks of age. His results on the formation of dominance patterns in both beagles and mongrels involved comparison of the mean bone possession time for the dominant individual in each condition, but without a report of individual differences within each condition.

In none of the above studies has the ontogeny of dominance been investigated within a litter of canids, nor has there been a comparison of the development of dominance for different individuals within one litter of pups. Fox (1972) has used the bone-in-pen test as a test of dominance in wolf cubs where individual differences were reported for the age interval between $7\frac{1}{2}$ and $9\frac{1}{2}$ weeks, within each of three litters. Fox reported, however, that the use of all pairwise combinations as a dominance test was inadequate for the wolf, since the cubs shared rather than fought over the bone. Likewise, Zimen (1975) has suggested that the bone-in-pen test is inadequate as a method for determining "Social Rank Order" (SRO) of a wolf pack, since it only indicates ordinary food aggression, which is not always identical with existing SROs.

The bone-in-pen test was used in my studies to measure the development of competitive dominance in three litters of German shepherds, and in individuals from each litter. For each litter, pups were ranked on total bone possession time, taken from trials where each pup was placed with each of his littermates and a bone for 10 minutes. The rank orders, scaled from highest to lowest on total possession time, were then compared with rank orders established from field-observation data, where the development of social dominance (Wright, in press) could be investigated for each litter. By describing the results of both methods of investigation, one can determine what kind of relationships exists for the development of both kinds of dominance, competitive and social.

REARING ENVIRONMENT

The pups from Litter 1 were born and reared at a kennel located at the Miami University Environmental Science Center, located about 8 kilometers northwest of Oxford, Ohio. The kennels occupy an isolated section of the Environmental Science Center, so that exposure to other dogs and to people not involved in the study was easily controlled.

Figure 6-1 shows the kennel in which Litters 2 and 3 were born and reared. It is located about 1 kilometer from the Berea College campus in Berea, Kentucky, and was built with specifications similar to the Miami University kennels. Pups from the three litters had constant access to the approximately 90-square-meter grass runs that allowed the pups within each litter to interact freely and move about, while remaining isolated from other dogs and people. A small window was cut in the metal shed, on the side of the area of observation, at the Berea kennels.

No specific instructions were given to the caretakers of hand-reared pups, except that they were to keep the pups away from the kennels and other areas used for canid testing. Litters 1 and 2 were reared in the summer months, whereas Litter 3 was reared during the fall.

METHOD: EXPLORATORY BEHAVIOR

A mobile 2.5- × 1-meter wooden arena (see diagram in Figure 6-2) placed on a concrete floor marked with 30-centimeter squares was used for all exploratory behavior testing. The enclosure was bisected diagonally with a 1-meter high partition that had a small opening at the center to allow access to either side. One side of the box, the start side, was empty, and four complex objects were equally spaced against the walls of the opposite, complex side.

Each trial was conducted for 10 minutes, during which four observers took one or two of the following measures: latency to the complex side entry (LAT); time spent in the complex side (COM); number of explorations of each object (EXP); number of vocalizations (VOC); number of 30-centimeter squares crossed on each side of the chamber (ACT); and side-to-side crossings (ARX).

Simmel and Eleftheriou (1977) conducted a study on exploratory behavior and activity in mice from which the arena and variables of my studies were derived. A factor analysis of their results revealed two factors: The first involved the initial responses to novel and complex stimuli (stimulus reactivity); the second involved behavior relating to locomotor activity. LAT and COM had high loadings on Factor I (stimulus reactivity) and almost no

Figure 6-1. Setting of kennel site at Berea, Kentucky.

loadings on Factor II (locomotor activity). ARX loaded highly on Factor I, but also fairly high on Factor II. For Factor II, two other variables had high loadings, but almost no loadings on Factor I. These variables included total locomotor activity (ACT), and another measure that I did not use since it involved an apparatus that would have been impractical to use in these studies. In addition to their Factor I, I included EXP, which Simmel and Eleftheriou could not use, but which was conceptually consistent with the behavioral category of stimulus reactivity.

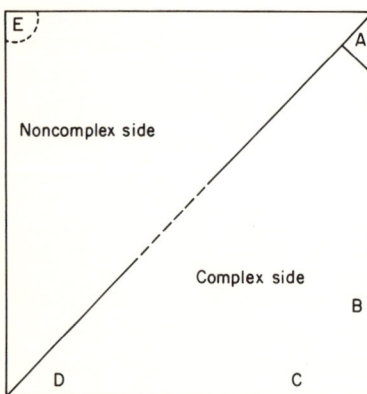

Figure 6-2. Exploratory behavior enclosure. *For Litter 1, all tests ($5\frac{1}{2}$, $8\frac{1}{2}$, $11\frac{1}{2}$ weeks) and Litter 2, $5\frac{1}{2}$ weeks:* A = metronome behind plastic barrier; B = cage with mouse; C = mirror (75 cm × 37 cm); D = empty mouse cage; E = start area. *For Litter 2, $8\frac{1}{2}$ weeks:* A = puppet moving vertically on string; B = wind-up clock; C = mirror; D = rat cage with used litter. *For Litter 2, $11\frac{1}{2}$ weeks:* A = voices of crowds on cassette tape; B = balloon moving vertically on string; C = mirror; D = used kitty litter. *For Litter 3, $5\frac{1}{2}$ weeks:* A = metronome; B = window; C = mirror; D = rat cage with used litter. *For Litter 3, $8\frac{1}{2}$ weeks:* A = mirror; B = wind-up clock; C = bag of horse dung hanging from wall; D = rat cage on wooden box.

Tests were conducted for each individual at approximately $5\frac{1}{2}$, $8\frac{1}{2}$, and $11\frac{1}{2}$ weeks of age (Litter 3 was only observed through 9 weeks). For Litters 2 and 3, some of the complex objects and the floor area were changed for the later tests, to help control for prior familiarization with the objects.

I computed a stimulus reactivity index (SR) for each litter, based on the four variable scores for each pup. Each variable was arbitrarily weighted equal to all other variables, and the index consisted of each pup's average rank on all variables (SR = [LAT + COM + EXP + ARX]/4). Ranks were computed from the data collected for each subject on each variable and testing session. A pup scoring a perfect high average ranking relative to his littermates (e.g., 1.0) would fit the following criteria: the lowest score on LAT and the highest score on COM, EXP, and ARX. For LAT and COM, a time greater than 6 seconds (1% of trial time) was arbitrarily selected as necessary for a score to be called "different"; for EXP, the necessary difference was "greater than 2 explorations."

A similar index was computed for locomotor activity (LA) based on individual rank averages from ACT and ARX scores (LA = ARX + ACT/2) for each litter and test session. A difference in one crossing per minute constituted a difference in rank for ACT, and one side-side crossing was sufficient for the ARX variable.

In addition to computing each pup's rank relative to his littermates on the two indices, a behavioral log was written to help clarify ongoing reactions to the test chamber and objects (e.g., constantly jumps at walls, stares into mirror, sleeps in corner, etc.).

RESULTS: EXPLORATORY BEHAVIOR

Litter 1

For Litter 1, subjects numbered 1, 2, and 4 were males and 3 and 5 were females. A sixth pup (a female, Sophie) was removed from the litter at 2 days of age and hand-reared away from the others. All five litter-reared pups remained together until the termination of the study at $11\frac{1}{2}$ weeks, and were handled only when necessary, for example, for weighing, puppy shots, and transferring to and from the test apparatus. The pups were raised until weaning by their biological mother, which was removed when they were $6\frac{1}{2}$ weeks old.

At $5\frac{1}{2}$ weeks of age, the scores were already indicative of individual differences for Litter 1 (see Figure 6-3). Pup 1 had a LAT time of 1 second, whereas Pup 3 never left the start side and either sat or laid down (awake) without moving for the entire session. Pup 1 was consistently ranked first on

Figure 6-3. Exploratory behavior differences appear early. Here at around 4 weeks of age, one pup is clearly less neophobic than his littermates.

most variables, whereas 3 and 4 never crossed to the complex side and were consistently ranked last. The SR indices can be found in Table 6-1.

At $8\frac{1}{2}$ weeks, Pup 3 had still not crossed from the noncomplex side and was ranked last, while Pup 1 was still scoring high on most variables, along with Pup 2.

The $11\frac{1}{2}$-week index showed that although Pup 3 had finally crossed to the complex side of the arena, she still ranked low compared with her littermates on most variables. Pup 5 had changed from second at the first session, to fourth at $11\frac{1}{2}$ weeks, only slightly higher than 3, largely due to her score on ARX (59% more crossings than the second-ranked Pup 4, for that variable). Pup 4, however, was ranked last with Pup 3 at $5\frac{1}{2}$ weeks, but was tied first (with Pup 2) at the final session, an indication of a strong change in stimulus reactivity for Pup 4, compared with that of his littermates. So, although Pup 3 remained "reactive" relative to her littermates over the 6 weeks, two pups (4 and 5) made noticeable changes from the first session to the $11\frac{1}{2}$-week test.[2]

[2] More information can be conveyed by rank comparisons between individuals and across sessions than by individual raw score comparisons across sessions. For example, a pup may perform similarly at $5\frac{1}{2}$ and $8\frac{1}{2}$ weeks and rank first at $5\frac{1}{2}$ weeks but fifth at $8\frac{1}{2}$ weeks. The informative comparison would concern his locomotor activity performance relative to the

TABLE 6-1
Stimulus Reactivity within Litter Ranks[a]

Litter and pup number	$5\frac{1}{2}$ Week		$8\frac{1}{2}$ Week		$11\frac{1}{2}$ Week		$11\frac{1}{2}$ Week[b]	
	Rank average	Index	Rank average	Index	Rank average	Index	Rank average	Index
Litter 1								
1	1.375	1.0	2.125	1.5	3.0	3.0	3.250	3.0
2	2.75	3.0	2.125	1.5	2.625	1.5	2.75	1.5
3	4.50	4.5	5.0	5.0	3.50	5.0	3.625	4.5
4	4.50	4.5	2.375	3.0	2.625	1.5	2.75	4.5
5	1.875	2.0	3.375	4.0	3.250	4.0	3.625	4.5
(6)							5.0	6.0
	1 > 5 > 2 > 3 = 5		1 = 2 > 4 > 5 > 3		2 = 4 > 1 > 5 > 3		2 = 4 > 1 > 5 = 3 > 6	
Litter 2								
1	4.0	4.0	4.125	4.0	4.125	4.0		
3	4.0	4.0	4.875	5.0	4.75	5.0		
6	1.875	2.0	2.375	3.0	1.625	1.5		
7	4.0	4.0	1.875	2.0	2.875	3.0		
9	1.125	1.0	1.75	1.0	1.625	1.5		
	9 > 6 > 7 = 3 = 1		9 > 7 > 6 > 1 > 3		9 = 6 > 7 > 1 > 3			
Litter 3								
1	4.625	5.0	5.625	7.0				
2	8.25	9.0	8.25	9.0				
3	7.75	8.0	8.0	8.0				
4	2.285	3.0	3.625	4.0				
5	6.875	7.0	5.0	6.0				
6	4.0	4.0	3.125	2.0				
7	6.375	6.0	3.0	1.0				
8	1.875	1.0	3.50	3.0				
9	2.375	2.0	4.875	5.0				
	8 > 9 > 4 > 6 > 1 > 7 > 5 > 3 > 2		7 > 6 > 8 > 4 > 9 > 5 > 1 > 3 > 2					

[a] Rank Average = LAT + COM + EXP + ARX/4.
[b] Based on six pups.

Locomotor Activity. Within-litter changes for locomotor activity were more moderate over the three test sessions. Most of the pups changed only one rank during the 6 weeks, while Pup 5 showed the greatest change, from third at $5\frac{1}{2}$ weeks to first at $11\frac{1}{2}$ weeks. Pup 3 was ranked last for all sessions,

---

changes in locomotor activity shown by his similarly reared littermates (rank comparison), rather than merely a report of his similar raw scores for both sessions. It is interesting to compare one pup's performance within the context of other members of the same litter similarly reared and of the same age.

TABLE 6-2
Locomotor Activity within Litter Ranks[a]

Litter and pup number	$5\frac{1}{2}$ Week		$8\frac{1}{2}$ Week		$11\frac{1}{2}$ Week		$11\frac{1}{2}$ Week[b]	
	Rank average	Index	Rank average	Index	Rank average	Index	Rank average	Index
Litter 1								
1	1.0	1.9	1.75	2.0	2.5	2.0	2.5	2.0
2	2.0	2.0	1.25	1.0	3.5	3.5	3.5	3.5
3	4.25	4.5	5.0	5.0	4.5	5.0	4.5	5.0
4	4.25	4.5	4.0	4.0	3.5	3.5	3.5	3.5
5	3.5	3.0	3.0	3.0	1.0	1.0	1.0	1.0
(6)							6.0	6.0
	1 > 2 > 5		2 > 1 > 5		5 > 1 > 2		5 > 1 > 2 =	
	> 3 = 4		> 4 > 3		= 4 > 3		4 > 3 > 6	
Litter 2								
1	4.0	4.0	4.5	4.5	4.5	4.5		
3	4.5	5.0	4.5	4.5	4.5	4.5		
6	1.5	1.0	1.25	1.0	1.0	1.0		
7	3.25	3.0	2.5	3.0	3.0	3.0		
9	1.75	2.0	2.25	2.0	2.0	2.0		
	6 > 9 > 7		6 > 9 > 7		6 > 9 > 7			
	> 1 > 3		> 1 = 3		> 1 = 3			
Litter 3								
1	4.25	4.5	2.5	1.0				
2	7.5	8.0	8.75	9.0				
3	9.0	9.0	6.75	7.0				
4	2.0	1.0	3.0	2.0				
5	3.25	2.0	4.0	4.0				
6	5.5	7.0	3.5	3.0				
7	5.25	6.0	4.25	5.0				
8	4.0	3.0	7.25	8.0				
9	4.25	4.5	5.0	6.0				
	4 > 5 > 8 >		1 > 4 > 6 >					
	9 = 1 > 7 >		5 > 7 > 9 >					
	6 > 2 > 3		3 > 8 > 2					

[a] Locomotor Activity = ARX + ACT/2.
[b] Based on six pups.

which is consistent with her SR rankings (fifth) for the three test periods. The LA indices can be found in Table 6-2.

The greatest difference in rankings on the two indices at any single session was that of Pup 5. Her SR rank was fourth at $11\frac{1}{2}$ weeks, compared with first for locomotor activity.

The indices for Litter 1 indicated that the development of exploratory behaviors begins to differentiate in individuals as early as $5\frac{1}{2}$ weeks of age.

For example, the stimulus reactivity rank averages (Table 6-1) for Pup 1 (1.375) and Pups 4 and 5 (4.50) at $5\frac{1}{2}$ weeks indicated some differences and consistencies in scores on the four variables that made up the index. SR and LA indices did not involve independent measures, but they did reflect behaviors that could develop differently relative to other litter members. For example, within-litter changes over the 6 weeks of testing for exploratory behaviors occurred in a similar direction for both indices (e.g., Pup 1), in a different direction for stimulus reactivity and locomotor activity (e.g., Pup 5), or remained identical and unchanging during the entire 6-week period (e.g., Pup 3).

Log Reports, Exploratory Behavior.   The log data coincided with the subjects' ranking on the indices. At $5\frac{1}{2}$ weeks, Pups 3 and 4 remained in the start side of the arena, and moved to one corner, either sitting or lying there for the entire session. Pups 1 and 5 explored all of the objects and sniffed, pawed at, or tried to interact with their image in the mirror. Pup 2 crossed to the complex side, but never approached the mirror, and continuously shook while being cautious in his approach to the mouse and cage.

At $8\frac{1}{2}$ weeks, the behavior of Pup 3 remained the same, but Pup 4 actively explored all objects. Pups 1, 2, and 4 were clearly the most exploratory.

The $11\frac{1}{2}$-week log data showed that Pup 2 was very interested in the metronome, but it also explored the other objects, especially the mouse and mirror. Number 2 sat calmly facing the mirror, and casually placed its front legs on top of it. Pup 4 was more anxious in its explorations, and continually howled as it sat facing or trying to "get into" the mirror. Pup 1 liked the mirror, tried to "get into it" and moved about anxiously like Pup 4, but explored objects less and made several escape attempts which twice resulted in landing on top of an object. Pup 5 was very active and spent time walking quickly about both sides of the arena. It knocked over the metronome and would frequently howl as it anxiously pawed at the mirror, or climbed at the top of it. Pup 3 finally crossed to the complex side and cautiously approached the mouse and mirror. It sniffed at the metronome, knocked it over, cried and howled, and then sniffed the mirror, vocalizing repeatedly. Pup 3 eventually tried to "get into" and on top of the mirror and sat by it while watching the mouse. According to log data, Pup 2 seemed least "reactive" to the complex objects, although the SR index showed Pups 2 and 4 at equal ranks.

The log data were generally supportive of the rankings for exploratory behavior, with the possible exception of Pup 1 at $11\frac{1}{2}$ weeks. Pup 1 made more escape attempts than the others and may have been anxious about being in the arena per se, but not necessarily more anxious as a result of exposure to the specific objects.

Sophie (Pup 6, taken from the litter at 2 days of age) was placed in the arena once, at $11\frac{1}{2}$ weeks. Tables 6-1 and 6-2 indicate that she was relatively inactive (LA = 6) and also ranked low on the stimulus reactivity index (SR = 6). Sophie's initial responses to the arena were to make several jumps at the sides in an attempt to escape. Pup 6's reactions to the objects, once it crossed (latency = 2 minutes) consisted of sniffing the mirror and mouse and behaving in a clumsy, yet alert manner. Sophie growled and barked at the mouse several times while backing away from it, signaling otherwise "dominant" intentions. None of the litter-reared pups growled or barked at the objects. Sophie was clearly more interested in the mouse than the mirror and did not make any attempts to interact with her image. When it was not backing away or cautiously approaching the mouse, Sophie would stand or lie behind another object and look at, or bark at, the mouse. Pup 6's initial responses to the objects, compared with the litter-reared pups, involved a different kind of vocalization, more attention focused toward the mouse than the mirror, and low rankings on both indices.

Litter 2

The exploratory behavior differences shown between Sophie and the litter-reared pups led me to investigate further the rearing variable for Litter 2. Although the litter was initially large enough for rank comparisons, four pups died prior to the halfway point of the study. This left only five pups to compare on exploratory behavior over the three test sessions: Two pups were litter-reared (Pups 1 and 3), one was hand-reared alone (Pup 9), and the other two were hand-reared together (Pups 6 and 7). The hand-reared pups were taken from the litter at 7 days of age and reared by two assistants. The two litter-reared pups were weaned at $4\frac{1}{2}$ weeks of age, due to their mother, a vicious bitch, that made it very difficult for us to get close to the puppies. Pup 1 was male; Pups 3, 6, 7, and 9 were females. Tests were conducted on all pups at $5\frac{1}{2}$, $8\frac{1}{2}$, and $11\frac{1}{2}$ weeks of age, but with new floor placements for the test arena, and some changes in the objects for each session (see Figure 6-1).

The most striking result for Litter 2 involved the consistency with which the hand-reared pups scored higher than the litter-reared pups for both stimulus reactivity and locomotor activity. Pups 6, 7, and 9 were ranked first, second, or third on both indices for all three test sessions (although Pup 3 tied with Pup 7 for third rank at $5\frac{1}{2}$ weeks).

At $5\frac{1}{2}$ weeks, the two litter-reared pups and Pup 7 never left the start side of the box. Pup 9 (hand-reared alone) was first ranked for stimulus reactivity and scored much higher on LAT (247 seconds) and COM (91 seconds) than the second-ranked Pup 6 (450 seconds and 15 seconds).

Pups 6 and 7 changed ranks with each other for the SR index at $8\frac{1}{2}$ weeks, while Pup 9 remained ranked first. Pups 1 and 3 ranked fourth and fifth, with Pup 3 still not leaving the noncomplex side for the entire session. The LAT score (196 seconds) and COM score (52 seconds) of fourth-ranked Pup 1 were still different from the hand-reared pup's scores that ranked third for each of those variables (LAT = 28 seconds, COM = 435 seconds).

The $11\frac{1}{2}$-week SR index had Pups 9 and 6 ranked first (rank average = 1.625), Pup 7 third, and Pups 1 and 3 fourth and fifth, respectively. Pup 3 finally left the noncomplex side (LAT = 103 seconds, COM = 70 seconds) and was ranked last, or next to last with Pup 1 on all four variables that measure stimulus reactivity.

Locomotor Activity. The locomotor activity index showed similar high rankings for the hand-reared pups. Ranks were consistent for rearing conditions and across test sessions: $6 > 9 > 7 > 1 = 3$. The relationships between the SR and LA ranks for individuals in Litter 2 were less variable than for the Litter 1 subjects. Except for a difference of two ranks for Pup 6 at $8\frac{1}{2}$ weeks (third on SR, first on LA), the indices were different by one rank at most for each pup for all sessions.

Log Reports, Exploratory Behavior. The log data for Litter 2 show that Pups 1, 3, and 7 behaved similarly at $5\frac{1}{2}$ weeks. Most of their sessions were spent either looking up at the top of the arena, jumping at the side to escape, standing in a corner with tail tucked, or lying down. Pups 3 and 7 looked toward the entrance to the complex side, but did not enter. Pup 6 (ranked second on SR, first on activity) was more active than were the other pups and never tucked her tail like her three littermates.

Pups 1 and 3 remained conservative in their exploratory behaviors at $8\frac{1}{2}$ weeks. Pup 7 showed different behaviors from his $5\frac{1}{2}$-week performances, however, and made 30 explorations, tied first with Pup 9. Pups 6 and 9 also behaved like Pup 7 and not only approached and looked at objects, but also pawed, sniffed at, and bit objects during their trials. So the $8\frac{1}{2}$-week trials showed distinct behavioral differences between the hand-reared and litter-reared pups, in both the indices and the log reports, with Pups 6, 7, and 9 being much more exploratory than were Pups 1 and 3.

The $11\frac{1}{2}$-week logs showed that Pups 1 and 3 were still hesitant in their approaches to the objects. However, compared with Pup 3's submissive postural approach to the mirror, Pup 7's second approach to the mirror was one of assertion, with tail raised. Five other object investigations of Pup 7 were also to the mirror, but with no noticeable change in her "normal" body posture. Pups 6 and 9 seemed much more exploratory than the others and investigated all objects. Some explorations involved "nosing," or biting at the balloon (Pups 6 and 9), sniffing the kitty litter (Pup 9), sitting with head cocked in front of the tape recorder, pawing it (Pup 6), and like Pup 7, approaching the mirror assertively and with tail raised (Pups 6 and 9). All five pups were similar in that they made escape attempts by raising up on the sides of the arena throughout the session. However, hand-reared pups (especially 6 and 9) were more active and assertive in their investigations than were the litter-reared Pups.

Litter 3

Due to the small number of subjects in Litter 2, Litter 3 was used to investigate further the effects that the rearing variable had on the pups' exploratory behaviors. Some of the objects and the arena floor area were changed between sessions, as in the Litter 2 study (see Figure 6-1). Pups 1–5 were litter-reared; Pups 6–9 were hand-reared alone. Since Pup 9 from Litter 2 was the only subject hand-reared alone from that litter and was also consistently ranked first on SR, I decided to hand-rear the Litter 3 pups alone, to maximize the possibility of finding a reliable difference between the two rearing conditions, if one really existed. The hand-reared pups were taken from the litter at 2 weeks of age, and the litter-reared pups were weaned at 5 weeks. Pups 1, 2, and 9 were males, whereas 3, 4, 5, 6, 7, and 8 were females. The $5\frac{1}{2}$-week session was conducted 1 day prior to their 6th-week birthday. Due to the adverse weather conditions and my assistants' leaving for Christmas vacation, the study was terminated when the pups were 9 weeks old.

The $5\frac{1}{2}$-week SR index for Litter 3 shows that there was no clear effect of hand-rearing versus litter-rearing on those behaviors that were measured (see Table 6-1).

In general, all pups from this litter had high exploratory behavior scores for being exposed to the arena for the first time: All pups entered the complex side within 90 seconds (LAT); all pups remained in the complex side for at least 69 seconds (COM); all pups made at least nine side–side crossings per minute (ARX); and all pups made at least 13, 30-centimeter-square crossings per minute (ACT). (One possible explanation for the higher scores may center on the effect of the temperature on the activity variables. Litters 1 and 2 were conducted in the summer, where the pups were taken from temperatures of 80° and 90°F to be tested. Litter 3 was conducted in the fall, when temperatures for the $5\frac{1}{2}$-week [late November] and $8\frac{1}{2}$-week [mid-December] tests were in the 30s. The excessive heat of the summer may account for the relatively lethargic activity of Litters 1 and 2; the extremes in temperature also makes any comparison of raw scores between the litters of questionable value.) In spite of the high scoring on most variables for all pups, the hand-reared pups ranked in the top five of six positions for LAT and COM, with Pup 4 (litter-reared) occupying the remaining rank for both variables. (Pup 1 tied for fifth with Pup 7 on ACT.) Ranks on EXP and ARX were varied within each rearing condition.

The $8\frac{1}{2}$-week index for stimulus reactivity showed a significant effect for the hand- versus litter-reared variable ($U = 1$, $p = .016$). The rearing conditions had a pronounced effect on the COM variable, with all hand-reared pups increasing their scores from $5\frac{1}{2}$ weeks, and all litter-reared pups, except Pup 5, decreasing their scores, so that the four hand-reared pups occupied the first four ranks on COM at $8\frac{1}{2}$ weeks. An almost equally strong effect concerned the EXP variable, with all litter-reared pups either decreasing their scores or remaining the same compared with their $5\frac{1}{2}$-week performances. The hand-reared also occupied the first four ranks for EXP at $8\frac{1}{2}$ weeks. The only consistent rankings on SR for both sessions were for Pups 2 and 3, who were ranked eighth and ninth at $5\frac{1}{2}$ and $8\frac{1}{2}$ weeks. The greatest change in rank was for Pup 7, who changed from sixth ranked at $5\frac{1}{2}$ weeks to first at $8\frac{1}{2}$ weeks (see section entitled "Log Report" for explanation).

Locomotor Activity. Locomotor activity was unaffected by the rearing condition as indicated by both the $5\frac{1}{2}$- and $8\frac{1}{2}$-week indices. Large changes occurred for Pup 8 (five ranks) and Pups 1 and 6 (four ranks) between the two sessions; Pup 8 decreased in LA rank and Pups 1 and 6 increased in rank. The hand-rearing condition thus seemed to allow for greater variability in the development of locomotor activity (e.g., Pups 6 and 8) when compared with changes in stimulus reactivity for Litter 3.

Log Reports, Exploratory Behavior. Log data for $5\frac{1}{2}$ weeks showed that all pups investigated the objects, including touching or "nosing" the mirror, except Pup 7. (At 3 minutes into the session for Pup 7, a large sheet of cardboard that covered a window above the arena fell into the complex side. This event probably influenced the pup's scores and its relatively low ranking on both indices for the $5\frac{1}{2}$-week session.) Pups 6 and 9 (hand-reared) were the only ones to approach the mirror with their tails up, in an assertive manner.

At $8\frac{1}{2}$ weeks, all pups, except Pup 9, approached the mirror first after crossing over to the complex side. Pups 2, 3, and 4 approached it in a low crouched position. Pup 9 approached the mirror on his seventh of 18 explorations. Pups 9, 8, and 6, all hand-reared, approached the mirror assertively with their tail raised and wagging. Pup 7 lay down in front of the mirror, gazing quietly at her reflection for 3 seconds, a very nonreactive behavior for $8\frac{1}{2}$ weeks. As in the other two litters, the log data seemed supportive of the indices rankings for both sessions.

Interlitter Comparisons and Breed Characteristics

Changes in LAT scores can be compared for the $5\frac{1}{2}$ to $8\frac{1}{2}$ tests for all three litters since prior familiarization with specific objects would not be apparent (for Litter 1) until a pup had crossed to the complex side at $8\frac{1}{2}$ weeks. One pup (Pup 9 of Litter 3) increased his latency score (took longer to cross), five pups remained the same (two pups did not cross at either session, three pups crossed within 13 seconds of being placed in the arena both times), and 13 pups decreased their LAT times from their $5\frac{1}{2}$-week score. Thus, on initial exposure to novel situations, German shepherds are certainly not more neophobic at $8\frac{1}{2}$ weeks of age than they are at $5\frac{1}{2}$ weeks.

The score changes between the first two sessions on COM and EXP did not show any consistent differences between Litters 2 and 3, but did reflect a consistent rearing-condition effect. (No comparisons can be made to Litter 1, due to the use of the same objects and floor area for all three sessions.) Table 6-3 lists the individuals by rearing condition for Litters 2 and 3 and gives the direction of score change for each on COM and EXP. All seven hand-reared pups increased their scores, whereas five out of seven litter-reared pups either did not change, or decreased their scores on both variables. The

TABLE 6-3
Comparison of Stimulus Reactivity Score Changes from the $5\frac{1}{2}$- to $8\frac{1}{2}$-Week Tests for Litter-Reared and Hand-Reared Subjects, Litters 2 and 3[a]

	Subject	COM	EXP
Litter-reared	1	+[b]	+[b]
	3	o[c]	+[c]
	1	−	o
	2	−	−
	3	−	o
	4	−	o
	5	+	o
Hand-reared	6	+	+
	7	+	+
	9	+	+
	6	+	+
	7	+[b]	+[b]
	8	+	+
	9	+	+

[a] + = increased score from first to second session; o = remained the same; − = decreased score from first to second session. A designation of *increase* or *decrease* in score for each variable meets the same criteria necessary for a score to be called *different*, used for indices rankings.

[b] Increased from zero at $5\frac{1}{2}$ weeks.

[c] Pup remained in noncomplex side for both the $5\frac{1}{2}$- and $8\frac{1}{2}$-week sessions; she stuck her head through the entrance to look at an object four times at $8\frac{1}{2}$ weeks.

trends show that the hand-reared pups became less neophobic during the 3-week interval, whereas the litter-reared pups did not.

Finally, there are a number of possible explanations for why the hand-reared pups in Litters 2 and 3 ranked differently in relation to their littermates than did Sophie to hers (Litter 1): Sophie was exposed only once to the arena at $11\frac{1}{2}$ weeks, compared with three different exposures for the other pups; she was taken from the litter at 2 days of age, compared with 1 week and 2 weeks, respectively, for Litters 2 and 3; her home environment may have been different than were those of the other pups (I do not have information concerning that possibility).

METHOD: COMPETITIVE DOMINANCE

Twenty-four hours after the exploratory behavior tests, pups from Litters 1 and 3 were placed in the bone-in-pen test (see Figure 6-4) for two 10-minute trials each. The following day, two more tests were run for each pup so that all pairwise encounters occurred once for each individual, at $5\frac{1}{2}$, $8\frac{1}{2}$, and $11\frac{1}{2}$ weeks of age. (Litter 3 was tested only at the first two sessions.) In addition to

Figure 6-4. Bone-in-pen test at $11\frac{1}{2}$ weeks. The same setting was used for all bone-in-pen tests.

keeping times of "alone" and "shared" possession for each subject, observers wrote a log for each trial, noting the occurrence of vocalizations or agonistic behaviors for each pup. An indication of whether or not "complete dominance" had been established (Scott & Fuller, 1965) was also recorded at the end of each trial (i.e., if a pup kept possession of the bone for at least 80% of the trial time and was able to repossess it at will). Each pup's bone-possession time was transformed to a percentage based on alone possession times for each 40-minute session. A competitive dominance index was used to compare the percentages by rank for each 40-minute session so that the pup with the highest score ranked first.

Five pups from Litter 2 were given the bone-in-pen test once, at $11\frac{1}{2}$ weeks of age, 24 hours prior to the exploratory behavior test. The hand-reared pups, 6, 7, and 9, were placed in the kennel with Pups 1 and 3 2 days before the dominance test, so that all pups would have some exposure to each other before the tests were conducted. Tests were also conducted for Pups 1 and 3 at $5\frac{1}{2}$ weeks of age (and again 3 days later to test for reliability) and at $8\frac{1}{2}$ weeks in addition to the $11\frac{1}{2}$-week session.

RESULTS: COMPETITIVE DOMINANCE

Litter 1

At $5\frac{1}{2}$ weeks, pups from all 10 dyads shared the bone for at least 12 seconds per dyad ($\bar{X}$ = 119 seconds; SD = 116 seconds). Pup 2 never possessed the bone alone, but was allowed to share it with each of his four littermates, especially with Pup 3, for a total of 252 of 2400 seconds possible. The 2 versus 3 trial involved 205 seconds of sharing between the two least competitive pups. Pup 1, however, only shared the bone for 12 seconds with Pup 2, and also established complete dominance over Pup 2 during the $5\frac{1}{2}$-week session. The dominance index showed the following relationships based on alone-possession times: 5 (70%) > 1 (53%) > (30%) > 3 (21%) > 2 (.4%).

At $8\frac{1}{2}$ weeks, the total bone-sharing time for all pups decreased from 1187 seconds (at $5\frac{1}{2}$ weeks) to 887 seconds. If mean sharing time is computed for only those dyads that did share (7 of 10), there was a slight increase in sharing time ($\bar{X}$ = 127 seconds per dyad; SD = 119 seconds per dyad). Sharing-only occurred in Dyad 2 versus 4 (for 2), and in Dyad 3 versus 1 (for 3). These two pups ranked lowest at $5\frac{1}{2}$ and $8\frac{1}{2}$ weeks. The alone-possession rankings showed the following relationships: 4 (58%) > 1 (44%) > 5 (37%) > 2 (33%) > 3 (12%). No trials resulted in complete dominance during this session.

Bone sharing at $11\frac{1}{2}$ weeks decreased from the earlier sessions both in mean time per dyad and in number of dyads sharing the bone ($\bar{X} = 24$ seconds per dyad; SD = 16 seconds per dyad, for 3 of 10 dyads). Pups 3 (in 3 versus 4) and 5 (in 5 versus 2) were allowed to share the bone by their opponent, but never to possess it. "Sharing," in both dyads, involved a tug-of-war in which the opponent pup eventually controlled the bone for the duration of the trial. For participants of the third dyad that shared the bone (1 versus 3), sharing did not involve a tug-of-war, and each pup possessed the bone alone for at least 60 seconds. This trial was characteristic of the $5\frac{1}{2}$-week sessions, in which most pups alternated possession of the bone with little antagonism. So actual sharing of the bone at $11\frac{1}{2}$ weeks was only demonstrated in this dyad, by the lowest ranking pups. The $11\frac{1}{2}$-week competitive dominance hierarchy reflected Pup 1's lack of competitiveness: 4 (77%) > 2 (72%) > 5 (67%) > 3 (22%) > 1 (2%). Thus, the two lowest ranking pups at $11\frac{1}{2}$ weeks had relatively docile temperaments compared with the competitiveness demonstrated by the top ranking pups. Pups 4 and 2 established complete dominance over Pup 3 during this session, and Pup 5 never let Pup 3 share or possess the bone alone. Similarly, Pups 2, 4, and 5 kept Pup 1 (ranked fifth) from possessing or sharing the bone during their trials with it at $11\frac{1}{2}$ weeks.

Litter 2

The two consecutive trials at $5\frac{1}{2}$ weeks for Pups 1 and 3 indicated that Pup 3 was slightly more possessive of the bone than was Pup 1, but that most of the trial time was spent in sharing (first trial = 530 seconds shared, second trial = 418 seconds shared). Likewise, at $8\frac{1}{2}$ weeks Pup 3 possessed the bone more than did Pup 1, still with a considerable amount of sharing (340 seconds shared), but not as much as either session at $5\frac{1}{2}$ weeks. This trend was similar to the decrease in bone sharing for three of seven dyads of Litter 1.

The $11\frac{1}{2}$-week session showed a reversal in alone possession times for Pups 1 and 3 (3 = 1 second, 1 = 400 seconds), and a decrease in sharing time (186 seconds) compared with sessions at $5\frac{1}{2}$ and $8\frac{1}{2}$ weeks. The 186 seconds was more than twice the sharing time of any of the other nine dyads, even the dyad of Pups 6 versus 7 (hand reared together), which ranked second in sharing time at 90 seconds shared. It is possible that exposure to the hand-reared pups in the kennel prior to the test influenced Pups 1 and 3, since the usually passive Pup 1 attacked Pup 3 about 3 minutes into the session after some initial bone sharing. The test for complete dominance, however, resulted in both pups sharing the bone, after the 10-minute trial. Thus, dominance was incomplete.

Pup 9 (hand-reared alone) had the least total sharing time, which was less than one-fourth of the total sharing time by Pup 6, the next lowest ranked pup. An index of sharing time for the five pups at $11\frac{1}{2}$ weeks showed the following relationships, with first rank indicating most time spent in bone sharing: $3 > 1 > 7 > 6 > 9$. Their competitive dominance index, based on the total time the bone was possessed alone for each subject, was not the reciprocal of the sharing index, but was consistent for the highest and lowest ranked pups: $9 > 7 > 1 > 6 > 3$. Pup 9 established complete dominance over Pups 1 and 3 during this session and was clearly the most dominant pup of the five. Complete dominance was also established for two other dyads, 6 over 3 and 1 over 6. The most consistent differences in competitive dominance behaviors were between the hand-reared alone pup (9) and both litter-reared pups (1 and 3).

Litter 3

The tests for competitive dominance for Litter 3 consisted of pairing the hand-reared pups (6–9) with each other, and the litter-reared pups (1–5) with each other at $5\frac{1}{2}$ and $8\frac{1}{2}$ weeks of age. An index, based on alone possession time, was constructed for each rearing condition at each test session.

Unlike the hand-reared pups for Litter 2, Pups 6–9 had not been exposed to each other prior to their first bone-in-pen test. The possession times and log reports for these hand-reared pups reflected a greater concern for social investigation than for bone possession at $5\frac{1}{2}$ weeks. Of 6 different dyads, only 2 pups had combined times (alone and shared) exceeding 50% of the 10-minute trial time (compared with 15 pups from 10 litter-reared dyads for Litter 3). None of the dyads shared the bone for more than 25 seconds and members from 6 versus 8 and 7 versus 9 neither shared the bone nor possessed it alone during the 10-minute trial.

Pup 6 ranked first with 508 seconds of alone possession time, whereas Pup 8 ranked last with 25 seconds at $5\frac{1}{2}$ weeks. The following index was based on percent of total trial time spent in alone-possession of the bone for the hand-reared pups: 6 (28%) > 9 (25%) > 7 (22%) > 8 (1%).

For the $8\frac{1}{2}$-week tests, still only 3 pups from 6 dyads possessed the bone for more than 50% of the trial (compared with 11 pups from 10 dyads for the litter-reared). Dyads 6 versus 8, 7 versus 9 (which also did not share at $5\frac{1}{2}$ weeks), and 6 versus 9 did not share the bone during their $8\frac{1}{2}$-week sessions. The pups were still more involved in social interactions than with the bone as indicated in the log reports. For example, after initially possessing the bone 86 seconds into the session, Pup 8 left the bone and play-bowed in front of Pup 6, who ignored her. Pup 8 then pawed at 6's muzzle; Pup 6 growled and snapped at 8. This sequence repeated itself and ended in Pup 6 snapping, growling, and wrestling Pup 8 to the ground, with Pup 8 continuously growling and baring her teeth while on her back. Pup 6 eventually walked away from 8, but still ignored the bone. When Pup 8 repossessed the bone, her tail was tucked under her, while 6 paced back and forth in the pen with her tail raised. As in the other hand-reared dyads, the bone seemed to attract less attention and competition than did social investigation or fighting. For $8\frac{1}{2}$ weeks, the hand-reared SR = 9 (54%) > 7 (20%) > 8 (17%) > 6 (1%).

The litter-reared pups, however, behaved more like the pups from Litter 1 than like their hand-reared littermates, especially at $5\frac{1}{2}$ weeks. Only one dyad shared the bone for less than 25 seconds, whereas the other nine dyads shared for at least 20% of the time trial ($\overline{X}$ = 248 seconds, SD = 113 seconds) during the first session. One pup only shared the bone and never possessed it for Litter 1 in four different dyads, compared with three pups from the litter-reared and no pups from the hand-reared of Litter 3. The $5\frac{1}{2}$-week alone-possession percentages for the litter-reared pups were structured in the following index: 3 (28%) = 5 (28%) > 4 (26%) > 2 (21%) > 1 (7%).

At $8\frac{1}{2}$ weeks, differences between the alone possession percentages increased from $5\frac{1}{2}$ weeks, whereas sharing times decreased for 9 of 10 dyads that did share. The following index was constructed from alone-possession times: 1 (86%) > 3 (45%) > 5 (37%) > 2 (10%) > 4 (2%). Although there were differences in sharing time and other social behaviors between the hand- and litter-reared pups, there were also similarities: The most competitively dominant pup from each condition had an identical alone possession percentage at $5\frac{1}{2}$ weeks (28%); the range of alone percentages were similar (h.r. = 27 percentage points; l.r = 21 percentage points); and both groups showed greater individual differences at $8\frac{1}{2}$ weeks (range = 53 and 83 percentage points) compared with $5\frac{1}{2}$ weeks for alone-possession times. So the two groups behaved similarly on the alone-possession measure, but what they did while not in possession of the bone was very different: The litter-reared pups' toleration of close social proximity encouraged a great amount of sharing, whereas the hand-reared pups reacted by fighting or involving themselves in other behaviors used to establish social dominance.

The similar competitive behaviors of the litter-reared and hand-reared pups of Litter 3 were not shared by Litter 1 pups: At $5\frac{1}{2}$ weeks, three Litter 1 pups had alone-possession percentages greater than 28% (70%, 53%, and 30%); the range of alone-percentages was initially greater (69 percentage points); and the pups were less different in dominance at $8\frac{1}{2}$ weeks (range = 46 percentage points) than at $5\frac{1}{2}$ weeks. Rank changes from $5\frac{1}{2}$ to $8\frac{1}{2}$ weeks for Litter 1 were at most two positions, whereas Pup 1 changed from fifth place (7%) to first (86%) for the litter-reared, and Pup 6 changed from first (28%) to last place (1%) for the hand-reared, indicating much greater variability in Litter 3 regardless of rearing condition, compared with Litter 1.

STIMULUS REACTIVITY AND COMPETITIVE DOMINANCE

Inspection of the Litter 2 rankings for stimulus reactivity and competitive dominance indicates that, for the $5\frac{1}{2}$ and $11\frac{1}{2}$ week tests, the two most competitive pups were also the ones that scored highest on the SR index, even though the ordering of the highest ranking pups changed over the two sessions. Those pups in Litter 1 that preferred novel objects were also the ones that were able to possess a desirable object in a competitive situation. The relationships were not as strong for the lower ranking subjects at any of the sessions.

The pups in Litters 2 and 3 did not show similar correspondences between the two indices. The bone-in-pen test was conducted only at $11\frac{1}{2}$ weeks for Litter 2. The hand-reared alone pup, 9, scored highest on both the competitive dominance and SR, but the second-ranked pup was different for each index. For Litter 3 no relationship existed between the two indices at either $5\frac{1}{2}$ or $8\frac{1}{2}$ weeks for either the hand-reared or litter-reared pups.

If a relationship actually exists between SR rankings and those for competitive dominance, then the Litter 3 pups (litter-reared) should have behaved similarly to those of Litter 1. However, the differences may reflect slightly different procedures between the two litters; recall that the objects and chamber were changed for each test session for Litter 3, but the same objects and enclosure was used for Litter 1.

Although this explanation may not account for the lack of correspondence at $5\frac{1}{2}$ weeks, it may have had an influence on the $8\frac{1}{2}$-week rankings for Litter 3. Another possibility involves the differences in climate, discussed previously, to which the two litters were exposed during rearing.

SOCIAL DOMINANCE: LITTER 1

Social dominance was investigated developmentally for Litter 1 while the pups were interacting in their rearing environment from $3\frac{1}{2}$ weeks to $11\frac{1}{2}$ weeks of age. A total of 60 hours of behaviors was sampled in two $\frac{1}{2}$-hour sessions from $3\frac{1}{2}$ to 5 weeks and one $\frac{1}{2}$-hour session from 5 to $11\frac{1}{2}$ weeks (due to the pups' increased activity during the latter period).

The units of behavior that were extracted from the videotaped sessions were based on behaviors that occur frequently during a pup's development (based on information taken from Bekoff, 1972; Fox, 1971a, 1971b; Rheingold, 1963). In addition to the descriptive units, a behavioral Gestalt was recorded that clarified the meaning of the signals and helped place the behavioral units in a particular context (e.g., play, investigatory, agonistic, etc.). Table 6-4 lists the behavior categories used to classify the various units of behavior. The following is an account that demonstrates how behaviors were assigned to categories, taken from an interaction of Pup 2 with Pup 3: "2 approaches and bites 3 on the neck and shakes—3 whines, tail tucked, ears backed; 2 gets 3 down on ground by neck, 3 whines." The interaction was clearly agonistic in nature, and Pup 2's behaviors were classified in Category F, Agonistic—assertive, whereas Pup 3's behaviors were classified in Category G, Agonistic—submissive. A less clear interaction was the following: "2 muzzle bites, scruff bites 5—5 tries to escape—2 scruff bites 5, 5 walked away." In this interaction it was not clear that the "muzzle and scruff bites" were agonistic; without a further description, these behaviors could be categorized as J, Play fight or agonistic (unclear)–assertive. However, a further description of the situation was given: "2 attacks 5, play-fighting." The behaviors (muzzle and scruff biting) then were clearly classified in Category C, Play fight—assertive. If no clarifying statement was given, it was assumed that the observer could not determine by merely watching the interaction whether, for example, the behaviors took place in an agonistic or play situation; thus, the need for Categories B, E, J, and K. If there was any doubt concerning the appropriateness of a category for identifying behaviors (e.g., Play fight—assertive versus Agonistic—assertive),

TABLE 6-4
Categories for Behavioral Units

Code	Behavior category
A	Play
B	Play fight
C	Play fight—assertive
D	Play fight—submissive
E	Play fight or agonistic (unclear)—submissive
F	Agonistic—assertive
G	Agonistic—submissive
H	Remains the same, self-maintenance, stops
I	Investigatory
J	Play fight or agonistic (unclear)—assertive
K	Ambivalent (rolls on back, sits up, stands up, lies down, sits down)
W	Lies, sits on top of
@	Walk away, move away
+	Play solicit

the behaviors were classified in the more inclusive category (e.g., E, J, and K). In other words, all behaviors classified in F were clearly of an Agonistic—assertive nature; all behaviors classified in G were clearly of an Agonistic—submissive nature.

The behavior categories were coded and used in a computer program that gave a behavior matrix, that is, a sum of the behaviors (as categories) emitted during a particular time interval by a particular subject. For example, "when subject 1 emitted a behavior classified in Category F, subject 2 emitted a behavior classified in Category G." If this sequence repeated itself five times during a taping session, the computer printout would read "when subject 2 emitted behavior Category F, subject 5 emitted behavior Category G, 5 times." I began the analysis for the primary socialization period when the subjects were $3\frac{1}{2}$ weeks old.

If social structure results from the accumulation of dominance—subordinance relationships, and these relationships are determined as an outcome of agonistic encounters, then one way to investigate the formation of social structure is to determine what each subject does during agonistic encounters. Specifically, when a subject is "being agonistic," it is important to know if his behaviors are usually assertive or submissive. Some individuals may be involved in more agonistic encounters than are others, but the determination of a litter social hierarchy depends on how the subject behaves when it is being agonistic. One way to determine a subject's assertiveness is to quantify the subject's assertive behaviors in relation to the total number of agonistic behaviors it emits that are clearly assertive or submissive.

I computed an "agonistic—assertive" score based on a subject's assertive behaviors (Category F) divided by his assertive and submissive behaviors (Categories F and G) and multiplied by 100. The percentage indicates what portion of its behaviors, while being agonistic, were assertive; the figures were calculated for the time intervals $3\frac{1}{2}$–$5\frac{1}{2}$ weeks, $5\frac{1}{2}$–$8\frac{1}{2}$ weeks, and $8\frac{1}{2}$–$11\frac{1}{2}$ weeks.

Results

During the $3\frac{1}{2}$–$5\frac{1}{2}$ week period, Pup 2 was more assertive than any of the other pups: 2 (92%), 1 (69%), 3 (66%), 5 (65%), 4 (62%).

A comparison of these data with the $5\frac{1}{2}$-weeks bone-in-pen test data indicated that dominance established in a rearing environment where many pups were present and involved in different life processes and dominance established during a competitive encounter (such as the bone-in-pen test) were two different kinds of dominance. The competitive dominance hierarchy at $5\frac{1}{2}$ weeks showed the following relationships (with dominance index percentages): 5 (86%) > 1 (67%) > 4 (59%) > 3 (51%) > 2 (11%). Recall that for Pup 2, possession of the bone involved sharing only, and Pup 1 was completely dominant over Pup 2 during their session. In contrast, Pup 2's dominance behavior in one setting was completely opposite to its dominance behavior in the other setting. It would be difficult to argue that both tests were measuring the same thing.

During the $5\frac{1}{2}$ to $8\frac{1}{2}$ weeks time interval, the assertive scores showed less variation for the litter as a whole (largely due to Pup 2's score), with Pups 1 (82%), 3 (81%), 4 (75%), and 5 (74%) increasing in assertiveness and Pup 2 decreasing in his assertive percentage (84%), but still remaining most assertive compared with all other pups. During the $8\frac{1}{2}$-weeks bone-in-pen test, however, Pup 2 increased his dominance percentage (from 11% to 43%) while still remaining last (tied with Pup 3) in his hierarchy. Only Pup 4 increased both his assertiveness and dominance scores at the $8\frac{1}{2}$-weeks test (Pup 4 social assertiveness = 62% → 75%, dominance index = 59% → 71%). All other subjects' scores changed in opposite directions during the $8\frac{1}{2}$-weeks test, again indicating the development of two separate kinds of dominance.

During the last 3 weeks of the socialization period, the social dominance relationships increased in range of percentages: 5 (96%), 2 (95%), 4 (82%), 3 (75%), 1 (60%).[3] During this period social relationships began to solidify, actual fighting between litter members decreased, and the social hierarchy became more apparent. Comparisons of these data to the $11\frac{1}{2}$-weeks bone-in-pen test showed some concordance: Pups 2 and 5 scored quite closely in both the social and competitive dominance settings, whereas Pups 3 and 1 ranked fourth and fifth in both social and competitive dominance.

A comparison of the development of dominance in each setting, however, would still indicate that a different sort of dominance was being measured in the rearing environment (social dominance) apart from the sort that was found in the bone-in-pen test (competitive dominance).

The interaction frequencies of $3\frac{1}{2}$ to 4 weeks of age fit fairly well with the final $8\frac{1}{2}$ to $11\frac{1}{2}$ week assertiveness scores for social dominance. The ordered frequency scores indicated the following: 2 (109 behaviors) > 5 (93) > 4 (53) > 3 (48) > 1 (19). Quite similarly, the assertive-score index at $11\frac{1}{2}$ weeks was: 2 (95%) = 5 (96%) > 4 (82%) > 3 (75%) > 1 (60%). If these relationships exist for other litters, perhaps social dominance is influenced

---

[3] Although Pup 5's assertive percentage was greater than was Pup 2's, log reports indicated that Pup 2 was the most assertive member of the litter by $11\frac{1}{2}$ weeks (see Wright, in press). This was the only instance in which the assertive percentages were not supported by log reports.

Figure 6-5. An example of socialization. The first time the hand-reared alone pup was returned to her littermates, the well socialized pups (barely visible at far right) responded to her assertive posture by vacating the feeding area.

by the relative number of interactions in which each pup is involved during the beginning of the primary socialization period. See Figures 6-5 and 6-6 for examples of dominance behavior.

The development of social dominance was not investigated for Litter 2 (due to the early mortality of three litter-reared pups) or Litter 3 (due to fall weather conditions). I have just completed collecting data on a litter of seven beagles (five litter-reared, two hand-reared), however, in which I investigated the development of competitive dominance, social dominance, and exploratory behaviors through 9 weeks of age. It will be interesting to learn whether breed differences exist for the development of these behaviors.

CONCLUSIONS

The ontogeny of two different kinds of dominance, competive and social, has been demonstrated in German shepherd pups through $11\frac{1}{2}$ weeks of age. Those pups that ranked highest on the competitive dominance index also ranked highest on the SR index, even when pups changed ranks during the 6-week testing period.

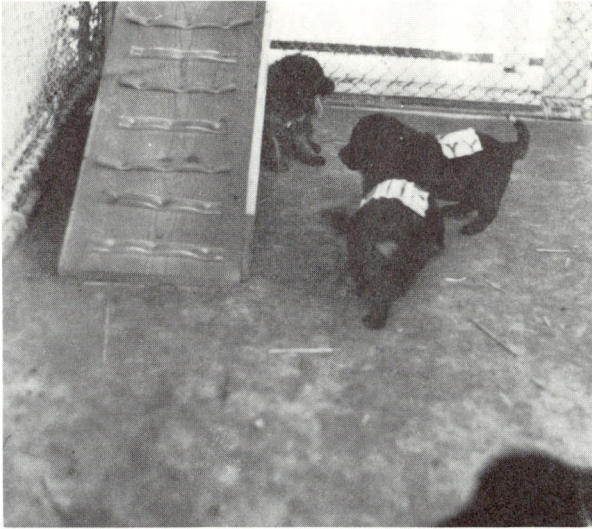

Figure 6-6. Social dominance was measured in a setting that allowed pups to approach, avoid, or escape from littermates.

This relationship was not found for Litters 2 and 3; for those litters, however, it is possible that the SR rankings were influenced by the pups' reactions to novel objects and settings for each test session (unlike members from Litter 1, who were exposed to the same objects and settings for all tests), and by exposure to adverse weather conditions during rearing (for Litter 3).

Scores on the stimulus reactivity variables were influenced by different rearing conditions. Pups that were taken from their mother and hand-reared within 2 weeks after birth consistently ranked higher on the SR variables than did their littermates. All hand-reared pups increased their scores on two of the SR variables between the $5\frac{1}{2}$- and $8\frac{1}{2}$-week sessions, whereas most litter-reared pups' scores decreased or remained the same. Other differences between the hand- and litter-reared pups were observed in the competitive dominance tests.

Similarities as well as differences were observed between rearing conditions and between litters for dominance and exploratory behaviors. The ontogeny of these behaviors differentiate early and vary not only within the litter, but within the individual, at least from $5\frac{1}{2}$ through $11\frac{1}{2}$ weeks of age.

REFERENCES

Bekoff, M. 1972. An ethological study of the development of social interaction in the genus *Canis:* A dyadic analysis. Unpublished Ph.D dissertation, Washington University.

Bekoff, M. 1977. Quantitative studies of three areas of classical ethology: Social dominance, behavioral taxonomy, and behavioral variability. In B. A. Hazlett (Ed.), *Quantitative methods in the study of animal behavior.* New York: Academic Press.

Bekoff, M. 1978. Behavioral development in coyotes and eastern coyotes. In M. Bekoff (Ed.), *Coyotes, biology behavior, and management.* New York: Academic Press.

Fox, M. W. 1971a. *Integrative development of brain and behavior in the dog.* Chicago: University of Chicago Press.

Fox, M. W. 1971b. *Behavior of wolves, dogs, and related canids.* London: Jonathan Cape.

Fox, M. W. 1972. Socio-ecological implications of individual differences in wolf litters: A developmental and evolutionary perspective. *Behavior, 41,* 298–313.

Fuller, J. L. 1970. Genetic influences on socialization. In R. A. Hoppe, G. A. Milton, & E. C. Simmel (Eds.), *Early experiences and the processes of socialization.* New York: Academic Press.

James, W. T. 1949. Dominant and submissive behavior in puppies as indicated by food intake. *Journal of Genetic Psychology, 54,* 151–164.

James, W. T. 1951. Social organization among dogs of different temperaments, terriers and beagles, reared together. *Journal of Comparative and Physiological Psychology, 44,* 71–78.

Lockwood, R. 1975. "Dominance" in wolves: Useful construct or bad habit? Paper presented at Animal Behavior Society Meeting, University of North Carolina at Wilmington.

Rheingold, H. L. 1963. *Maternal behavior in mammals.* New York: Wiley.

Scott, J. P., & Fuller, J. L. 1965. *Genetics and the social behavior of the dog.* Chicago: University of Chicago Press.

Scott, J. P., & Marston, M. W. 1950. Critical periods affecting the development of normal and maladjustive social behavior of puppies. *Journal of Genetic Psychology, 77,* 25–60.

Simmel, E. C., & Eleftheriou, B. E. 1977. Multivariate and behavior genetic analysis of avoidance of complex visual stimuli and activity in recombinant inbred strains of mice. *Behavior Genetics, 7,* 239–250.

Wright, J. C. In press. The development of social structure during the primary socialization period in German shepherds. *Developmental Psychobiology.*

Zimen, E. 1975. Social dynamics of the wolf pack. In M. W. Fox (Ed.), *The wild canids.* New York: Van Nostrand Reinhold.

Author Index

Numbers in italics refer to the pages on which the complete references are listed.

Subject Index

A

Acceleration, 88
Accommodation, 86
Adaptation, 83, 85–87
  social, 83
Adrenocortical reactivity hypothesis, 58
Agonistic behavior, 10–11, 201–202
Alternation of generations, *see* Metagenesis
Anthropocentrism, 58
Arousal hypothesis, 49
Attachment
  mother-infant, 113, 132
  site, 25
  social, 25
Audiogenic seizures, 10

B

Behavioral development, 16–32
  dog as example, 16–27
  mammals, 27–32
Behavioral epigenesis, 82
Biological neutrality, 65–66
Bladder training, 154
Bone-in-pen test, 182
Brain chemistry studies, 6–8, 48–49

Breast feeding
  advantages of, 158
  extra contact and, 150, 159–160, 163
  mother's position and, 132

C

Causation
  proximate, 87
  ultimate, 87
Cesarec–Marlee Personality Scale, 156–157
Classical conditioning, 19–20
Cognitive theory, 102–103
Communication, crying as example of, 113
Conditioning, *see* Classical conditioning; Instrumental conditioning
Critical periods, 99
Crying in infants, *see also* Communication, crying as example of
  releaser mechanism, 149
  type of care and, 148–149

D

Dependent variable, validity of, 67
Deprivation, 99–102

215